François Truffaut

Annette Insdorf

A TOUCHSTONE BOOK
Published by Simon & Schuster Inc.
New York • London • Toronto • Sydney • Tokyo
Revised Edition

Touchstone
Simon & Schuster Building
Rockefeller Center
1230 Avenue of the Americas
New York, New York 10020

First Touchstone Edition, 1989

Published by arrangement with the author.

Manufactured in the United States of America

10 9 8 7 6 5 4 3 2 1 Pbk.

Library of Congress Cataloging in Publication data

Insdorf, Annette.
    François Truffaut / Annette Insdorf.—Rev. ed.
        p.   cm.
    "A Touchstone book."
    Includes bibliographical references.
    1. Truffaut, François—Criticism and interpretation. I. Title.
PN1998.3.78157 1989
791.43′0233′092-dc20   89-21635
                                          CIP

ISBN 0-671-67166-9 Pbk.

For my parents

Contents

Preface

THIS BOOK GROWS out of my deep affection and respect for the films of François Truffaut. It is from my teaching of "The French New Wave" and other courses in cinema at Yale that the study developed, and I see my role before the reader as continuous with my function before a class: to communicate and justify through close analysis my enthusiasm for the aesthetic and experiential richness of the subject. I address primarily those who are already aware of Truffaut's talent and achievement and wish to explore the thematic and stylistic concerns that have emerged from his films. I hope this approach results in the tone of sympathy that characterizes Truffaut's attitude toward his medium, his mentors, his material, and his performers.

Truffaut's films constitute what he once termed "cinema in the first person singular," and I have therefore tried to retain the personal context, effect, and purpose of his efforts. The first chapter serves as an introduction to the French New Wave and Truffaut's transition from critic to director. After connecting three "Charlie" characters who are central to this movement in film history—Chaplin, Orson Welles' Charlie (Citizen) Kane, and Charlie Kohler of *Shoot the Piano Player*—I move in Chapters 2 and 3 to Truffaut's relationship to his mentors, Alfred Hitchcock and Jean Renoir. Here I discuss the films of his "Hitchcockian" period in the mid-1960s, *The Soft Skin*, *Fahrenheit 451*, *The Bride Wore Black*, and *Mississippi Mermaid*, and his more "Renoirian" endeavors: Part 1 of Chapter 3 contains close analyses of *Stolen Kisses* and *Bed and Board*, Part 2 of *Jules and Jim* and *Two English Girls*, and Part 3 an extended comparison of *Rules of the Game* and *Day for Night*.

The first section of Chapter 4, "Are Women Magic?", deals with the images of women and love throughout his films, while the second part pays special attention to *The Story of Adèle H.* and *The*

Man Who Loved Women. Chapter 5, "Les Enfants Terribles," is an exploration not only of the importance of children in his work, but of his ongoing concern with the crucial acquisition of language in childhood. Chapter 6, "Cinema in the First Person Singular," traces the autobiographical strain in his films, with the second section focusing on *The Man Who Loved Women.* Here I address myself to Truffaut's growing preoccupation with literary texts and the depiction of the creative process. Chapter 7, "Images on the Run," offers close analyses of his last five films.

The translations from French are my own, except where noted, and the films are identified by their American titles. For the use of stills, I wish to acknowledge Les Films du Carrosse, Janus Films, New World Pictures, and the Museum of Modern Art Film Stills Archive. Suzanne Schiffman and Josiane Couëdel were extremely helpful in arranging special screenings in Paris, as was Jeannie Reynolds at Yale Audio-Visual. I appreciate the academic and personal support of Harold Bloom, David Cast, Warren French, Jay Holman, Crosby Kemper, Sam Oberfest, Lillie Mae Rose, David Stannard, and Donald Yacoe. For the new edition, I must express appreciation to Bob Bender, Georges Borchardt, Monique Holeck, Madeleine Morgenstern, Paul Wagner, and Michael Webb.

I am particularly grateful to Cecile Insdorf, David Lapin, Doug McKinney, and Edward Baron Turk, whose criticism and suggestions proved invaluable during revision of the manuscript. Finally, special thanks to my students for inspiration, and to François Truffaut for his accessibility and kindness.

ANNETTE INSDORF
New York, New York

Chronology

1932   François Truffaut born in Paris, February 6, the only child of Roland Truffaut, an architect, and Janine de Montferrand, a secretary; is sent to live with grandmother till eight years old.

1951   Enlists in the army for three years; then deserts on the eve of departure for Indochina. Released in 1953 for "instability of character" after six months in prison and hospital.

1953   Enters the Service Cinématographique of the Ministry of Agriculture. When he is fired after a few months, André Bazin enables him to begin writing film criticism for the recently founded *Cahiers du Cinéma*. Later he also becomes a film reviewer for *Arts*.

1955   Makes *Une Visite*, a short 16mm film, with Jacques Rivette and Alain Resnais.

1956   Assistant to Roberto Rossellini for two years; works on three of his unreleased films.

1957   Marries Madeleine Morgenstern, daughter of film producer and distributor Ignace Morgenstern, on October 29.

1958   *Les Mistons* shown at Brussels and wins an award. Makes *Une Histoire d'eau* with Godard. Because of his articles attacking the Cannes Film Festival, Truffaut is banned from the Festival.

1959   *The 400 Blows* wins the Grand Prix at Cannes. Birth of daughter Laura. Script of *Breathless*, directed by Godard.

1960   *Shoot the Piano Player*.

1961   *Jules and Jim*. Birth of daughter Eva. Produces, co-scripts, and supervises *Tire au flanc*, directed by Claude de Givray.

1962   *Antoine and Colette*, sketch in *Love At Twenty*.

1964   *The Soft Skin*.

1966   *Fahrenheit 451*. Publication of *Le Cinéma selon Hitchcock*.

1967 *The Bride Wore Black.*
1968 *Stolen Kisses.* The Langlois Affair: when the French government dismisses Henri Langlois, head of the Cinémathèque Française, Truffaut helps to organize protests, until Langlois is reinstated. Along with Godard, is involved in closing down the Cannes Festival because of May 1968 uprising.
1969 *Mississippi Mermaid.*
1970 *The Wild Child. Bed and Board.*
1971 *Two English Girls.*
1972 *Such a Gorgeous Kid Like Me.*
1973 *Day for Night.* Wins Oscar for Best Foreign Film.
1975 *The Story of Adèle H.* Publication of *Les Films de ma vie.*
1976 *Small Change.*
1977 *The Man Who Loved Women.* Stars in *Close Encounters of the Third Kind,* directed by Steven Spielberg.
1978 *The Green Room.*
1979 *Love on the Run.* American Film Institute tribute/retrospective in Washington and Los Angeles to celebrate Truffaut's 20th anniversary in filmmaking.
1980 *The Last Metro.*
1981 *The Woman Next Door.*
1983 *Confidentially Yours.* Birth of daughter Josephine with Fanny Ardant.
1984 Publication of the definitive version of *Hitchcock-Truffaut.* Dies October 21 of brain cancer.

About the Author

Annette Insdorf is known primarily as a film professor, critic, lecturer, translator and television personality. She is Director of Undergraduate Film Studies at Columbia University, where she holds the title of Professor as well as Chairman of the Doctoral Program in Film and Theater. She taught film history and criticism at Yale University from 1975 to 1988.

Dr. Insdorf is the author of *Indelible Shadows: Film and the Holocaust*, published by Random House in 1983 to critical acclaim (updated version Cambridge University Press, 1989).

She is a frequent contributor to *The New York Times* Arts and Leisure Section, and her articles have appeared in *The Los Angeles Times, The San Francisco Chronicle, Premiere, Film Comment, Elle, Cineaste, The Boston Globe, American Film* and *Rolling Stone.*

On television, Dr. Insdorf has served as host for "TéléFrance Ciné-Club" (a national cable-TV program); for "Years of Darkness" (an 8-week series of films about the World War II experience shown by WNET/PBS); and for WNYC-TV. A popular panel moderator, translator, film festival traveler, and lecturer, she offers numerous lecture series at New York's 92nd Street Y.

She was born in Paris, France, and went on to receive her B.A. (summa cum laude) from Queens College, and her M.A. and Ph.D. from Yale University, where she was a Danforth Fellow. In 1986, she was named *Chevalier dans l'ordre des arts et des lettres* by the French Ministry of Culture.

Dr. Insdorf is the Executive Producer of Tom Abrams's "Shoeshine," nominated for an Academy Award for the Best Live-Action Short Film of 1987. The ten-minute movie starring Jerry Stiller also won the Grand Prize (Short Film category) at the Montreal Film Festival. In addition, she served as Executive Producer of "Short-Term Bonds," a nine-minute film by Michael Lengsfield, winner of a CINE golden eagle; and of "Performance Pieces"—a short film directed by Tom Abrams, starring F. Murray Abraham—which was named Best Fiction Short at the 1989 Cannes Film Festival.

1

From "Cinéphile" to "Cinéaste"

IMAGINE (or if you are lucky, remember) the thrill of being a child at the movies—especially if you manage to sneak in, and especially if you are playing hooky. François Truffaut's critical writings and films suggest that he has never forgotten the shivers of delight inherent in the early movie-watching experience: the escape into darkness and surprises, the screen that overwhelms with people larger than life, and then the growing realization that film is less a substitute for life than a frame for a more intense and moving picture of it.

Truffaut's early film-going experiences were flavored by what we might call "sinema": not only were his excursions into the darkness clandestine, but they were accompanied by a growing awareness of sexuality. A fine example of this conjunction in the boy's mind (around the age of twelve) is his recollection of lost panties in the 4,500-seat Gaumont-Palace in Paris during the Occupation. He learned from his friend—whose mother worked at the famous movie theater—that after the last show every Sunday night, at least sixty pairs of panties would be found under the seats: "I hardly need to add that these sixty little weekly panties—we never failed to check the exact number . . . —made us dream in a direction that had little to do with the art of cinema or the ideas of Bazin."[1]

Nevertheless, Truffaut's first films prove that the kind of experience he recalls here has everything to do with filmic art. His first short film, *Les Mistons* (1958), and his first feature, *The 400 Blows* (1959), both depict the sexual awakenings of young boys. In the former, a group of *mistons* (brats) spy upon the young woman of their dreams, furtively and adoringly sniffing the seat of her bicycle (a moment which Truffaut eternizes through stopped images). We see Antoine Doinel in *The 400 Blows* at his mother's vanity table, toying with her perfume and eyelash curler; later he is fascinated by her legs as she removes her stockings. And a subsequent Doinel

Top: Jean-Pierre Léaud, Jean Cocteau, and Truffaut at Cannes in 1959. Bottom: Truffaut, Léaud, and Henri Langlois during the shooting of Stolen Kisses.

15

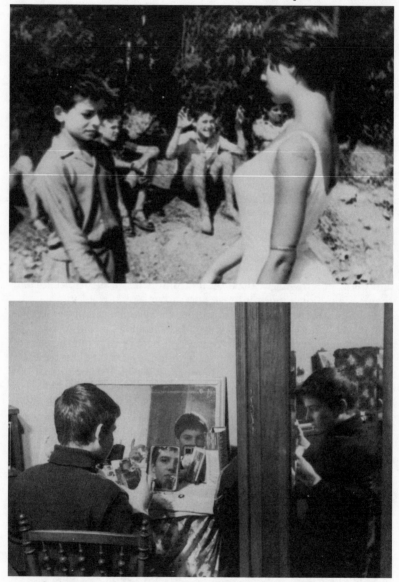

The fascination with women: *Les Mistons* (top); *The 400 Blows* (bottom).

Antoine and René in *The 400 Blows* with Bergman's Monika.

film, *Stolen Kisses* (1968), is about characters who spend their time spying upon each other. If we consider these themes while recalling the great theorist André Bazin's essay, "Theater and Cinema," in which he says, "Alone, hidden in a dark room, we watch through half-open blinds a spectacle that is unaware of our existence and which is part of the universe,"[2] we can see an aspect of the continuum between Truffaut's film-watching and film-making: the degree to which the movies provide stimulation/sublimation, making the spectator a voyeur.

Inseparable from this identity in solitude is the existence of a *community* of voyeurs—the audience in which strangers are not only aware of each other, but become united in shared emotions. Truffaut tells us that his first memory of the cinema takes him back to 1939 when, at the age of seven, he sees Abel Gance's *Paradis Perdu*. It is wartime both on and off the screen, and the theater is filled with soldiers on leave (accompanied by their girlfriends or mistresses). The coincidence between the situation of the characters and that of the spectators is so intense that everyone is crying—hundreds of white handkerchiefs dotting the darkness—and the little boy is engulfed in the "unanimité émotionnelle" that washes through the audience.[3]

Among experiences such as these, Truffaut became a cinéphile—a passionate lover of film—thus illustrating Jean Cocteau's maxim, "A child's eyes register fast. Later he develops the film." A neglected child whose only real home was the movie theater, he would see favorite films as many as ten times, even memorizing the sound-track. He kept a diary in which he listed all the films he saw, with stars next to those seen most often. (Jean Renoir's *Rules of the Game* accumulated twelve.[4]) And then in 1947, at the age of fifteen, he started a ciné-club "with the pretentious but revealing name of 'Cercle Cinémane' " (*FV*, 15). This enterprise was doomed to failure because it was in competition with the ciné-club of Bazin, but it did give him the opportunity to make the latter's acquaintance. Their meeting has tremendous resonance for both personal and film-historical reasons. Although Bazin was only thirteen years older than Truffaut, he became a substitute father to the boy. When Truffaut was arrested because of his club's unpaid bills (and like Antoine in *The 400 Blows* was locked up with thieves and prostitutes and then transported by police van to a delinquents center), Bazin negotiated his release and assumed responsibility for him. And most significantly, he channeled Truffaut's passion into profession by in-viting him to write about film. Truffaut says of this period, "It was the first happy time of my life . . . watching films, talking about them, and to top it off, I was getting paid for it!" (*FV*, p. 30).

Bazin was already known as one of the most sensitive and articu-late of film critics, one who addressed himself to the aesthetic poten-tial of the medium within the context of ethical concerns. Truffaut declares in his Foreword to the second volume of *What Is Cinema?*,

André Bazin wrote about film better than anybody else in Europe. From that day in 1948 when he got me my first film job, working alongside him, I became his adopted son. Thereafter, every pleasant thing that happened in my life, I owed to him. (II, v)

Truffaut would be deeply influenced by Bazin's generosity of spirit, critical intelligence, and focus upon the director as the dominant creative force in film. A humanist in the best sense of the word, Bazin wrote with informed affection about everything from deep-focus photography to the entomology of the pin-up girl. His pre-dilection for the former offers a clear picture of how his sensitivity to film technique relates to his fundamental respect for human beings. Whereas the Soviet theorists and filmmakers had given cinematic primacy to montage (editing, cutting, or the creation of meaning through the juxtaposition of shots), particularly insofar as it lends itself to manipulation and didactic intent, Bazin emphasized deep-focus photography, which maintains the integrity of the shot and restores faith in the camera over the cutting room. Bazin in "The Evolution of the Language of Cinema" was among the first to comprehend the impact of this technique upon the spectator's response. Composition in depth is seen as egalitarian in the sense that everything in the frame exists with equal clarity, thereby giving the spectator a choice: our eyes are free to roam from foreground to background and around. It is closer to the way we perceive in off-screen life, and it reintroduces ambiguity into the structure of the image.

Whether celebrating masters of depth-of-focus, Orson Welles and Jean Renoir, or tempering the dominance of Sergei Eisenstein, Bazin (like Truffaut after him) was evolving what he called "an aesthetic of reality," an approach that recognizes film's unique capacity to capture and reproduce "real" experience. This was not merely an adherence to realism, but to a process that transcends mimesis, and presents "common" individuals and events in all their generally ignored complexity and beauty. In his article, "An Aesthetic of Reality: Neorealism," for example, Bazin claims that faithfulness to everyday life is the basic material of the æsthetic of Italian film. Particularly in the work of Roberto Rossellini and Vittorio De Sica, he finds "a revolutionary humanism," rooted in the portrayal of ". . . concrete reality in itself multiple and full of ambiguity." Bazin applauds the way that people in neorealist art are individuated and that "nobody is reduced to the condition of an object or a symbol that would allow one to hate them in comfort without having first to leap the hurdle of their humanity."[5]

Truffaut not only worked as an assistant to Rossellini in 1956,[6] but his critical writings also seek out the "ring of truth." He praises directors such as Jean Renoir and Ingmar Bergman for the overwhelming reality of their characters and fluid emotional situations, for their presentation of the intimate relationships among love, pain, celebration, and loss. In *The Cinema of François Truffaut*, Graham Petrie's impression of the director's art weaves these Bazinian influences together:

The sensitive viewer of a Truffaut film will find himself making constant and subtle re-adjustments of his standard assumptions and preconceptions; he will emerge with a new awareness of the incongruous rhythms of life, of the inextricable mingling of beauty and sadness in evervday experience, but he will feel that he has discovered these for himself. [7]

Bazin founded *Cahiers du Cinéma* in 1950—the first major magazine to treat film (the medium, the directors, and the individual motion pictures) with the seriousness, respect, and passion traditionally reserved for the other arts. It brought together the leading French critics/film enthusiasts of the time—Truffaut, Jean-Luc Godard, Claude Chabrol, Eric Rohmer, and Jacques Rivette—and became one of the two focal points of the movement known as the New Wave. The other center was the Cinémathèque under the direction of Henri Langlois, where the film fanatics spent the better part of their waking hours under the spell of motion pictures from every nationality and period. They devoured the silents, the talkies, the German Expressionists, the Italian Neorealists and, most ravenously, the American studio films that had been banned during the Occupation. Here they learned to love directors like Howard Hawks and John Ford, the American masters who were virtually ignored in this country until the French critics made a case for their artistry in the pages of *Cahiers du Cinéma*. The Cinémathèque made them aware and enamored of genres—Westerns, musicals, gangster films, "film noir" (detective/psychological/thrillers)—and of the Hollywood studio system: the genre conventions and production methods were seen as necessary limitations that defined the possibilities of personal expression for American directors.

The critics in what was to become the French New Wave noticed thematic and stylistic consistencies among the films of individual directors and elevated identifiable personal signature to a standard of value. They championed the director as the "auteur," the creator of a personal vision of the world which progresses from film to film. Paradoxically enough, their limited knowledge of English made them uniquely equipped to appreciate individual cinematic style: the American films often had no subtitles, thereby inviting a closer look at how meaning is expressed through visual texture, composition, camera movement, and editing. The cinéphiles' exuberant respect for auteurs who were previously considered craftsmen (at best) generated great controversy; Andrew Sarris reminds us how Truffaut was repudiated by non-*Cahiers* people: "Truffaut's greatest heresy, however, was not in his ennobling direction as a form of creation, but in his ascribing authorship to Hollywood directors hitherto tagged with the deadly epithets of commercialism."[8] Truffaut and Company were nicknamed "hitchcockohawksiens" since they championed directors like Hitchcock and Hawks as auteurs of the highest order.

The attention to the director and the renewed exploration of film as an essentially *visual* medium constitute two major foundations of the New Wave. These points of emphasis can be better understood in relation to previous trends in French cinema. Perhaps the most important single document in this regard is Truffaut's famous attack on classic French film, "Une certaine tendance du cinéma français," which appeared in *Cahiers du Cinéma* in January, 1954. The target was what he termed "la Tradition de la qualité," the French postwar films that were adapted from novels and were heavily dependent upon plot and dialogue. These films of "psychological realism" by directors such as Claude Autant-Lara, Jean Delannoy, and René Clément were seen as stunting the growth of filmic art since they did not exploit or even lend themselves to the visual possibilities of cinema. The key figure was the scriptwriter (the director was "the gentleman who adds the pictures"), and Truffaut singles out for blame the successful writing team of Jean Aurenche and Pierre Bost since they manifest "1. A constant and deliberate care to be *unfaithful* to the spirit as well as the letter; 2. A very marked taste for profanation and blasphemy." Aurenche and Bost are defined as essentially literary men, and Truffaut reproaches them "for being contemptuous of the cinema by underestimating it." They are also taken to task for giving the public "its habitual dose of smut, nonconformity, and facile audacity," and for manifesting the trait that Truffaut would always manage to avoid in his own films—the desire to be superior to their characters.[9]

Above and beyond these "littérateurs" (whose work is also pugnaciously termed "le cinéma de papa"), Truffaut proposes "un cinéma d'auteurs," praising the directors who often write and invent what they shoot. Jean Renoir, Robert Bresson, Jean Cocteau, Jacques Becker, Abel Gance, Max Ophuls, Jacques Tati, and Roger Leenhardt reveal the limitations of the verbally dominated "antibourgeois cinema." Truffaut's concern with realism led him to denigrate the use of literary dialogue, elaborate studio sets, polished photography, and big-name stars. In the same manner that his own films would exemplify, his critical writings paid homage to the directors who ennobled ordinary experience, vulnerable individuals, daily language, and common emotions.

Truffaut's article is credited by Andrew Sarris, the first and most articulate promulgator of the auteur theory in the United States, with the polemical stance of the term "auteur." In the introduction to his seminal book in film history, *The American Cinema*, Sarris lucidly discusses the "politique des auteurs" and Truffaut's centrality to its development: "Truffaut was involved in nothing less than changing the course of the French cinema" (p. 29). This is not to say that he merits unqualified praise: the auteur theory has been abused nearly as often as it has been used fruitfully. Certain directors—such as John Huston—were unjustly accused of mediocrity, and criticism often degenerated into a question of taking sides for or against individual directors. Bazin's article, "On the Politique des Auteurs," warned against the excesses of this principle, the danger of an "esthetic cult of personality." While stressing that we need an auteurist approach in film, where artistic creation is more vulnerable, he concludes with a plea for a more judicious application:

But its exclusive use would lead to another peril: the negation of the work to the profit of the exaltation of its *auteur*. We have tried to show why mediocre auteurs were able, by accident, to make admirable films, and how, in turn, genius itself was menaced by a sterility no less accidental. The *politique des auteurs* will ignore the first and deny the second. Useful and fecund, it then seems to me, independently of its polemical value, to have been filled out by other approaches to the cinematographic fact which restores to the film its value as an oeuvre. This is not at all to deny the role of the auteur, but to restore to it the preposition without which the noun is only a lame concept. '*Auteur*,' without doubt, but *of* what?[10]

Truffaut is not exempt from this warning. He confesses that after the Liberation, "because of a taste for exoticism, a thirst for novelty, romanticism, evidently also because of a delight in contradiction, but surely through love of vitality, we decided to love everything as long as it was from Hollywood" (*FV*, 293). He is justifiably persuasive when he writes lovingly of Jean Vigo's *Zero for Conduct* or Max Ophuls' *Lola Montes*; he appears on occasion merely idiosyncratic when he waxes eloquent over Samuel Fuller or Robert Aldrich.

But in every case, he is seeking the personal touch—the man behind or inside the work—the manifestation of a human sensibility molding an art form to communicate its obsessions. In this sense, Truffaut follows in the footsteps of critic/filmmaker Alexandre Astruc who declared in 1948:

The cinema is becoming a means of expression like the other arts before it, especially painting and the novel. It is no longer a spectacle, a diversion equivalent to the old boulevard theatre . . . it is becoming, little by little, a visual language, i.e. a medium in which and by which an artist can express his thoughts, be they abstract or whatever, or in which he can communicate his obsessions as accurately as he can do today in an essay or novel."[11]

His call for a "new wave" was answered when in 1959, twenty-four French directors made their first feature films, followed in 1960 by forty-three more first features. In the intervening decade (1949-59), Truffaut and his colleagues were setting the stage for the creative explosion of the late 1950s. Astruc had been proposing that direction was no longer a means of illustrating a scene, but an act of writing: "The filmmaker/author writes with his camera as a writer writes with his pen."

The New Wave critics were able to apply and develop this notion, partially because of the technical innovations during the fifties. The advent of lightweight equipment made it possible to shoot with a handheld camera that is virtually a fluid extension of the filmmaker's body. Less expensive camera methods introduced a visual freedom (for example, the cultivation of cinematic roughness) that permitted more identification between camera and director— and, consequently, between camera and audience. As James Monaco points out in his excellent study, *The New Wave* (1976), these critics insisted on

a personal relationship between filmmaker and film viewer. Movies must no longer be alienated products which are consumed by mass audiences; they are now intimate conversations between the people behind the camera and the people in front of the screen. It is immediately clear that the ethics of the *politique des auteurs* owed a great debt to Bazinian moral realism. (p. 8)

The personal relationship finally made creative demands upon the critics, and 1959 boasted Truffaut's *The 400 Blows*, Godard's *Breathless*, Chabrol's *Les Cousins*, Rivette's *Paris Belongs To Us*, and Resnais' *Hiroshima mon amour*. (Alain Resnais is generally considered part of the New Wave, with the difference that he did not begin his film career as a critic.)

Bazin's association with both Italian Neorealism and the New Wave symbolizes the intimate connections between the movements, for the French critics/filmmakers made virtues of necessities similar to those of their Italian mentors: young, independent, and without studios, they resorted to on-location shooting, the use of nonprofessional or relatively unknown performers, and an address to daily experience. These traits led to the elements that best characterize most New Wave films: spontaneity and improvisation.

The films of Truffaut and his comrades move according to inner quirks more than rigid plot; an excellent example is his second feature, *Shoot the Piano Player* (1960), whose "storyline" is less significant (or even traceable) than Truffaut's idiosyncratic treatment of characters and events. For instance, the film has a deliberate visual roughness; Raoul Coutard's photography (also crucial to *Breathless*) is grainy rather than polished. The camera is alive and nervous, reflecting the characters' personalities. The style is therefore as desirous of freedom as the individuals. The word that comes to mind is one of André Gide's favorite terms—*disponibilité*—a palpable freedom of the character, camera, and film itself to go where they like. Consider the scene in *Shoot the Piano Player* when Charlie is about to ring Lars Schmeel's bell for his audition. Rather than accompany him inside at this climactic moment, Truffaut follows an attractive young woman with a violin case—someone we do not yet know and will not see again. The camera remains with her as she goes outside, as if she might have some dramatic effect on the story, but when she moves out of the frame, we are left with the sense of a fortuitous encounter, the possibility of an acquaintance that will never be realized. *Shoot the Piano Player* continually surprises us in this fashion, deliberately disrupting tone; it disorients and improvises and flies—in the best tradition of American jazz. The implication in many of Truffaut's films is that both aesthetics and ethics are processes of improvisation: nothing is given, all must be created fresh.

In fact, the connection between the French New Wave and movements in jazz is rich and deep if we consider narrative and melody as analogous processes. There is something basically accessible and communal about them for they tell the "story"; they are the content. But because the New Wave and jazz are rooted in spontaneity and improvisation, the *treatment* becomes an integral, if not dominant, part of the experience. A possible counterpart to Truffaut might be the pianist/composer Keith Jarrett who, like the director, is responsible for the score and the performance, creates intensely personal art, and even dedicates his albums in the manner of Truffaut with his films. To understand his music, at least on one level, as a blend of Debussy (lyricism and harmony) and Miles Davis (discontinuity and fragmentation) might help us to see Truffaut between Renoir and Godard; it is interesting that Jarrett and Truffaut have recently moved closer to the former or more "classical" strain. Both force the audience to experience their art emotionally through rhythm—visual (montage) and visceral (percussion)—and texture, which enrich the theme. The "characters" of music are instruments (which, like film roles, need actors to bring them to life), and the story can be expressed only through these individuals as they interact or perform solo, obey structures, or soar freely. The instruments and the characters have lines to speak through the agency of performers.

Jarrett's relation to the piano should be like that of Truffaut to the camera, but the equation goes only so far due to the existence of a cinematographer. However, if we accept with Truffaut that the rawest material of film is human emotion (as opposed to the view that stresses celluloid), then perhaps Jarrett's handling of the piano finds its analogue in Truffaut's relationship to his actors. *Day for Night* is in a sense "live jazz" since it permits us to watch how Truffaut plays his actors to elicit varied tones and deeper resonance. We see the filmmaking as well as the movie, the process as well as the product. With the score and the screenplay as blueprints rather than absolutes, both artists can incorporate grace notes/fleeting characters; they can utilize syncopation—the "offbeat" or unexpected emphasis, but predicated on an underlying order. The foundations of *Day for Night* and *Arbour Zena* (Jarrett's superb album of 1976), for example, are strong and flexible enough to sustain flights of fancy, such as Alphonse on a go-kart or Jan Garbarek on tenor saxophone. Truffaut and Jarrett exemplify how you can improvise if you know the score.

Both the French New Wave and jazz, for all their freedom and experimentation, are respectful of tradition; Truffaut and Jarrett are as allusive as they are innovative. Inseparable from the youthful, firsthand, impulsive attitude of New Wave films is an awareness of film history that becomes an intense cinematic self-consciousness. *Shoot the Piano Player,* which calls attention to itself as a motion picture, is the work of a *cinéphile.* Abrupt shifts in tone make us conscious of watching a film; the most delightful instance is the audacious inset when one of the gangsters swears, "May my mother drop dead if I'm lying," and we suddenly see an old woman keeling over. But the self-reflexive quality is primarily noticeable in the rich allusiveness of New Wave films. Some viewers feel these references to be in-jokes for the elite; more to the point is Vincent Canby's impression that "the quotations are always relevant to the multi-levelled films Truffaut makes with such seeming effortlessness, yet they aren't essential to the primary pleasures. They are dividends."[12] They are really acts of homage to the tradition, directors, and films that formed New Wave sensibilities.

For instance, in *Shoot the Piano Player* we find the iris techniques that call back to silent film: an oval of Schmeel fading out between Charlie and Theresa in bed, or the three ovals of Plyne (specifically recalling Abel Gance's visual experiments) as he sells his employees' addresses to the gangsters. In addition, the family consists of four brothers, one of whom is named Chico: this takes on more resonance when we realize how much Truffaut loved the Marx Brothers. He even said that Charlie was named because of Charlie Chaplin,[13] and we need only look at Charles Aznavour next to Charlot (Chaplin's nickname) to catch the shared vulnerability and combination of comedy and pathos. Other New Wave films are more blatant about references, often bursting with movie posters, marquees, and conversations about everything from Gene Kelly to *Johnny Guitar.* In *Shoot the Piano Player* too we see a truck with an advertisement for *Cahiers du Cinéma* on the back!

But the way that *Shoot the Piano Player* is most fruitfully allusive is through its connections to American "B" films of the forties. Like his friend Jean-Luc Godard whose early films use thriller material as a point of departure (*Breathless* is as much rooted in American film as Belmondo's self-image in Bogart's persona), Truffaut was fascinated with the image of America as it filtered through low-budget films of the period. He once called *Shoot the Piano Player* "a respectful pastiche of the Hollywood B-films from which I learned so much,"[14] and it does in fact constitute a cinematic continuation of the critical affection he displayed in *Cahiers du Cinéma* and *Arts.*

But if *Shoot the Piano Player* and *Breathless* are variations on American genres such as the gangster film and detective thriller, the accent definitely falls on pastiche rather than plot. The stories of these films leave much to be desired as far as plot development or coherence are concerned.

What is *Shoot the Piano Player* about? Visually, it is a "film noir"—dark, couched in shadows, urban enclosures, with figures on the run. Verbally, it is rather comic, with the dialogue of the gangsters more farcical than threatening. Truffaut confessed in an interview, "the idea behind *Le Pianiste* was to make a film without a subject, to express all I wanted to say about glory, success, downfall, failure, women, and love by means of a detective story. It's a grab bag. . . ."[15] And perhaps the most amazing aspect of the film is the way it moves, jumping from comedy to tragedy, ridiculous gangsters to real guns, comic timidity to an impotence of action that kills the two women Charlie loves. The film is as unpredictable as experience itself—crazy at some moments, poignant at others; all that is certain is movement and change.

If the gangster film or "film noir" had a tight form (genre conventions as strict as those of a sonnet in poetry) *Shoot the Piano Player* is a glorious exercise in free verse, creating its own form. It begins fairly straightforwardly: a man is running down a dark street among shadows and headlights. He bumps into a lamppost and falls. A stranger who is passing by picks him up and proceeds to tell him about his wife and kids, about the high proportion of virgins in Paris, and after he has finished his story, our victim resumes his running. The stranger never returns; this was a chance encounter that does little for the plot but plenty for the tone. It is a realistic touch that captures the fluidity of experience, the way that a person enters our lives for a moment and then disappears. To return to the analogy with poetry, instead of rhyme we are given a parenthesis, a personal aside that exists for its own sake, and for what it tells us about how we live.

The first two minutes of the film establish that we are on the uncertain ground of mixed tones, that we are being catapulted from crime melodrama to comedy to love story, and that the movie is not conforming to any of our assumptions. It unsettles us and forces us to experience it in its own terms. Truffaut leads us to an awareness of how close laughter and suffering can be and how experience is more complex than the terms with which we label it.

This aesthetic and moral position (amoral with respect to con-

ventional standards, but loyal to its own values of tolerance) took
shape during his years as a critic. For example, in *Arts* 598 (1956) he
praises Renoir for "the bitterness of the gay moments, the clownish-
ness of the sad," and calls attention to the qualities in Jacques Becker's *Casque d'or* that would become so apparent in his own films:
"*Casque d'or*, sometimes funny and sometimes tragic, proves finally
that, through the refined use of change of tone, one can move
beyond parody, look at a picturesque and sorrowful past, and then
revive it with tenderness and violence" (*FV*, 196). Becker had been
assistant to Renoir; therefore, it is not surprising that Truffaut also
recognizes in his work the primacy of character, an element that
unifies the work of all three directors. When he writes about
Touchez pas au grisbi, Truffaut claims, "Becker is saying to us,
'What interests me first is characters' " (*FV*, 198). In a similar vein,
he singles out John Ford: "What I like in the work of Ford is that he
always gives priority to the characters" (*FV*, 87). This is not merely
an infatuation with quirky personality; rather this priority points to
how *individuals* will be the source, material and goal, the manner
and the matter, of Truffaut's films. As Don Allen points out, "his
'landscape' is reduced to the human level; his portraits are concerned with the minute fluctuations of confidence, timidity, affection, desire."[16]

In a manner reminiscent of James Agee's film criticism for *Time*
and *The Nation* in the 1940s, Truffaut's articles focus on the quality
of human experience within the films, and the effect upon it after
the lights go on. Although Truffaut goes beyond Agee in his concern
with cinematic form ("when I was a critic I thought that a film, to be
successful, must express simultaneously an *idea of the world* and an
idea of the cinema" [*FV*, 17]), both critics are especially sensitive to
the way movies condition our perceptions and self-images through
identification with characters.[17] For instance, they share a deep love
for Chaplin, about whom Truffaut can claim, "Without either wish-
ing or realizing it, Chaplin helped people to live" (*FV*, 17). He
proceeds to place Charlot's work in a biographical context (an approach practiced fruitfully by Agee with directors like Jean Vigo and
Preston Sturges). Our appreciation and understanding of Chaplin
are deepened when we consider the following:

Charlie Chaplin, abandoned by his alcoholic father, lived his first years in
the fear of seeing his mother dragged to the asylum, and then after she *was*

taken away, in the terror of being carried off by the police; it was a little nine-year old tramp who defaced the walls of Kensington Road. . . . When Chaplin will enter the Keystone world to make chase films, he will run faster and farther than his colleagues from vaudeville because if he is not the only filmmaker to have described hunger, he is the first to have lived it, and this is what the spectators of the entire world will feel when the reels begin to circulate in 1914.[18]

Like Agee (and Bazin), Truffaut is no less interested in the social foundations and implications of the films, particularly since the social and the personal constantly feed upon each other. It is no coincidence that two of the films he mentions most often in his criticism are *The Great Dictator* and Ernst Lubitsch's *To Be Or Not To Be*, both of which depict the horror of war, but through dark humor at the expense of the Gestapo "personality." In the latter, Jack Benny plays a Polish actor impersonating Nazi officers (!), incarnating what Lubitsch suggests are the dominant traits of the Reich: vanity and fear of superiors. In *The Great Dictator*, Truffaut sees how the source of issues is personality or "identity." Building upon Bazin's excellent article about the way *The Great Dictator* is "a settling of accounts with Hitler, who deserved this lesson for having had the double impudence to appropriate Charlot's moustache and having raised himself to the level of the gods," Truffaut proposes that, in 1939, Hitler and Chaplin were indeed the most famous men in the world: "In repressing Hitler's moustache to reinstate the myth of Charlot, Chaplin destroyed the myth of the Dictator" (*FV*, 76). This leads Truffaut to a perceptive reading of Chaplin's body of films, which he divides into a concern with two figures: the vagabond and the most famous man in the world. Truffaut finds the question raised by the first image to be "Do I exist?" while the second attempts to respond to it with "Who am I?" He concludes that the work of Chaplin, taken in its totality, "revolves around the major theme of artistic creation: identity" (*FV*, 86).

It is not difficult to see the connection between this reading of Chaplin and almost any Truffaut film, from *The 400 Blows* to *The Story of Adèle H.* (via *Shoot the Piano Player, Fahrenheit 451, The Wild Child*); all of these center on characters in the act of creating their identities (Antoine through his "anti-social" experiences, Adèle through her diary), or responding to other people who attempt to form them (Charlie with Theresa and Lena, Montag in

Fahrenheit 451 with Clarisse and Linda). Like Charlot, Truffaut's characters tend to be outsiders, momentarily controlling the worlds they enter—as when they are in love—but ultimately powerless, and alone. They are bundles of energy and pain, triumph and loss. Charlie in *Shoot the Piano Player* is a touching example of a Truffaut male who is somewhere between vagabond (Charlie the piano player) and the most famous man in the world (Edouard Saroyan, the concert pianist). At the beginning of the film, we meet a man who is fragmented: his brother calls him Edouard, but he says to call him Charlie like everyone else. This split in outer definition is then mirrored by an inner split: we often hear his internal monologues on the soundtrack, but in conflict with his externalized behavior. This takes poignant shape when he is walking with Lena (Marie Dubois), agonizing over whether to touch her hand, while we are presented with extreme close-ups of his clenched fists. And, of course, just when he musters up the courage to ask her out for a drink, he finds she has disappeared.

Charlie's timidity is a question of timing: he is too late with Lena, and more tragically, too late in the flashback with Theresa. There again, his inner voice yells, "Take her in your arms, forgive her," but he abandons her. Moments later, he runs back in, but it is too late and she has jumped to her death. Truffaut displays an understanding of how identity is dependent upon time, that it is not so much what we do as *when* we do it. Physical surroundings take second place to psychological movement: "I know it's a bit unusual, but I don't like landscapes or things. I like people; I'm interested in ideas and feelings."[19] There is the suggestion in his films that people can choose their space; characters and vehicles are constantly moving through a succession of spaces but are controlled and defined by time (consider the frenetic opening sequence of *The Soft Skin*). It doesn't matter where most of them go (are Pierre and Nicole any different when they escape from Paris?) since their inner landscapes are always part of the baggage; what matters is whether they timed it correctly: in *Jules and Jim*, Catherine and Jim's arrivals and letters—one beat off, or the violent end of *The Soft Skin* because Pierre gets to the phone a minute too late. Space exists, of course, but time is inexorable.

For Charlie, action and intention do not come together in time—except when he is playing his old honky-tonk tune, which has perfectly regular rhythm. Within his music, time is a given, a space

Credit: Janus Films

Shoot the Piano Player: Charlie Kohler/Edouard Saroyan (top); "the gangsters" (bottom).

to be filled by regular pulses. But when it comes to people, he
misses too many beats. The significant exception is with the
prostitute Clarisse: their encounter is uncomplicated, and this is
underlined by a metronome ticking predictably before they frolic in
bed. He can't bring himself to press the impresario's bell, and enters
only because a woman opens the door to leave. This scene illustrates
the way Truffaut incorporates *temps-mort,* the moments of indeci-
sion which force us to experience time the way the character does.[20]
Charlie wants to be kind to his boss, Plyne, but ends up murdering
him in self-defense. He loves Theresa and then Lena, but is indirectly responsible for the deaths of both.

In an illuminating article entitled "Through the Looking Glass,"
Roger Greenspun helps us see that Truffaut creates a stylistic
analogue for the split in Charlie's identity. Despite the seeming lack
of structure in *Shoot the Piano Player,* the film is tightly based in
correspondences and mirror images, which also serve to suggest
that life repeats itself. The outer frame of the film is the present with
a love story between Charlie and Lena, a waitress. The inner frame
is the flashback with a love story between Edouard and Theresa,
also a waitress. The third party in the outer story is Plyne, whose
interest in Charlie's girl parallels that of Schmeel in the past. Both
men give Charlie a job and both claim they know what is wrong with
him (fear and timidity). Edouard runs out on Theresa because she
has become (in her words) soiled, a dirty old rag; he runs to the
defense of Lena because Plyne has called her soiled (which also
points up the similarity between Charlie and Plyne in their extreme
view of women). Theresa plunges to a dark death, Lena falls to her
death in the snow. Greenspun adds that in the past we have "a
romantic tale of dedicated love and brilliant success supported by a
grimy business deal" and in the present, "an obscure and sordid life
briefly illuminated by a recklessly romantic dream."[21]

The doubling even extends to Theresa's personality, as she tells of
how Lars Schmeel worked like a spider, cutting her in two—heart
and body. Now she looks for the old Theresa but finds only a new
one. This unfaithful mirror is visually reinforced by the numerous
mirrors used throughout the film. Charlie is partially seen through
the mirror that hangs above him in the cafe; the fragmentation of his
relationship with Theresa is enacted before the mirror in their bedroom; toward the end, Charlie will stare at his reflection in the
cracked mirror hanging in the kitchen of the cabin. This theme of

doubling coexists with the circularity of the film, the fact that the last images we see are Charlie being introduced to the new waitress, and his haunting face in closeup as he falls back into the mechanical tune.

The last shot of *Shoot the Piano Player* bears a resemblance to the endings of other Truffaut films. *The 400 Blows* ends with the boy escaping from reform school, running toward the sea, and when he reaches the water, a freeze-frame of his face expresses uncertainty. Truffaut's third film, *Jules and Jim* (1961), ends with Jules walking away from the coffins of his wife and best friend, with what appears to be a combination of loss and relief. All three endings blend freedom and ambiguity as we leave a male character who has gone through harrowing experiences; there can be no certitude about where he will go from here. Greenspun goes so far as to call them "emblems of life's possibilities exhausted," although perhaps they are rather survivors who have managed to endure severe trials. All three are alone, not very heroic, but certainly worthy of our sympathy. Antoine and Charlie are presented in extreme close-up which forces us into intimacy with the character. Chaplin was usually able to move away from the camera, twirling his cane; Charlie Kohler cannot take advantage of such mobility, and retreats behind his piano (and the more abstract realm of twirling his melody). In both cases, the instruments have become extensions of the protagonists' bodies, emblems of their identities.

The extent to which Truffaut was consciously working out such a parallel is uncertain; however, if one is dealing with the films of a cinéphile, it is fairly safe to assume that a cinematic sensibility, informed by bits from thousands of beloved movies, permeates the work. This can take the obvious form of the dream sequences in *Day for Night*, in which the director Ferrand (played by Truffaut) is haunted by the image of a little boy stealing the stills of *Citizen Kane* from a movie theater. Or it can be the more subtle connections between *Citizen Kane* and *Shoot the Piano Player*, such as the use of music as a narrative device, to link scenes and to give them an emotional tone. Truffaut claims he knew *Citizen Kane* by heart, more as a record than a film, particularly through the overlapping music that would signal new scenes: "Before *Citizen Kane*, nobody in Hollywood knew where to put the music in films. In this sense, *Citizen Kane* is the first—and only—great radiophonic film. Behind each scene, there is a conception of sound that gives it its color . . ."

(*FV*, 296). Equally influential might be the ambiguous presentation of a central figure who is alternately sympathetic and destructive, adored and alone. Charlie Kane and Charlie Kohler both have numerous identities; Charlie's timidity and Kane's aggressiveness are two sides of their common need for the one thing they want but cannot sustain: love.

Even the very telling of the story through flashback in *Shoot the Piano Player* harks back to *Citizen Kane*. One could argue that any film with a temporally fragmented narrative is therefore indebted to Welles. Precisely, Truffaut would claim. For in his article, "Citizen Kane, Le Géant Fragile," he declares that this film was most responsible for turning the greatest number of people into filmmakers. Welles' influence is described as "indirect and subterranean" (*FV*, 294) [22]—and well it might be for Truffaut who had seen *Citizen Kane* at least thirty times! This film's impact on the New Wave is all the more comprehensible when we realize the extent to which it is visually innovative and totally *personal*. Truffaut is able to compare Welles' visual style to that of Chaplin, since both organize technique "around the physical presence of the auteur-actor in the center of the screen" (*FV*, 298). Truffaut would make this an organizing principle for himself by starring in the *The Wild Child, Day for Night*, and *The Green Room*.

One can sense in this essay and throughout Truffaut's criticism a hunger for intimacy with the director, a desire for the artist to make himself present through the film—if not on screen, then through personal touches. We learn that even as a child, he felt a great need to enter *into* the films—a need which he fulfilled by sitting increasingly closer to the screen (*FV*, 14). His articles transform the act of passive movie-watching into a process of communication, and in writing about the film, he becomes an integral part of that process. He admits in an interview, "I would invariably review a film while thinking of its director. I wanted to try and touch him . . . above all to convince him."[23] In this sense, film watching, film reviewing and filmmaking become one continuous conversation. (His criticism is often as much concerned with telling the director what to do with his next film as with persuading the audience what to do with the present one!)

In the same essay, he definies the "critique de cinéma" as one who is inclined to analyze his own pleasure (*FV*, 299). Criticism is acknowledged to be an ultimately subjective act, rooted in the degree of interaction between film and spectator, or between cinéaste and cinéphile. In a major article (*Arts,* May 15, 1957), Truffaut declared, "Tomorrow's film will resemble the man who makes it, and the number of spectators will be proportional to the number of friends of the director." Criticism therefore becomes a means of increasing this number of friends.

However, this portrait of Truffaut as sympathetic critic is incomplete, even if it is the aspect he presents in his collected articles, *Les Films de ma vie.* In fact, he was as ruthless as he was respectful, as cruel with French *metteurs-en-scène* as he was courageous with American "auteurs." Because he loved the cinema so passionately, he felt it his duty to condemn anything that hindered its growth. His colleague Jacques Doniol-Valcroze said in 1958, "In a few years François Truffaut has become the most famous of the young film critics. What many muttered under breaths he dared to say out loud. . . . He has firmly kicked the conformist backside of the French cinema."[24] *L'Express* went farther and called him "a hateful *enfant terrible* who put his foot in his mouth with unbearable self-conceit" (*400 Blows,* 222). His reputation was based upon pieces in *Arts* and *Cahiers du Cinéma* which continued with uncompromising fervor the line of attack of "Une certaine tendance du cinéma français." Each week, readers were told that the French commercial products could not measure up to the standards of Renoir, Vigo, Ophuls; plots were trite, dialogue uninspired, acting stilted, and charm absent.

At this time, he was growing sensitive to plot construction since he had to recount the story of each film for *Arts.* After the predominantly visual experiencing of the American films, he moved into an awareness of basic narrative material, as he was forced to reconstruct it via plot and dialogue. Admitting that he had formerly been so intoxicated "with the idea of 'cinema' that I could see nothing but a film's movement and rhythm," he now views this period as corresponding with "what must be the experience of a scriptwriter." And because he became so conscious of the dangers within scripts—the inherent tendency toward triteness—he later turned as a filmmaker to improvisation on the set as a means of counteracting these dangers.[25]

Truffaut has softened since the fifties, for his reviews are no longer the admonishments of a frustrated director. As soon as his first feature was completed, he was able to confess, "I have become more indulgent—that is to say, I have lost all intention of reforming cinema . . . I only want to make good films" (400 Blows, 234). He can now acknowledge his poor judgment of John Ford, for example: "As a critic, I didn't like him and I certainly wrote two or three nasty articles. I had to become a director and turn on the TV to find *The Quiet Man* before I could measure my blindness" (FV, 31).[26] His articles during the 1960s and 1970s are still aggressively affectionate with fresh talent, still insistent that cinema possesses and must develop its own language, still humble toward the old masters, but no longer can he be called "the grave-digger of French cinema." His pleasure in a contemporary film like Claude Berri's *Le Vieil Homme et l'enfant (The Two of Us)* (1967) stems from principles familiar to us from his own films and those of his mentors: "If one feels an intense pleasure in seeing this film, it is because it leads us from surprise to surprise, we can never anticipate the following scene and, when it arrives, we love it and recognize it as true while being astonished at the madness it conceals" (FV, 348). And he still criticizes where necessary: even in 1971 he needs to point out that

too many scenarios throughout the world are considered in terms of the literary effect they will have in producers' offices; they constitute something like novels in pictures; pleasant to read . . . but . . . the logic of cinema has its own rules, which have not yet been well explored or stated. (FV, 281)

And in 1977, he laments the general decline of his former school, the American cinema, though he singles out for praise Alan J. Pakula's *All the President's Men* and the work of Milos Forman, and he appears as the star of Steven Spielberg's *Close Encounters of the Third Kind.*[27]

Nevertheless, we should be aware that by the early seventies, the same man who had equated cinema with primarily visual expression twenty years before has altered his definition a bit. The former champion of the "caméra-stylo" now says in an interview of 1970 that he learned during *Fahrenheit 451* how "dialogue was more important in a film than I had realized. It is, in fact, the *most* important thing."[28] After making a few films, he defined his medium as a combination of the literary, the musical, and the visual.[29] He is now more sensitive to the soundtrack and, as we can see from *The Story of Adèle H.* and *The Man Who Loved Women*, is increasingly drawn to voice-over commentary. In a recent interview, he likens this verbal narration to music, and calls it a means of bringing the spectator into the character's confidence. Moreover, he acknowledges his attachment to "forms of narration which interest few people these days because the fashion is direct confession."[30] Has Truffaut therefore become as cinematically reactionary as his former targets? The evidence points to the contrary. He has rather returned to the stage that preceded the addictive Cinémathèque screenings: when he went to the movies to experience intense emotions above and beyond admiring "the film's movement and rhythm," when form was more of a means than an end. If he seems less enamored of the camera, it may be because he is more in love with his characters. His own response is that the camera is less visible in his films because "I have become more interested in my characters, in their situations, and in what they say."[31]

The underlying impulse seems continuous with all his happiest film experiences: a desire for contact. The cinéphile whose words existed to bring him closer to the director is now the cinéaste whose characters exist to bring him closer to the public. Many of his films end on a note of direct address to the audience: the eloquent faces of young Antoine Doinel or Charlie in close-up, implicating us in their fate; Bernard the prop man speaking for the crew of *Day for Night,* inviting us into their pleasure; Adèle reciting triumphantly from the waves, challenging us in her obsession. Truffaut creates complex emotional bonds between his characters and ourselves and, to the degree that we enter into intimacy with them, we become "friends" of Truffaut. We return to the charm and poignancy of his films because of what they reveal about these characters, and about the director, and—perhaps—about those couples in the balcony of the Gaumont-Palace.

2

The Hitchcockian Strain

TRUFFAUT RECOUNTS in *Les Films de ma vie* how he saw his first two hundred films illegally, illicitly, and with "a feeling of guilt that could only add to the emotions created by the film" (p. 14). One can therefore sense how he would have been especially susceptible to the cinema of Alfred Hitchcock; for the "Master of Suspense" is also the master of presenting and producing paranoia, anxiety, and the guilt of the voyeur who at once watches and wills violence. If Hitchcock leads "respectable" adult audiences (who have paid for their tickets and are not hiding from school) to identify with his guilty characters, we can imagine his powerful effect on Truffaut: ". . . the work of Alfred Hitchcock, which is entirely devoted to fear, seduced me from the beginning . . ." (*FV*, 14). The seduction would become a lasting relationship, with Truffaut—consciously and unconsciously, stylistically and thematically—incorporating Hitchcock into his own films. And the written document that best celebrates this union is his book-length interview (together with Helen Scott), *Le Cinéma selon Hitchcock* (1966, English translation by Helen G. Scott in 1967, *Hitchcock*).

Here Truffaut is the admirer/questioner, and he often places himself in the role of student: "In Hitchcock's work a film-maker is bound to find the answers to many of his own problems, including the most fundamental question of all: how to express oneself by purely visual means" (*H*, 8). Truffaut takes Hitchcock as his "master" not merely because of Hitchcock's virtuosity, but also because the two directors are in agreement over the basis, process, and goal of cinema: arousing emotions. Both have come under attack for making films that are facile, intellectually lightweight, and socially insulated. But we must consider that they are less interested in abstract concepts than in compelling images, less interested in society than in individual situation, less in transient politics than in

39

Julie Kohler (Jeanne Moreau) in The Bride Wore Black.

Credit: The Museum of Modern Art / Film Stills Archive

universal and permanent emotions. And many critics have failed to realize that the playfulness of their films is not without its complexity. Nonetheless, it is apparent from the body of Truffaut's work that there is a basic incompatibility between his vision and Hitchcock's; just as the romantic in Antoine Doinel plays at being a detective in *Stolen Kisses*, the cinematic romantic in Truffaut plays at being a "master of suspense." Ultimately neither succeeds: they get too involved with the characters they are following.

The key to Hitchcock's emotional richness is suspense—not merely shock technique, but a process invested with moral significance. Hitchcock is careful to distinguish between surprise, which is momentary, and suspense, a prolonged state of heightened anticipation, which depends upon the public's being informed about the situation. Truffaut adds that "the whodunit" is a question of *what*—"you simply wait to find out who committed the murder" (*H*, 52)—while suspense is a question of *how*—knowing what to expect, the public waits for it to happen (*H*, 63). Truffaut's succinct phrase, "the art of creating suspense is also the art of involving the audience," should recall his ongoing concern with the active participation of the viewer. A Hitchcock film is for him "a three-way game in which the audience, too, is required to play" (*H*, 11); but anyone who has seriously looked at his own responses to *Psycho*, *Rear Window*, *Strangers on a Train*, or *Shadow of a Doubt* knows that in "playing," the audience is morally implicated in the events and emotions on the screen. For as soon as we identify with a character (something that Hitchcock always elicits through devices such as subjective camera and close-ups)—Anthony Perkins' Norman Bates, James Stewart's photographer, Farley Granger's Guy, Joseph Cotten's Uncle Charlie—our involvement in his actions cannot be brushed aside. Hitchcock builds suspense so that we are set up to expect violence . . . and we are often disappointed when it does not materialize.[1]

Consider *Rear Window* (1954) in which James Stewart is confined to a wheelchair and watches across his Greenwich Village courtyard all that is happening in other apartments. He comes to believe that a neighbor is a murderer and waits for the act to verify his deductions. We wait, we *will* it with him; the Hitchcockian complexity of response demands that we see ourselves as voyeurs. It should come as no surprise that Truffaut displays sensitivity to this aspect of *Rear Window*:

FT: Would you say that Stewart is merely curious?
AH: He's a real Peeping Tom. . . . Sure, he's a snooper, but aren't we all?
FT: We're all voyeurs to some extent, if only when we see an intimate film. And James Stewart is exactly in the position of a spectator looking at a movie. (*H*, 159–60)

Truffaut had already proposed such an interpretation in 1954, during that period in which he demanded that a film express simultaneously "an idea of the world and an idea of the cinema." The filmic self-consciousness so characteristic of the New Wave is nourished by *Rear Window*, for "the courtyard is the world, the reporter-photographer is the filmmaker, the binoculars become the camera lens. And Hitchcock in all this? He is the man by whom we are glad to know we are despised" (*FV*, 107).

What are we to make of this last sentence? Is Truffaut suggesting that Hitchcock appeals to a masochistic impulse in the audience? Do we want to be caught in our voyeuristic activity, to confess our sins in the darkness, both to thrill in the crime and then partake of the punishment?[2] Although Truffaut does not develop his suggestive remark, the descriptions of his own childhood movie-going point to an anxiety about the voyeuristic impulse that cinema fulfills or the vicarious quality inherent in the medium. Is this then the ambivalence of a cinéphile who thinks he should be engaged in some action rather than sitting in a theater, doing rather than watching and, on a more personal level in 1954, directing rather than writing?

In a probing article entitled "Truffaut, Hitchcock and the Irresponsible Audience," Leo Braudy agrees that Hitchcock emphasizes the moral dimension of voyeurism, but he faults Truffaut the interviewer for shying away from larger thematic and structural implications to concentrate on technical details. Although Braudy seems a bit harsh—and we will return to the possible reasons for Truffaut's "skirting of psychological themes and preoccupations" (if these are in fact evasions)—he offers a brilliant analysis of *Psycho* which develops Truffaut's perceptions. He studies how Hitchcock leads us out of detachment and irresponsibility into compelling identification with ambiguous characters. Through the gradually increasing use of a subjective camera, we are first involved with Marion (Janet Leigh), who is an adulteress and a thief, and then with Norman (Anthony Perkins), a Peeping Tom. Braudy shows how the director is then able to manipulate our sympathy for a character who will turn out to be a deranged murderer:

We follow Norman into the next room and watch as he moves aside a picture to reveal a peephole into Marion's cabin. He watches her undress and, in some important way, we feel the temptress is more guilty than the Peeping Tom. . . . Whether we realize it or not, we have had a Norman-like perspective from the beginning of the movie . . . this time, like the first time, we know we won't be caught. We tend to blame Marion and not Norman because we are fellow-voyeurs with him, and we do not want to blame ourselves.[3]

Both Braudy and Truffaut are aware of the extent to which Hitchcock invites our sympathies by visual means, by exploring form to express content. Truffaut locates Hitchcock's "art" in the ability to create drama without recourse to dialogue, and lauds *Psycho*, for example, because "it's a half-silent movie; there are at least two reels with no dialogue at all" (*H*, 214).[4] His questions trace Hitchcock's genius for telling a story cinematically to his work in silent film: he had switched to graphic design after training to be an engineer, and he began his film career by writing and designing title cards. It is noteworthy that three of the most gifted directors in the history of cinema, Eisenstein, Buster Keaton, and Hitchcock, studied mechanics and engineering before they made their mark in film. They share a sensitivity to the dramatic rather than merely decorative potential of objects and a superb sense of timing which feeds into their montage.

Hitchcock exploited like few before him the manipulation of pieces of celluloid that results in the manipulation of the spectator's sympathies, the juxtaposition of shots that creates juxtaposition of emotions. By the time he made *Psycho*, he could boast that the audiences "were aroused by pure film" (*H*, 211). And what is pure film? To take the most violent, gripping and famous example—the scene where Norman stabs Marion to death in the shower—the director is pleased to explain, "Naturally, the knife never touched the body; it was all done in the montage" (*H*, 210).

It would be misleading, however, to suggest that pure cinema is merely montage. Visual storytelling is no less a function of the placement, angle, and movement of the camera. Hitchcock's perfection of devices or "parts of speech" such as subjective camera and close-ups is crucial to Truffaut, who is equally concerned with drawing the viewer close to his characters. For instance, four years after making *The 400 Blows*, he calls his first film Hitchcockian because "one identifies with the child from the first shot to the last."[5] We might feel uncomfortable with this assessment (does identification with a character necessarily signify Hitchcock?) but for Truffaut, Hitchcock's work constitutes a kind of textbook on the technical means to emotional ends. Years later, Truffaut maintained, ". . . in respect to form and the meaning of form, Hitchcock's films have aged the least."[6]

By the time Truffaut made his second feature, *Shoot the Piano Player*, he was influenced by Hitchcock's sense of film construction. The Master expresses less interest in plot than character and less concern with the "what" at the root of the suspense than the "how" of its presentation. Long before Truffaut would sacrifice rigid narrative for character study and emotional fluidity, Hitchcock was working in this direction by indulging in what he calls "the MacGuffin." The term is merely the pretext for the plot, "the device, the gimmick, if you will, or the papers the spies are after" (*H*, 99). *The 39 Steps* provides a fine illustration of the way "the MacGuffin" works: the plot supposedly centers on secret plans, but we become so involved with the meanderings of characters and suspenseful episodes that the original point of the title no longer matters.

In *The 39 Steps* we also find the Hitchcockian predilection, shared by Truffaut, for rapid changes of situation, abrupt shifts in tone. Robert Donat, as the innocent hero who is being hunted by both the police and the villains, escapes from the police station and finds himself at a political rally where he is mistaken for the guest speaker. He is forced to deliver a ridiculous speech, and the dramatic intensity of the thriller yields to the comic as he receives cheers from his audience. We are catapulted from suspense to humor and back. In this fashion, the films of both directors chip away at the complacency of passive movie-goers; the immediacy and intensity of emotional counterpoint demand alertness throughout the film (and, by implication, after the film is over as well). A most effective device in this regard is Hitchcock's red-herring technique, whereby apparently sinister situations turn out to be harmless, while the ordinary reveals danger where it is least expected (suspense and surprise, respectively). Hitchcock also enjoys injecting (or revealing?) malice in settings that are ordinary or incongruous, the classic example being the scene in *North by Northwest* where Cary Grant finds himself in a sunny cornfield when a plane enters from out of nowhere to mow him down.

In Truffaut's universe, death is also present when and where least expected: Gérard's climbing accident in his first film *Les Mistons*; the "accidental" killings of Plyne and Lena in *Shoot the Piano Player*; the sudden drive off the bridge that drowns Catherine and Jim; the murder of Pierre by Franca in a crowded restaurant at the end of *The Soft Skin*; the shock of Alexandre's death in *Day for Night*. And in the films that center on premeditated murder (*The Bride Wore Black, Mississippi Mermaid, Such a Gorgeous Kid Like Me*) we are no less disoriented since the "murderers" are more appealing than the "victims." Many viewers tend to remember only the lightness and lyricism of Truffaut's work, often forgetting the more "Hitchcockian" realms it explores. Thus, when he proposes to his mentor, "it might be said that the texture of your films is made up of three elements: fear, sex and death" (*H*, 240–1), he is pointing to threads in his own fabric as well.

Four films he directed around the time of the interview–book with Hitchcock—*The Soft Skin* (1964), *Fahrenheit 451* (1966), *The Bride Wore Black* (1968), and *Mississippi Mermaid* (1969)—are his most "Hitchcockian" in terms of theme, tone, and technique. On a surface level, they are related to Hitchcock in their use of the Master's collaborators. Bernard Herrmann, who composed for many of Hitchcock's films, was asked to do the score for *Fahrenheit 451* and *The Bride Wore Black*. William Irish (also known as Cornell Woolrich), who wrote the story from which *Rear Window* is adapted, provided the source novels for *The Bride Wore Black* and *Mississippi Mermaid*. On a deeper level, these four films share an atmosphere of paranoia, with guilt, vengeance, and murder the dominant elements.

When *The Soft Skin* was released after the resounding success of *Jules and Jim*, André Téchiné's review in *Cahiers du Cinéma* stated, "*La Peau douce* speaks to us of distances,"[7] and there are indeed numerous spaces—between characters and audience, among characters, within them. The credit sequence signals how to "read" the rest of the film: we see the interlacing hands of a man and a woman, but without the context of faces, bodies, or voices, an impersonal quality results. This is no longer the world of *Jules and Jim*, in which a triangle is connected by warmth, friendship, and a panning camera that sustains and encloses deep emotions. Truffaut moves instead into a story of contemporary adultery that depends upon Hitchcockian principles of editing and visual storytelling to convey its sense of fragmentation.

Pierre Lachenay (Jean Desailly) is a successful writer and lecturer, married to an attractive woman, Franca (Nelly Benedetti). While traveling to lecture on Balzac, he meets a young stewardess Nicole (Françoise Dorléac). Timid and gauche at first (shades of Charlie and Jules), he succeeds in engaging her affections, but they encounter a series of practical difficulties. Under the impression that things will go more smoothly for them away from Paris, Nicole accompanies him to Reims where he is to introduce a film; however, his old friend latches onto him and Pierre proves too weak to get away. He tries to establish a permanent relationship with Nicole, but she leaves him in the half-built apartment he found for them. When Franca learns of the liaison through photographs in his pocket, her passionate nature leads her to track Pierre down to a restaurant where she shoots him with his rifle.

As with *Shoot the Piano Player,* plot summary is wholly inadequate to the experience of this film, since it is the visual texture and rhythm of cutting that create the mood and punctuate the nature of relationships. The desire and emotions of the three characters are relatively absent from the dialogue, but emerge through the more Hitcockian means of looks and objects. Difficulties of verbal communication are reflected in the presence of glass which affirms distances while giving the illusion that it erases them: at the airport, Pierre and Franca greet each other through a wall of glass; the two times that Pierre and Nicole embrace in the car, we see them through the windshield; Pierre communicates with his secretary via a mirror in which they can see each other, but not themselves. These surfaces are like language in the film—meant to facilitate communication, they are clear, but at a remove from deeper contact. A space always exists between the mirror and its contents.

The opening sequence has the quality of cracked glass: we are shown Pierre's frenzied activity in bits and pieces which do not cohere until we learn that he is on the verge of missing his plane for Lisbon. By means of quick cutting, he is propelled through an urban jigsaw puzzle, at the mercy of subway, taxi, traffic lights, elevator, keys, and doorbells, respectively. When Pierre then tells his wife the reason he is rushing, he introduces what Hitchcock defined as suspense, since we become involved and anxious for him to get to

Soft skin against hard glass: Pierre and Franca.

Nicole and—at one remove—Pierre

the airport on time. The presentation of his ride to Orly is a perfect illustration of Truffaut's understanding of Hitchcock. In the introduction to the interview, he remarks,

A man leaves his home, hails a cab and drives to the station to catch a train. This is a normal scene in an average picture. Now, should that man happen to look at his watch just as he is getting into the cab and exclaim, "Good God, I shall never make that train!" that entire ride automatically becomes a sequence of pure suspense. Every red light, traffic signal, shift of the gears or touch on the brake, and every cop on the way to the station will intensify its emotional impact. (*H*, 9)

The montage conveys the jigsaw texture of Pierre's world as we are bombarded with images that connote tense acceleration: jump cuts, a danger sign, close-ups of the hands of the driver on wheel and horn, sections of the car's interior, a foot on the gas pedal, and the windshield (through which Pierre sights the airport, but cannot yet reach it). He runs for the plane, and we breathe a sigh of relief at his departure.

The jagged nature of the movement and the proliferation of objects suggest a dehumanized world in which individuals are not necessarily in control. It is like Hitchcock's arena in which objects are charged with power, functioning as extensions of and vehicles for the characters' emotions and, ultimately, as arbiters of their fate. Hitchcock's films ascribe to *things* a revelatory power, as with the glass of milk in *Suspicion*, the ring in *Shadow of a Doubt*, the cymbals in *The Man Who Knew Too Much*. Film—by virtue of the close-up—can portray objects as overwhelmingly as actors, often making them stars of the drama. *The Soft Skin* contains a cast of light switches, portions of car dashboards, sections of airplane controls, elevator parts, gasoline pumps, camera buttons, dials, doors, and assorted electric paraphernalia. These "extras" of modern technology constitute a mixed blessing: they facilitate mobility (both geographical and emotional) at their best, but also demand the character's attention for fueling, filling, and handling, while remaining impervious to his desires. In fact, one could say that the car and the telephone are the leading actors in *The Soft Skin* for they control the film's relationships and events.

The car appears to be the male principle: we associate it with Pierre from his suspenseful ride to the airport, to his kissing Nicole in the front seat, to his cowardly incapacity to refuse his friend a ride to Paris, to his sudden driving away with Nicole in the night. The automobile is the vehicle for his activity. The telephone, on the other hand, is the instrument of Nicole's personality. She calls Pierre in the hotel; she makes their next rendezvous possible by slipping him a matchbook with her telephone number; and the slightly disembodied quality of phone conversations (can a telephone reveal a whole person?) is symbolic of her character. Her voice travels on air waves, her body makes daily trips through the clouds, but we never see her become her own plane, flying as a complete woman. (Ironically enough, Pierre's wife Franca is a veritable jet.)

Perhaps because the phone has been the medium for Pierre and Nicole, it does not permit communication between Pierre and Franca and brings about his demise. From a restaurant, he telephones his wife's friend Odile and debates about calling Franca, unaware that she is about to come looking for him with a rifle. The scene is palpably Hitchcockian, for suspense mounts as his attempt to call Franca is prevented by another occupant of the phone booth. Truffaut's personal contribution to the situation is his knack for the detail that individuates a character. Pierre returns to his table and shifts his cigarettes from one pack to another. This gesture suggests that he is putting things in order, returning to Franca, making his life neat once more. Precisely at this moment Franca enters the restaurant, with the kind of passion that does not fit into rational organization, and shoots Pierre. In her act of combined love, vengeance, and despair, she becomes another Truffaut emblem of absolutism; she joins characters like Catherine, Julie Kohler, and Adèle H., each of whom demands all or nothing, perfect love or death.

Truffaut would develop these interlocking themes of the difficulties in communication and the role of objects in his next film, *Fahrenheit 451.* In this adaptation of Ray Bradbury's science fiction novel, the civilization of the future is so dehumanized that a giant television set is the "family" and an antenna is a substitute godhead. In this story of a society where books are forbidden, the firemen's job is to burn all the books they can find. (Truffaut's interest in this phenomenon is already visible in *Jules and Jim* where he includes a clip of the Nazi book-burners.) One of the firemen, Montag (Oscar Werner), who is about to be promoted, meets a young woman, Clarisse (Julie Christie); under her influence he begins to read and love books. His own wife Linda (also Christie) denounces him through fear and Montag is led to set fire to his Captain (Cyril Cusack). He escapes to a colony of "book-people"—a band of exiles, each of whom has memorized an entire book and has, therefore, become that book.

Hitchcock can be invoked once more since Truffaut's introduction to the interview-book lists dozens of directors and films influenced by the master and ends with his own *Fahrenheit 451.* Made in the same year as his book's publication, Truffaut's film explores the power of the word—but as a visual more than an oral entity. In a sense, the main characters are the books themselves. Truffaut even noted that he could not allow the books to fall out of the frame: "I must accompany their fall to the ground. The books here are characters, and to cut their passage would be like leaving out of frame the head of an actor" (*J*, 182). During the book-burning, close-ups of pages slowly curling into ashes look almost like fists of defiance. As in *The Soft Skin,* he suggests that the written word can capture and convey emotional depths, while the spoken is doomed to skim the surfaces. The stylistic analogue to this sentiment can be found in the film's subordination of the dialogue to visual expression. Like

Hitchcock with *Psycho*, Truffaut reduced the amount of dialogue: "Half of the film is strictly visual, which makes me truly happy" (*J*, 228).

Beginning with the credit sequence, the tension between what is seen and what is heard makes itself felt. The credits are spoken while the camera zooms in to a series of rooftops, each in a different color. Given a society that bans books, Truffaut withholds the printed word from us so that its first appearance will be a privileged moment. We see only a landscape covered with wires—a magnetic field in which the camera is drawn to center and freeze on one antenna after another. Following these establishing shots, the opening sequence is reminiscent of *The Soft Skin*: the nervous activity within the frame (the sweep of the red fire engine crosscut with a young man who is warned by phone to flee) and between frames (quick cutting) creates an atmosphere of anxiety. Visually evocative of storm troopers in their black uniforms and of Ku Klux Klansmen in the white robes they don for the burning, Montag and his men search the suddenly deserted house. They find a copy of *Don Quixote* hidden in a lamp (and behind a television screen, a library!). Then in a slow-motion shot that contrasts with the accelerated pace thus far and emphasizes their vulnerability, the books fall into a pile that will be ritually burned to ashes.

The film's first conversation (when Montag's Captain tells him of the impending promotion) establishes an essential part of the film's tone, which is again one of distance: he speaks to him as a third person—"What does Montag do on his day off-duty? . . . Montag might be hearing some exciting news"—so that the subject is objectified, removed from direct address. In a similar fashion, Montag's conversations with his wife deprive him of real presence: when he comes home, she looks at the TV while he speaks (she is watching a judo demonstration), their voices competing with the sound of the program. While they are talking, another element of distance is created by our seeing the TV screen rather than the characters. When they go to bed, the space between them is expressed by their separate activities: she takes a pill and watches the set, he looks at a comic book (which has no words!).

The most intimate form of human communication—sex—is presented as mere narcissism. Truffaut added to Bradbury's story haunting images of auto-eroticism on the train: a girl kisses her reflection in the glass, a woman caresses her fur collar, and then Linda is seen stroking her body before Montag comes home. (Even the comic echo of *The 400 Blows'* first classroom scene forms part of this pattern, for in the park scene the man who seems to have a lover's arms around his head turns out to be wrapped around himself!) The only time we see Montag and Linda kiss—when she playfully pulls him down with her on the bed—is attributed to the blood transfusion she has just undergone after taking an overdose of pills.

The film therefore constitutes a departure from Truffaut's typical material, namely relationships of love and solidarity. The tension and affection usually found between a man and a woman are relocated between individuals and books, for Truffaut presents the texts as concrete, sensuous objects, each with its own texture and human story. The equivalent for a tentative kiss in his other films is Montag beginning to read *David Copperfield;* the equivalent for the anguish of romance is the burning of the books (with the title referring to the temperature at which paper burns); the equivalent for lovemaking is the process by which the book-people learn their texts by heart—becoming the thing they love.

As *Day for Night* would be a tribute to the cinema, *Fahrenheit 451* pays homage to literature as artifact of human expression; Montag learns that "behind each of these books there is a man" (a discovery Truffaut made ten years earlier about a film and its auteur). But the manner in which the books take on life is less related to the lyrical sincerity of *Day for Night* than to a more Hitchcockian approach that juxtaposes banality and incongruity. At the end of his Journal, Truffaut makes clear that the idea of mixing tones and genres gives birth to his films: "In the case of *Fahrenheit 451,* it was a question of treating a fantastic story in an offhand way, making the fantastic seem banal and the banal seem odd" (*J*, 234–5). (For example, Truffaut considers Jacques Demy's *Umbrellas of Cherbourg* as science fiction because ordinary events have one twist: the characters sing instead of speaking!)[8]

The most compelling image that returns to the common its (often-forgotten) miraculous quality is that of Montag learning to read. By means of a subjective camera, we begin *David Copperfield* through his eyes, entering with him what might be termed a religious experience. The sacred quality of the encounter between man and book is heightened by his wearing a bathrobe which resembles that of a monk. By the light of the television screen (another touch of incongruity) he reads haltingly aloud while we see his finger accompanying each line (not unlike other Truffaut protagonists stroking a woman's profile or leg). The first words of the novel are, appropriately enough, "I was born," establishing a book as a record of one's life as well as the beginning for the reader. The camera moves into increasingly closer shots of the print, conferring upon it the status of a living being; the rhythm of the editing suggests the "heartbeat" of the text.

David Copperfield signals how literature is the process of recording and recounting, and it is tantamount to the power of memory for Montag. He later asks Linda when they first met and she cannot remember. (It is significant, therefore, that Clarisse will become a memoir, *Les Mémoires de St-Simon*.) Without the written word, continuity cannot be sustained. The books of *Fahrenheit 451* can be connected with the letters that proliferate through all of Truffaut's work for, in both cases, the printed word has threefold magic: it enters through the eye, rides through imagination/emotion, and remains in memory.

Montag's sense of personal history commences with this clandestine entry into art (perhaps not unlike Truffaut's boyhood refusal of social convention—school—for the heightened experience of sneaking into films). With an existential awareness that an individual is the sum of his actions and words, Montag creates a self through questions and choices. When the firemen search people during the following sequence in the park, he feels a book in a man's pocket; Truffaut reframes so that half the screen becomes black—a partial wipe that isolates the characters—and the music rises. Montag lets him go, and the screen's full space is restored. The wipe's appearance is like a graphic holding of the breath. We see Montag undergoing a transformation from the conformist values represented by Linda to the liberating risks and commitments symbolized by Clarisse. It is therefore noteworthy that Truffaut was one of the critics (along with Chabrol and Rohmer) who pointed out that Hitchcock's films usually center on a transfer of identity, such as the "exchange" of killings in *Strangers on a Train*. The point of departure for Hitchcock's transfer is usually crime (as in *I Confess*, when Montgomery Clift as the priest assumes the burden of guilt after hearing the killer's confession).

In *Fahrenheit 451*, Clarisse is the catalyst for Montag's conversion to "criminal" status. Because of her questions, he begins to think, implicates himself in her "guilt," and enters that great Hitchcockian

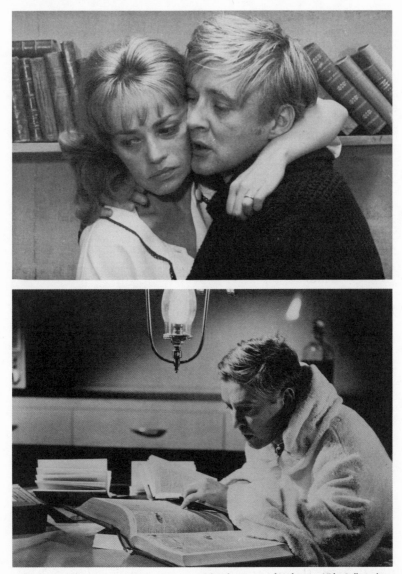

From love to literature: Oscar Werner with Jeanne Moreau in *Jules and Jim*, and with his books in *Fahrenheit 451*.

tradition of a man who is both the hunter and the hunted. This theme reaches its climax when Montag and his men ride out to search the house of a suspected book-possessor—and it turns out to be his own. Here, the character transformation is completed when he sets fire to his own bed, symbolically destroying the Montag who was defined by Linda. His movement into a more "Clarissian" identity is conveyed through powerful visual means that point to Hitchcock's direct influence. We watch Montag tossing and turning in a nightmare during which Clarisse lights a match in slow motion. (This image refers to a preceding scene in which the old lady with whom she lived refused to leave her books and insisted on burning along with them.) As he awakes, Montag's face is superimposed and fades into that of Clarisse in the same position, visually echoing an unforgettable shot in Hitchcock's *The Wrong Man* (1957), in which Henry Fonda plays a musician who has been mistakenly accused of robbery because of his physical resemblance to the real criminal. The latter walks by while Fonda is in a church, and his face in the glass is superimposed on Fonda's. Gradually, Fonda's face becomes his.

Hitchcock seems to hover in the background with respect to Truffaut's character depiction as well. Many of Hitchcock's films elicit a simultaneous attraction and repulsion for a character, and we often find villains who are more appealing than the heroes. He once quipped, "The more successful the villain, the more successful the picture" (*H,* 141). After casting Cyril Cusack as the fear-inspiring captain in *Fahrenheit 451,* Truffaut realized that the character would be "terribly sympathetic, and this is quite good. Thanks to this, we move away from melodrama and the role will be more alive" (*J,* 176). Montag, on the other hand, is one of Truffaut's least likeable male protagonists. In a Journal entry toward the end of filming, Truffaut writes that Cusack introduced humanity into his role whereas Montag now appears more of a bastard when he kills him; "But since I don't like heroes, everything is fine," he adds (*J,* 202).

There is a crucial element of ambiguity throughout the film with respect to all the characters and situations. For despite the need and love for books that Truffaut presents through Montag, the book-people, and the texts themselves, the Captain's condemnations are not without their ring of truth. Books do in fact make Montag and the other readers anti-social, unable to live with their surroundings. (Complementing the statement that literature "makes people want

to be something else" is a shot of *Madame Bovary*, itself a denuncia-
tion of romantic novels.) Montag becomes monomaniacal, obsessed
with reading, and cruel to Linda and her friends. And the Captain's
point about philosophy being even worse than novels—each book
asserting "I am right"—indicates as much about the presumptuous-
ness and vanity of certain writers as the desirable (to us) multiplicity
of perspectives they offer.

The last scene (which Bradbury called one of the most beautiful in
the history of film)[9] reinforces this ambiguity since the book-people
do not in fact talk to each other, they simply recite their lines. We
hear a babble of voices and we see a group of wandering bodies, but
there is no suggestion that this is a unified society that could affect
the "real world." As an alternative, it is attractive (emphasized by
the panning camera rather than the rapid cutting of the earlier
scenes), but ultimately unsatisfactory. The individual who has become *Wuthering Heights* or *Alice in Wonderland* may not necessarily be less of an automaton than the "cousins" who watch television.
The amount of self-absorption may not be less than that of the
women we saw stroking their bodies. The last shot of a still lake in
winter conveys the impression that what is underneath is frozen and
that, like the book-people, it exists primarily because of its potential
for reflection.

Nevertheless, ice melts: the book world can be seen as less of an
alternative than a valiant and incomplete effort at maintaining a
portion of civilization during a Dark Ages. They await a "Renais-
sance" in the springtime. Montag's escape is presented as a liberation, similar to that of Antoine in *The 400 Blows:* a tracking camera
accompanies his flight into freedom. The book he has chosen to
memorize is Edgar Allan Poe's *Tales of Mystery and Imagination.*
After having been a functionary of the state, he will now serve a
realm in the universe of art and free thought. He gives up his name
to become not an "homme-libre" (free man) but an "homme-livre"
(book man). He *is* free, but less as a human being than as an instrument for the text he has chosen to become.

Julie Kohler, the "heroine" of *The Bride Wore Black*, is similarly
free from all external restraints, but a slave to an idea, namely her
monomaniacal desire for revenge. This next film by Truffaut is considered his homage to Hitchcock, but is remarkably consistent with
his own work as well, even in other genres. Jeanne Moreau plays a
widow who murders five men. Midway through the film, a flashback

Credit: *The Museum of Modern Art / Film Stills Archive*

Book burning in *Fahrenheit 451*.

Charles Denner and Jeanne Moreau in *The Bride Wore Black*.

reveals that the victims were formerly friends; they had accidentally shot a young man who was emerging from the church where he had just been married—this man was Julie's husband. The theme of an inexorable and depersonalized force operating through Julie is introduced in the credit sequence: we see pictures of a woman, devoid of expression, being stacked mechanically one after the other. Like the credit sequence of *Fahrenheit 451*, the images suggest something enclosed, framed, inorganic, and the repetition of motion frozen into a still. Julie will incarnate these qualities in her ruthless quest to even the score, which in her terms is five to one.

A Hitchcockian "exchange" does, of course take place,[10] while our reactions to the characters are extremely ambivalent. Julie is perhaps the least sympathetic of Truffaut's heroines, particularly when she and we discover that the five men had no intention of harming her husband. But the film draws upon Hitchcock's complex interrelationships of guilt and innocence, villains and heroes, crime and audience empathy. We are drawn into a world where the men say they felt both "guilty and innocent," which may be the only way we can finally see Julie—and, through identification, ourselves. One could say that the exchange occurs before the action begins: Julie the woman has died with David; Julie the avenger has assumed the identity of David's ghost.[11] This is visually presented during the flashback, just after his death, through the exchange of rings: in an extreme close-up, Julie removes the signet ring from his hand and puts it on her own index finger. Later, she temporarily assumes the identity of a schoolteacher, Mademoiselle Becker, in order to infiltrate the home of her third victim.

Hitchcock's comment that all villains are not black and all heroes are not white[12] informs *The Bride Wore Black*, and Truffaut finds an effective visual equivalent for this moral perspective. Julie is seen in both the white gown of innocence and the black garb of anguish, but in most scenes she wears patterns that starkly combine both dimensions. In this color film, she wears *only* black and white; her clothes represent her absolutism—the purity of her motives, the darkness of her deeds. Black and white appear in sustained conflict on her body (the black glove that undercuts her white dress when she acts as a model, the white cape that qualifies her black dress as she prepares the second murder). Black stripes forcefully declare themselves on Julie's white dress, indicative not only of her internal struggle which surfaces toward the end, but also of the way good and evil are interwoven in the films of both directors.

The Julie Kohler of the film is presented in a more sympathetic light than the Julie Killeen of the novel, and the change of name should alert us to the resonances within Truffaut's work. In connecting her to Charlie Kohler of *Shoot the Piano Player*, we remember someone who has suffered because of the death of his wife and has attempted to change his identity into one that resists strong emotions. He defines himself by one honky-tonk tune, Julie by the strains of the Wedding March. Kohler also invokes "colère" (anger, madness), thereby rendering Julie's name continuous with her obsessive behavior. But if Charlie's problem was that he could not quite integrate intention and action because of timidity, Julie compensates by aggressively executing all her plans. The unique handling of each murder renders her an artist of sorts: she fulfills and therefore assumes a different role for each victim, and is consistently a convincing actress; she is also a fine *metteur-en-scène*, engineering props and movements for maximum effectiveness.

Our interest in the way she sets up the situations—and in her survival—is due to Truffaut's alteration of the novel according to Hitchcockian principles. Whereas Irish does not let the reader know the motivation for Julie's acts until the end of the book, thereby rendering it a mystery, Truffaut informs us through a flashback after the second murder, thereby introducing suspense. We are made to care less about *why* she kills them than *how* she does so. The novel is less capable of inviting our identification with her since it also devotes more attention to the detective who follows her. Truffaut prefers to present the events through Julie's point of view which becomes, to some extent, that of the audience through awareness of motives, subjective camera, and close-ups. In addition, whereas the novel revealed that she had killed the wrong men, Truffaut maintains a complex balance of sympathy by making them the right men, but not altogether guilty of the crime.

Julie's character in relation to her men will be explored in Chapter Four; but for the purposes of our attention to Hitchcock's influence on Truffaut, her methods merit discussion here. Her victims constitute a cross-section of male types, and each meets a death consistent with his character. The first is the vain Bliss (Claude Rich), whom she pushes off a balcony by tantalizing him with her scarf. There is less horror than humor in the scene since the camera does not follow the body but remains with her long white scarf as it floats down. The second is the pathetically romantic Coral (Michel Bouquet) whom she poisons. We meet him marking the level of gin in his bottle because he is suspicious of the maid but unaware that she waters it down. Julie adds something more fatal to the bottle from which he drinks. Third is the pompous politician Morane (Michel Lonsdale) who is locked in a closet and left to suffocate. Before the fourth murder, Truffaut humanizes Julie a bit when the real Mlle Becker is accused in her place and she calls the police to establish the teacher's innocence. This is followed by a scene in a confessional where she pauses to gather the strength to continue with her revenge and declares that she is dead already. The fact that Julie is now a potential victim herself adds a note of vulnerability to her and tempers the efficiency she has displayed. This is conveyed visually by the white scarf which hangs from the back of her neck like a noose. Her fourth attempt is then frustrated since the crooked car-dealer Delvaux (Daniel Boulanger) is suddenly arrested. Julie postpones their rendezvous and addresses herself instead to the artist Fergus (Charles Denner).

Here, Truffaut indulges in manipulating, misleading, and playing with the audience in a manner worthy of his master. Fergus is perhaps the most appealing figure since he is presented as a sensitive painter, bearing a physical resemblance to Antoine/Charlie/Truffaut (and we are led to think he may be spared when he proposes the quintessentially Truffautesque activity of going to the movies), and he is the only one who makes Julie lose her composure and miss her mark. Fergus is the sole man who tells her, "I love you," and takes from her the signet ring or symbol of revenge. But visual touches keep us in constant doubt. Hitchcock's remark about *Psycho*, "you turn the viewer in one direction and then in another; you keep him as far as possible from what's actually going to happen" (*H*, 206), is relevant here, for just as we assume that the knife in Morane's kitchen was a murder weapon, but it turned out to be for snipping the wires, so the razor in Fergus' apartment is ominous, but Julie merely cuts the painting with it. When she holds a bow and arrow (posing, appropriately, as Diana the Huntress), the quivering of the arrow suggests the uncertainty of her determination. At the same time, Corey (Jean-Claude Brialy), who had been present at Bliss' death, returns and we are momentarily tantalized by the possibility that he will realize her identity before she murders Fergus. Between his being "sure he's seen her somewhere before" and her own attraction to her victim, we think Julie will make an exception.

Truffaut places the camera behind Fergus who is painting in the foreground, with Julie aiming the bow and arrow in the background.

The suspense builds as the artist tells her to move the arrow more in his direction, for we are at that point in the position of potential victim. As we prepare for the whiz of the arrow, the doorbell rings, and Fergus is spared. A subsequent shot reveals that his reprieve was short-lived: the camera pans from a ringing telephone (Corey trying to warn Fergus about Julie) to his body on the floor, the arrow upright on his back.

If Fergus' death places us farther from Julie, the last murder swings the pendulum of our sympathy back to her side through protracted suspense. She attends the funeral in order to be caught and taken to the prison where she can find Delvaux. There, she manages to work her way into the kitchen where a close-up of a large knife prepares us for the end. In a similar fashion to *Shadow of a Doubt* or *Rear Window*, we wait for the violence, perhaps willing it, and then recognizing our own complicity in the action. In the last image of transference through which Julie divests herself of any lingering female attributes, she moves from the female section of the prison to the male, dispensing food. The camera remains on the hallway as she moves down and then around the corner. Truffaut has gradually built the intensity of the violence, culminating in the stabbing of Delvaux, which is the most directly brutal murder of the film though we see only the empty hallway. It satisfies our expectations in terms of plot, if not presentation. In the novel Julie is arrested before committing the fifth murder, but here the design is allowed completion; one is permitted the aesthetic pleasure of a job well done. Moreover, by leaving the most despicable victim for the last, Truffaut does not lead to total condemnation of Julie's activities. As Graham Petrie reminds us, "the point of the film is our simultaneous complicity with and revulsion from her, making us uncomfortably aware of potentials within us which we prefer not to acknowledge."[13]

Nevertheless, for all these Hitchcockian aspects, *The Bride Wore Black* does not succeed as a Hitchcockian film. For example, the visual punctuation mark between Julie's murders is a ride in a train or airplane, during which she crosses a name off the list in her little black book. The train recalls Hitchcock's fondness for this vehicle as the locale for climactic encounters, both amorous and violent. But where *Strangers on a Train, The Lady Vanishes, North by Northwest,* and *Shadow of a Doubt* make use of trains for the intersecting of motives, events, or individuals, Truffaut swerves from his model's aims by making the train a setting of *de*-dramatization rather than suspense. Unlike Hitchcock, he never lets us see a violent murder—the last knifing is presented as an off-screen scream—and perhaps demands a more intellectual than physical response. (He is also closer to the oblique way in which Renoir presents murders, as evidenced by the cutaway to a street song in *La Chienne* or to the train screech in *La Bête humaine*.) The recurring image of the train serves to heighten the sense of stasis in movement, of a passenger's suspension as the world speeds past. A shot of Julie's determined face next to a window through which we see the landscape whipping by, makes literal that she is a "still in motion."

Murder is also the basic material of *Mississippi Mermaid*, although the emphasis shifts from its facility to its difficulty since the story is one of love rather than revenge. The uncut version, longer by twenty minutes, is far more rich and persuasive as a love story. Louis Mahé (Jean-Paul Belmondo), a plantation owner on the island of La Réunion, waits at the port for Julie Roussel, his wife-to-be. He has never seen her since they "met" through the marriage ads of a newspaper. The woman who arrives (Catherine Deneuve) bears little resemblance to the photo of Julie, but he is delighted to find her more beautiful, and they marry. Despite certain suspicious aspects of Julie's behavior, they lead a relatively happy existence until she runs away with his money. It turns out that she is an impostor named Marion, and he pursues her to France. He cannot bring himself to fulfill his plan to shoot her after she recites her sorrowful life story and, acknowledging that he loves her, Louis kills instead the detective on her trail (Michel Bouquet). They escape to a cabin (the same one as in *Shoot the Piano Player*) where he realizes she is poisoning him, but is willing to die at the hands of the woman he loves. She then tries to keep him alive, and they walk away together in the snow.

In Truffaut's alteration of William Irish's novel, the characters become less simplistic: Marion is not as cruel, Louis not as naive. Truffaut explained, "that sort of woman isn't a tramp any longer, she's something much more comprehensible, and her victim is no longer entirely a victim. The black and white have become shades of grey. So despite myself, I weakened the contrast between the characters, at the risk of de-dramatising the subject a little."[14] The finality of Louis' death in the book is replaced by the open ending of the lovers' disappearance in the snow.

The credit sequence is again an integral component of the film's theme and texture. We see the personal column of a newspaper, indicative of men and women seeking companionship and placing us in the Truffautesque universe where the search for love is the point of all departures, while we hear the voices. They begin to overlap and become incomprehensible, reminiscent of the encapsulated book-people at the end of *Fahrenheit 451*, who also defined themselves through written and spoken words. The opening sequence then recalls the beginnings of *Fahrenheit 451* and *The Soft Skin* as it creates a mood of nervous anticipation (though we do not know the reason) through jump cuts behind a man driving a car. This atmosphere is sustained by numerous cuts as Louis searches the boat for his bride.

Suspicion then becomes the dominant tone by means of details that are vehicles for betrayal, and visual punctuation that creates tension. The wedding ring is too tight on her finger; she has voiced an aversion to coffee, but enjoys drinking it; the death of her canary elicits no sorrow from her; a small square of her on the left side of the frame widens to reveal the whole scene, and the fact that she is hiding. In the throes of a nightmare, she cries and clutches her throat; when she explains that she can't sleep in the dark, the camera participates in Louis' acquiescence by moving back to include the light which will now remain shining in the bathroom.

We share with Louis the suspicion that Julie is not whom she claims to be, and if we have seen *The Bride Wore Black*, the shared name (added by Truffaut) would intensify this sentiment; the shot of the just-married couple on the church steps also echoes that of Julie Kohler and her short-lived husband. They know each other only by the letters in which they both lied—the opposite extreme from *Fahrenheit 451* in which the characters are deprived of deep contact because removed from the written word. In this sense, their ancestry can be traced to Hitchcock's couples who move between the poles of suspicion and trust. Critic Molly Haskell's perception about 1940s films in general—that suspicion is its own magnet, exerting a strong and sublimated pull[15]—is especially relevant to Hitchcock in films like *Rebecca* (1940), *Suspicion* (1941), *Spellbound* (1945), and *Notorious* (1946) (Truffaut's favorite). Whereas Hitchcock's women are generally the potential victims, Truffaut reverses the roles in *Mississippi Mermaid* so that the woman is the mysterious and powerful force while the man must agonize over his fate at her hands. She is as elusive and inexplicable as the wild birds whose sound we hear each time Louis approaches her trunk.

The letter from and arrival of Julie's sister Berthe (Nelly

Borgeaud), presented with great emphasis through voice, printed page, and superimposed picture of her face, establishes that the transfer of personality in this film is literal. Her identification of the photograph confirms that Louis' wife was not Julie Roussel. Berthe and Louis suspect that Marion may have murdered Julie before assuming her identity. As in the three preceding films of Truffaut's Hitchcockian phase, photographs play a central role in the plot. The pictures of Pierre and Nicole alert Franca to their liaison; Linda betrays Montag by placing his picture in the information box; Julie is arrested because the police photographed Fergus' painting of her. Like books and letters, photographs capture and reveal, record and recount; they are both objects and persons, repositories of identity.

The photograph takes on even more resonance when the detective Comolli cuts out her picture: in close-up the scissor slices *Louis*, perhaps foreshadowing how he will become the object of pursuit later in the film. Like Montag, Louis has had the rug pulled out from under his feet and now enters the realm of nightmare. Both protagonists are haunted by images of linearity and speed, presented through fast tracking shots. Montag's mind flies through the monorail and school hallways, Louis' through road lines that converge, his face superimposed on a car moving through the country. Marion (and Adèle H.), on the other hand, have dreams of choking and sinking, suggesting inner depths rather than horizontal speed, madness more than pursuit.[16]

Louis finds Marion through an accidental glimpse of her dancing on television (again a moving photograph is revelatory) and tracks her down to a sleazy hotel where an iris shot of the gun in his hand establishes suspense. But in a reversal of Theresa's confession to Charlie in *Shoot the Piano Player*—where her feelings of split identity and guilt, combined with Charlie's inability to heed his deeper impulses, led her to death—Marion's story elicits Louis' compassion and declaration of love. However, their relationship then takes a turn toward the sexually abnormal often found in Hitchcock's films. On one level, Louis brings to mind James Stewart in *Vertigo* (1958), who realizes his love for the unstable woman he is trailing, or Sean Connery in *Marnie* (1964), about whom Hitchcock said he liked "the fetish idea. A man wants to go to bed with a thief because she is a thief . . ." (*H*, 227). Marion can be likened to Kim Novak's Madeleine/Judy in *Vertigo* (and it may be more than coincidental that Truffaut changed the name of his heroine to Marion/Julie) in her double identity and trickery of the man who loves her; but more centrally, Marion invokes Marnie in her neurotic sexuality.

Tippi Hedren's Marnie is a thief who changes identity after each robbery she commits; we learn that she has terrifying nightmares and that her need to steal is intimately connected to her frigidity. In Truffaut's film, Marion becomes incapable of making love after Louis finds her; however, after he shoots the detective, she wants him to make love to her with her clothes on. As is generally true of Hitchcock's blondes, there is a constant tension between the extremes of frigidity and nymphomania. One recalls the admittedly healthier examples of Grace Kelly in *To Catch a Thief* or Eva Marie Saint in *North by Northwest*, particularly when Hitchcock delivers his philosophy:

Sex on the screen should be suspenseful, I feel. If sex is too blatant or obvious, there's no suspense. You know why I favor sophisticated blondes in my films? We're after the drawing-room type, the real ladies, who become whores once they're in the bedroom. . . . Sex should not be advertised. An English girl, looking like a schoolteacher, is apt to get into a cab with you and, to your surprise, she'll probably pull a man's pants open. (*H*, 167)

Truffaut calls this "icy sexuality," wondering if the public doesn't prefer the more carnal and tangible women.

Snow White of the virginal visage is no less the temptress, the "mermaid"—half-woman, half-mystery—and the serpent (the mirror of the screen reveals that she can be foul as well as fair), and Truffaut literalizes these metaphors in the film's last sequence. In the cabin, Louis sees a comic strip of Snow White and a poison apple, from which he realizes that Marion is slowly poisoning him for his insurance policy. When he confronts her, she replies, "So you knew all the time," and breaks into tears and confessions of love for him. Our confusion and ambivalence about her are crystallized in Louis' declaration that it is "joy and misery" to look at her, and Truffaut's fairy tale ends with the two reunited (away from the social reality of La Réunion), to live ambiguously ever after. This denouement wreaks havoc with audience expectations and is, therefore, consistent with all the preceding sequences which permit no easy identifications or resolutions.

Since little about the distributed version of the film is satisfying, it ultimately falls short of Truffaut's other efforts. As in *Shoot the Piano*

Player, he pushed the disruption of tone and genre to an extreme, producing (in both cases) a daring artistic experiment and a commercial failure. One of the film's problems is its lack of cohesion; as Truffaut later realized, the sections he omitted from the novel for the sake of economy were probably necessary to plot development and plausibility. Another drawback is the casting, for audiences admitted that expectations are different for big-name stars: the public images of Deneuve and Belmondo got in the way of the characters. *Mississippi Mermaid* had been Truffaut's most expensive production, and its poor showing at the box office determined his conclusions: "Perhaps what I had tried to do before in *Tirez sur le pianiste* and *La Mariée était en noir*—combine an adventure story and a love story—worked less well here . . . as those who don't like it constitute 95%, I have to admit something went wrong."[17]

For Truffaut, a film that does not grab audiences is not great. As early as his review of *Rear Window* in 1954, he articulated his preference for "popular" rather than "elitist" art:

There are two kinds of directors: those who consider the public while conceiving and then realizing their films, and those who do not. For the former, the cinema is an art of spectacle, for the latter an individual adventure. . . . For Hitchcock as for Renoir, in fact for almost all American directors, a film is not successful if it is not a success, in other words if it does not touch the public. *(FV, 104)*

Almost ten years and three films later, Truffaut still found that "being popular art, all films should have popular appeal,"[18] although he went on to qualify his assertion by adding that he was speaking for his own films. We should guard against seeing this attitude as an endorsement of mere entertainment. There is first of all aesthetic rigor and quality: Truffaut pointed out,

It is this dosage of suspense and humor that has made Hitchcock one of the most popular directors in the world (his films regularly gross four times their cost), while it is his great discipline with respect to himself and his art that makes him, equally, a great director. *(FV, 105)*

On a deeper level, he quotes the Master's crucial remark from a 1947 Hollywood press conference:

I aim to provide the public with beneficial shocks. Civilization has become so protective that we're no longer able to get our goose bumps instinctively.

The only way to remove the numbness and revive our moral equilibrium is to use artificial means to bring about the shock. The best way to achieve that, it seems to me, is through a movie. (*H*, 149)

Truffaut believes that pleasing the audience is inseparable from some degree of "planned violence" upon it. We must be led to see and approve of something or someone we would normally refuse to consider—adulterers, murderers, or simply fools. The films of both directors are as much in the service of lucidity as diversion, of emotional flexibility as excitement, of moral openness as pleasure. However, the influence goes just so far and deep until we come to a fundamental distinction between Hitchcock and Truffaut. Hitchcock mentions that he would like to make a film about twenty-four hours in the life of a city, whose "theme might almost be the rottenness of humanity" (*H*, 241). This is a revealing statement, for his films finally offer little love for individuals and little respect for human experience.

Truffaut, the entertainer, visual storyteller, playful audience-manipulator, and explorer of dark moral and psychological realms, has obviously learned some lessons from Hitchcock. But these lessons are ultimately more formal than thematic. Truffaut's current appraisal of the Hitchcockian strain in his work is that it exists less in the thrillers than in *The 400 Blows* and *The Wild Child*. Hitchcock's influence can best be seen in the economy of shots, drama within the frame, and sympathy for weak characters.[19] Thematically, the Master's underlying pessimism would be tempered by the sympathy Truffaut found in Renoir's films. Restless behind Hitchcock's peephole, Truffaut would return to the window which is symbolic of Renoir's more expansive vision.

3

Renoirian Vision

From Renoir to Antoine Doinel

IN HIS INTRODUCTION to André Bazin's *Jean Renoir*, Truffaut
writes,

I am not far from thinking that the work of Jean Renoir is the work of an
infallible film maker. To be less extravagant, I will say that Renoir's work
has always been guided by a philosophy of life which expresses itself with
the aid of something much like a trade secret: *sympathy*. It is thanks to this
sympathy that Renoir has succeeded in creating the most alive films in the
history of the cinema, films which breathe forty years after they were made.
(pp. 8–9)

This comment lends itself to what is perhaps the most striking and
engaging aspect of Truffaut's own work. Both directors form part of
the "lyrical" tradition of French cinema, suffusing their often dark
visions with warmth and humor. The sympathy that one feels in
their work derives in part from the attitude of the director toward
his subject matter, characters, actors, and medium; beyond choices
of script and casting, these attitudes are expressed through camera
placement, camera movement, and montage. There is implicit affection in certain uses of the close-up, pan, or long take in the way that
we are brought closer to the characters, moving and remaining with
them longer.

For younger filmmakers like Truffaut, Renoir's films provided an
ongoing lesson in the primacy of the imperfect individual. It is
difficult to find either "heroes" or "villains" in his work—or in films
like *Stolen Kisses*, *Bed and Board*, and *Day for Night*. As the
marionette in the opening section of Renoir's *La Chienne* (1931)
proposes, "The characters are neither heroes nor villains. They are

Truffaut demonstrates discomfort for Jean-Pierre Léaud in Bed
and Board.

poor people like me, like you. There are three principals: he, she, and the other one, as always."[1] This puppet-show frame typifies how both directors distance us from their characters, thereby balancing sympathy with lucidity. Renoir's frames tend to be visual and theatrical, as in *Le Carrosse d'or* (1952) from which Truffaut's production company, Les Films du Carrosse, takes its name. Truffaut's frames are more often verbal and literary, like the voice-over commentaries of *Jules and Jim* and *Two English Girls*. These self-conscious devices which distance the audience from the work reflect how, within the films, art enables the characters to control their experience; because both filmmakers are concerned with the relationship between nature and art, their characters often oscillate between the conflicting demands of chaotic impulse and aesthetic order.

Stylistically, Renoir and Truffaut balance the rigor of frames with the looseness of their narrative texture. A fine article in *New Republic* focuses on the spirit of casualness that characterizes the films of these directors. Gerald Mast is right to point out how

this spirit has led many critics of both Truffaut and Renoir to dismiss several of the films (particularly the sunniest ones) as "minor" in comparison to the heaviest ones against which they are inevitably measured. But these comic works of acceptance, synthesis and sunshine (say, Renoir's *The River, The Golden Coach,* and *French Cancan* or Truffaut's *Stolen Kisses, Day for Night,* and *Small Change*) are perhaps as "minor" as *The Marriage of Figaro, A Midsummer Night's Dream,* or *City Lights.*[2]

In all of these works, the profundity is inseparable from the playfulness, and the magical aspects from the mundane.

As Renoir made the successful transition from silent to sound films, he tended to depict the miraculous quality within ordinary situations and individuals. In fact, Renoir is considered the precursor of Italian Neorealism. In *Toni* (1934), he laid the groundwork (with respect to both theme and a way of filming) by dramatizing a real incident of a peasant's crime of passion. He went on location to the south of France, used nonprofessional actors, did away with conventional makeup, recorded direct sound, and incorporated the music, customs, and faces of the region. Renoir said, "My aim was to give the impression that I was carrying a camera and microphone in my pocket and recording whatever came my way, regardless of its comparative importance."[3] In its address to the daily life of a poor and relatively uneducated segment of the population, *Toni* looks forward to the early work of Roberto Rossellini, Vittorio De Sica, and Luchino Visconti (who was an assistant to Renoir on this film). However, even in this Neorealist film, Truffaut has called attention to the "fantasy-like atmosphere surrounding the rather ordinary drama."[4]

Truffaut's Antoine Doinel cycle (*The 400 Blows, Antoine and Colette, Stolen Kisses,* and *Bed and Board*) reveals the extraordinary qualities of the "ordinary" situations and individuals of Truffaut's own experience. This is due, in part, to the particularly Renoirian freedom that the director gave his actors in general, and Jean-Pierre Léaud in particular, to create their roles. Whereas Hitchcock demands the subjugation of the actor to the script and overall conception (he once claimed, ". . . the best screen actor is the man who can do nothing extremely well"[5]), Renoir consistently altered scenario and plan according to the impulses and quirks of his actors. Even his method of rehearsal, the "Italian" practice he learned from Louis Jouvet, was geared to permit the personality of a performer to feed into the part. He would have his actors speak their lines as though reading a telephone directory, so that expression would emerge only after several readings of the text.[6] And whereas Hitchcock maintains fidelity to the decoupage or storyboard, in which every shot is pre-planned before the cameras ever begin rolling, Renoir believes that a script is simply a vehicle to be modified as one draws nearer the real intention. As would be true of Truffaut's Doinel cycle, his films owe relatively little to the pre-production stage that is so fundamental to Hitchcock; in Renoir's words, "the artisans of the film . . . are subject to the immutable law whereby the essence is only revealed when the object begins to exist."[7]

In his introduction to *The Adventures of Antoine Doinel: Four Autobiographical Screenplays,* Truffaut acknowledges Renoir's influence in this regard: "It was from Jean Renoir that I learned that actors are always more important than the characters they portray, or . . . that we should always sacrifice the abstract for the concrete" (*AD,* 13). In the course of shooting, Antoine Doinel became the "synthesis of two real-life people: Jean-Pierre Léaud and myself" (*AD,* 7), as Truffaut encouraged the young actor to use the words of his own vocabulary rather than sticking to the script. Ultimately, "Antoine Doinel began to move away from me to come closer to Jean-Pierre" (*AD,* 13), especially in *Stolen Kisses.* Truffaut confessed that Léaud was the raison d'être for the film. (Likewise, Renoir has admitted that he made *The Golden Coach* for Anna Magnani, *Elena et les hommes* around Ingrid Bergman, and *La Bête humaine* because Jean Gabin wanted to drive a locomotive.)[8]

It is this primacy of the individual, and of improvisation, that provides the most direct link between the two directors, particularly because these are not merely aesthetic decisions, but philosophical (and affective) ones. Given the greater risks implicit in this perspective, it would seem that Renoir and Truffaut have less control over the shooting and subsequently have to exercise more control in editing to accommodate and integrate the individual and unpremeditated moments. If Hitchcock's degree of command makes the film totally his creation, Renoir's feeling is that the director is comparable to a chef:

I am convinced that I and other directors are the only cooks capable of making a choice meal. But I also know that we can do nothing without the collaboration of our sauce-makers, roasting specialists, wine stewards, etc. . . . as well as the owner of the restaurant . . .[9]

Stolen Kisses was a response to the limitations imposed by Truffaut's previous Hitchcockian efforts:

Fahrenheit 451 and *The Bride Wore Black* did not allow for improvisation, since they dealt with abstract ideas. I now felt the need to come back to the concrete, to the familiar occurrences of everyday life. (*AD*, 10)

Antoine returns as a young man, about to be discharged from the army for "instability of character." He loves Christine Darbon (Claude Jade) and is drawn to her parents' warmth. After failing at a few jobs, he becomes a private detective. Antoine encounters the woman of his dreams in Fabienne Tabard (Delphine Seyrig), wife of the paranoid shoestore owner (Michel Lonsdale) who has hired him. He writes her a hopeless declaration of love, to which she responds with a visit to his room—and his arms. After he is fired, Antoine becomes a television repairman; Christine purposely breaks her TV set when her parents leave for the weekend. He comes to fix it and spends the night with her; they plan their future over breakfast. When they go out, a man who has been following Christine throughout the film offers her a bizarre declaration of love.

The apparent casualness of the narrative, the attention to details of urban life, the active camera, and the preoccupation with romantic love all point to Renoir's influence. The form is that of "a loosely written chronicle in which improvisation would have the final word" (*AD*, 10). There is consequently less dependence upon linearity and plot than upon density of incident and character (although Truffaut displays more concern with plot than his New Wave colleagues Godard or Rivette). As in *Shoot the Piano Player*, much of the film's cohesiveness stems from the way characters keep telling stories. Perhaps the most important story is the one that Fabienne Tabard relates to Antoine in order to illustrate her point that we are all unique and irreplaceable: "Before he died, my father motioned to his doctor to come closer. He whispered to him: 'People are wonderful' and died a few minutes later . . ." (*AD*, 200). It is significant that while she is saying this, we hear the sounds of the street filtering through the open window. Even the soundtrack fulfills Fabienne's respect for the "ordinary" and reinforces the realism of the scene.

Stolen Kisses brings to mind what Andrew Sarris aptly termed ". . . Renoir's vitally sloppy framing of dramatic action against a fluid background of extraneous life."[10] It is nonetheless tightly structured by a kind of "internal rhyme" or doubling, precisely of the kind that characterizes Renoir's *Rules of the Game*. The film begins and ends with an image of absolute, anachronistic, and impossible love: we first see Antoine behind Balzac's *Le Lys dans la vallée*, a nineteenth-century novel of repressed passion which Antoine will try to reenact with Fabienne, and we will leave him "visibly disturbed" after he hears the stranger tell Christine, "We shall never leave each other . . . not even for an hour . . . for I am definitive" (*AD*, 213). Just as Plyne in *Shoot the Piano Player* represented the extreme of Charlie Kohler's romanticism, this stranger is a caricature of Antoine. The relationship is visually established when a shot of the man following Christine succeeds that of Antoine following a tall woman in black.

In the early moments of the film, Antoine's naïveté is illustrated by his awkwardness on the stairs: he does not know how to get around in a brothel. Toward the end of *Stolen Kisses*, stairs mark the stage of his development, as the camera moves up step by step to reveal that he is in bed with Christine. Likewise, there are two encounters with prostitutes: the first is a disappointment because the woman won't remove her clothes and because he is anxious to keep the promise to his army buddies "to get laid at five on the dot."

The second time in the latter part of the film, the visit is for himself
—he is relaxed and tells the prostitute she can keep her clothes on.
Even a simple object like a vase assumes structural significance:
when Antoine bungles his first job as a night clerk in a hotel, a
cuckolded husband breaks a vase in a comic rage. Mme Tabard
"restores" this image before she steps into Antoine's arms: she says
that in the novels they both like, "the woman would take the key
and throw it out of the window, but for us this vase should be fine"
and drops his key in.[11]

Truffaut also uses repetition of writing motifs to signal Antoine's
growth. The protagonist's hyperbolic nature is suggested at the beginning when Christine says Antoine sent her nineteen letters in
one week! The act of penning his love is compressed when he composes the passionate *pneumatique* to Mme Tabard (in Paris, a letter
mailed by *pneumatique* would reach its destination within an hour
or two). In a remarkable montage sequence, we follow the process of
its delivery as it passes from Antoine's hands to other hands that pick
it up, stamp it, place it in a metal roll, then into a tube leading to an
underground pipeline that runs along the Paris sewerage system.
Through a series of quick cuts, the names of the streets click by. The
effects of Truffaut's attention to these details of urban communication are numerous: we see all of Paris participating in this relationship, and because we are drawn through the process, there is more
involvement on our part as well; the nervous system of Paris is
presented with rhythms that constitute a particularly urban aesthetic; we are made more aware of time—not merely the foreshor-
tened time in which the action takes place, but the historical and
romantic time to which street names like Rue La Fayette, Rue de la
Boétie, and Rue Richelieu allude. This presence of the past is especially appropriate given that Antoine's letter declares, "For a while I
dreamed that something might happen between us . . . but that
dream will die from the same impossibility that marked the love of
Felix de Vandenesse for Madame de Mortsauf in *Le Lys dan la vallée.*
Adieu" (*AD*, 197). In addition, Truffaut points to a paradox inherent
in modern civilization: the communication of even the most ethereal
sentiments depends upon the mediation of technology—romantic
content through impersonal, mechanical form—not unlike the
processes of cinema itself.

Antoine's third epistolary experience toward the end of the film
suggests that he is literally getting closer to his object and to his

feelings. He and Christine are having breakfast in the new intimacy following a night in her parents' bed. Antoine has something to tell her but "would rather write it down." He scribbles a few words, and they exchange a series of notes. The contents are not revealed to us but the outcome is clear: he puts the circular part of a bottle opener around Christine's ring finger. Through these three sequences, a gradual progression emerges: we are brought increasingly closer from the relative impersonality of merely hearing about the nineteen letters from their recipient to the involvement of watching the composition by the sender and the stages of its delivery to the witnessing of the entire process of communication. The message itself evolves from the painfully composed to the spontaneous, and each instance involves less distance, in space and time, until subject and object are face to face.

For Antoine's problem in *Stolen Kisses*, like that of numerous Renoir and Truffaut male protagonists, is that he may be eloquent via letter or telephone, but is inarticulate in the physical presence of the woman he loves. When he is alone with Fabienne in her apartment and she asks if he likes music, he blurts out, "Oui, Monsieur," and runs away. Like almost all the secondary characters in the film, Antoine wants love but doesn't know how to say so. As Truffaut found in *Rules of the Game*," all the characters have a sentimental problem to resolve."[12]

Truffaut takes basically Hitchcockian motifs of hiding and following, but weaves them into more Renoirian methods and concerns. Antoine's visual presentation externalizes the theme of hiding: he is first seen hidden behind a book; subsequently, his face will be blocked by a newspaper, trees, and doorways. When Fabienne enters his room, he pulls the blankets up to his nose. Moreover, the shots themselves are often constructed so that a part of the picture is hidden from view. When Truffaut repeatedly places the camera outside a doorway, he makes us aware that we are peering in on a world where there is more than meets our eyes. For example, when Christine and her father sit down to dinner, which we observe from outside the door, Antoine comes forward and closes the door on us. This camera set-up is later repeated in the detective bureau, first when Antoine is waiting for the boss to call him, and then when he and one of the other detectives are primping in front of the mirror. Sound plays a role in this context as well: after Antoine accidentally meets M. Henri in a cafe, they go outside and say goodbye, but the

The Renoirian courtyard in *Small Change.*

latter calls him back as an afterthought. We are still in the cafe, separated from the men by glass doors, and we cannot hear Henri's offer. Finally, when Antoine asks his boss to take him off the Tabard case, we are distanced through multiple framing of doors within doors.

While this perspective might recall the Hitchcockian specialty of the camera as voyeur, it is really a more Renoirian position, in that we are seeing only a part of a larger continuum of experience. The film offers the ultimate "grand illusion"—a segment of reality that is not created for us but exists in itself before and after we look at it. The shot that best communicates this notion is that of the camera in Christine's house slowly ascending the stairs in its search for Antoine and Christine: it enters the wrong room, discreetly exits, and then finds them in bed down the hall. Here Truffaut's "voyeuristic camera" serves to gently mock our voyeurism. It follows the young people to bed but remains outside the room. This recalls, for example, Renoir's *La Bête humaine* (1938), in which his inquisitive camera brings us right up to a window or door when a murder is about to take place, but then does not enter. While such a set-up suggests the power of the camera to participate, investigate, and reveal—to become another character—Truffaut's shot is curious, fallible, and modest. Scenes take place but that doesn't mean we will see them; lovers will kiss near an open door—but just beyond our vision. (They "steal kisses" from our view.)

If Hitchcock's vantage point can be likened to a peephole, Renoir's presence is symbolized by a panning and tracking camera whose mobility expresses a more open and fluid sense of experience. In films as early as *La Chienne* (1931) and *Boudu Saved from Drowning* (1932), Renoir was already deepening and expanding the frame through composition in depth and lateral panning; both of these methods alert the spectator to all that exists outside the immediate frame. As Bazin points out, such techniques are in the service of realism in that the screen seems to mask a part of the action which continues beyond its edges.[13] This affords the spectator a perspective closer to that of "real life," and suggests a continuum of which only a portion is being revealed.

In Renoir's cinema of the 1930s, these themes are graphically presented through the use of symbolic decor: the courtyard and the window are also stage and camera. The courtyard is the central setting—and metaphor—in two of his most important films of this era, *La Chienne* and *Le Crime de Monsieur Lange* (1936). In his exploration of the possibilities for communication and unity (in a word, community) as well as cinematic language, it functions as the equivalent in decor to depth-of-field in photography. The courtyard permits the characters to interact with their neighbors, and invites the audience to acknowledge how much more life there is beyond the immediate story. As in *Small Change*, the inclusion of "background" individuals suggests that everyone has his story, with each window a lens and each apartment a soundstage.

This perspective also informs *Bed and Board* (1970). Antoine and Christine Doinel live in an apartment that faces a courtyard. By means of windows, stairs, and the yard itself, Truffaut peoples the film with a myriad of characters who point to the generally unacknowledged lives that surround us (those, perhaps, whose stories consist in their not having a story). Antoine is an artist of sorts—he dyes flowers, improving upon nature with a palette of chemicals—and because his stand is in the middle of the courtyard, he is always "on stage," the center of attention for those inside and outside the building. When his flower business withers, Antoine joins a large American firm where he maneuvers miniature boats. Christine gives birth to a son, Alphonse; Antoine has an affair with a Japanese woman, Kyoko. He moves out of his home after a fight with Christine, but then becomes increasingly bored with Kyoko, and returns to the *domicile conjugal*.

The tone established at the outset of the film is one of camaraderie: people greet Antoine as they move in and out of the frame, neighbors stick their heads out of windows and offer advice, and the cafe in the courtyard bustles with activity. We are shown how the bar unifies characters when the telephone rings: the proprietor shouts that it is for Antoine, who jumps over crates to come in through the window and answer. The call is for his wife and he yells for a neighbor to tell Christine to come down. Her phone conversation is presented in a deep-focus shot that recalls Renoir's layering of experience; in the foreground she speaks to her mother, but her words are drowned out by the argument we see in the background as two women scream about the noise of the garbage pails. Between these two planes, a customer sits at a table, a mirror above his head opening up yet another perceptual level. Truffaut thus leads us to experience the texture of modern life the way the characters do: we must actively discriminate among the sounds and images and choose what is most essential.

This approach also reinforces the context in which the main characters must be seen. In the preceding films of the cycle, Antoine is essentially alone and outside warm, stable relationships. His need for a family—which has now been fulfilled by Christine and her parents—is heightened by the solitary male characters who punctuate *Bed and Board:* the neighbor who has not left his apartment for twenty-five years, the moocher who constantly takes advantage of Antoine, the "strangler" who turns out to be a television performer, and the drunk who comes to the cafe because he is looking for a fight. And if these men suggest what Antoine might have been, his musical neighbors provide the model for what he and Christine will become. Like Renoir in his "courtyard" films, Truffaut includes in the building a personage whose presence is constantly evoked by the soundtrack. From the little pianist in *La Chienne* and the flute-player in *Boudu,* we move in *Bed and Board* to the opera singer and his Italian wife. In front of Antoine's door, or on the stairs, we hear constantly the sound of his vocal exercises; the music is not incidental but an integral part of the characters' lives.

The tenor and his wife are introduced as a comic couple: they are late for the opera, he paces nervously before the apartment, she is still not ready, he throws her bag and coat down the stairs, he begins to descend, and she follows in a flurry. This humorous bit is repeated later in the film, and we are led to understand that this is always how he gets her out of the house on time. Although they exist in the background of the film, their pattern surfaces in the epilogue: Antoine is seen pacing back and forth, he throws Christine's things over the banister, she dashes out, and these neighbors help her on with her coat. The wife looks up at her husband and sighs happily, "Now, they're in love!" His reaction, a series of three facial expressions, is emphasized by Truffaut through freeze-frame close-ups; they suggest amusement, skepticism, and mockery, thereby providing a question mark within the film's "happy" ending. His face intensifies the note of real ambiguity with respect to Antoine's acceptance of and entry into bourgeois domesticity. But then again, the wife had been able to utter to Christine, "Life is beautiful," her husband's shenanigans notwithstanding. She and her tenor unite affirmation and irony, an appropriate blend for the future of Antoine Doinel.

These final reaction shots are a crucial device throughout *Bed and Board*. Like depth-of-field and the courtyard itself, it is used in a Renoirian attempt to unify characters. Truffaut incorporates a wealth of reaction shots, thus creating a world in which people are aware of and respond to each other. There are the men who react to Christine's shapely legs (an old codger murmurs, "I'd lay her badly but I'd lay her gladly"); the dweller's responses to Antoine's flowers, to the strangler, or to the birth of Alphonse; the older people who pause on the stairs at the bizarre sounds emerging from Antoine's apartment, looking at each other and up at the source; and the intercutting of both Antoine's and Christine's faces when they watch the impersonator on TV. The predominance of this technique also relates to and undercuts Kyoko since she is the only one who does not lend herself to reaction shots: her inscrutable features never change. Her face is beautiful but it lacks expressive power: she looks the same when she is attracted to Antoine as when she leaves him a note that reads "Drop dead!" This message as well as her love notes hidden in tulips—which open and reveal her feelings to none other than Christine—show that her most intense emotions require the mediation of the written word. Antoine's realization that "she is another world" is what initially attracts him but ultimately separates them. Kyoko's idea of romance, "If I ever commit suicide with someone, I'd like it to be with you," does not amuse Antoine.

Despite the recurring use of reaction and depth shots, the *difficulties* of communication exemplified by Antoine and Kyoko is actually one of the prime concerns of the film. For even when connective devices are employed, they point to a lack of understanding, or distance between individuals—the inability to enter another character's frame. The most striking example of this limitation is the first time that Antoine and Kyoko see each other at the hydraulics plant. Truffaut crosscuts between a square insert of Kyoko on the left (with the right side of the screen dark) and one of Antoine on the right (with the screen dark on the left). On the soundtrack is a mysterious strain, reminiscent of the "siren song" in *Stolen Kisses* that accompanies Antoine's first glimpse of Fabienne. In both cases, the music introduces "an apparition." By the fourth crosscut, we feel not only the attraction between Antoine and Kyoko, but the fact that they do not share the frame; the suggestion is that they fill in each other's blank space. This can be contrasted with the dinner scene at Christine's parents' home, in which Antoine and Christine are consistently presented in a two-shot that reinforces their identity as a couple.

Nevertheless, even Antoine and Christine have distances in their togetherness which become more palpable throughout the film, particularly when they become parents. Immediately after the birth of Alphonse, the proud father proves insensitive to Christine's needs when he has himself photographed with the child. She asks him to go, he feels shut out, she feels stifled; the only clue she gives to her anger is, "I waited for the baby by myself." It is now Antoine's turn to be alone, wandering the streets (as he did in *The 400 Blows*) because he has no one to whom he can announce his paternity. His unfulfilled yearning for human contact is expressed—as often in Truffaut's work—through the presence of glass barriers in this sequence: we see him through the window of a cafeteria where he eats in solitude, then standing outside the glass door of a bar which he does not enter, and finally in a telephone booth, where his inability to get out of his encapsulation—visually and thematically—is most poignantly presented. When he calls his friend Jean Eustache (the film director for whom Léaud would star in *The Mother and the Whore*), he is not at home and Antoine can only leave a message.

Antoine and Christine are also increasingly separated in bed. Even at the beginning, he announces that naked men are repulsive and jumps into bed fully clothed for the night. In the second half,

Antoine poses with Alphonse (note how Christine is relegated to the background, hardly in focus).

Is Kyoko posing for Antoine? *(Bed and Board)*

At a restaurant with Kyoko, Antoine is fed and bored.

we see him reading *Les Femmes Japonaises* while Christine is en-
grossed in Nureyev's autobiography. Each is alone with his or her
fantasy, much like the shot of Montag and Linda who share little
more than the bed in *Fahrenheit 451:* Montag looks at a comic book
(with no words) while his wife is glued to the TV set. Another
example of this distance can be seen when Antoine and Christine
talk from separate windows that face each other. During their conversation, Truffaut pans the gap between the two windows, a space
that is broken by vertical bars which suggest imprisonment. This
corresponds to the repeated shot of the inside of the Doinels' door:
it is contorted with locks, knobs, bolts—the trappings of modern
enclosure. When Antoine leaves Christine, she is framed by this
door, with tears in her eyes, as she eats a chocolate bar—an image of
impotence at a moment when both characters are locked within their
stubbornness.

Even the comic incidents and characters of the film contribute to
the theme of language or the problems of communicating. Whereas
Renoir's *Grand Illusion* explored the tragic problems that result
from the lack of a common language, *Bed and Board* points to the

comic consequences. The most extreme—and grotesquely funny—example of this difficulty is Monsieur Max, the American businessman who becomes Antoine's boss. When Antoine's flowers fail, he answers a newspaper advertisement for a "dynamic, English-speaking young man" to work in a major American hydraulic company. Through a mixup, Antoine is assumed to be the candidate described in a letter as "completely fluent in the language of Shakespeare." During his interview, Monsieur Max not only mutilates the French language while Antoine can't speak English, but he won't listen to his secretary who is trying to tell him of the mistaken identity. They respond to each other with their own stock phrases: Antoine comes out with lines that he must have learned in some English textbook while Monsieur Max recites homilies that are familiar to all his employees:

M. MAX: Well . . . the problem for our employees here is transportation. Do you have a car?

ANTOINE (in English): I am not in a hurry. I prefer to cross the town. (*AD*, 260)

Each of these characters, to one degree or another, points to two fundamentally Truffautesque perceptions: how much they need others, and how difficult it is to reach them. The minor female characters are as frustrated and incomplete as the males. Ginette, the waitress in the cafe, stalks Antoine in vain, unable to realize her declaration, "I want you and I'll get you!" Monique, the secretary in the hydraulic company, confesses to Antoine, "When I'm alone at night, I'm scared. I'd even marry a lamppost . . . if it could talk!" Truffaut's symbol for these sentiments is the telephone, whose presence helps to structure the film. At the beginning, Christine's father has pulled connections for Antoine and Christine to have a telephone (a far more difficult acquisition in France than America). Antoine's thank-you note—"Dear Senator: Thanks to you, it took me eight days to get what the average Frenchman spends years waiting for!"—results in the couple's argument, during which he exclaims that he doesn't want a phone.

CHRISTINE: That's right, you don't give a damn, but when we're bored, we can get in touch with friends on that phone!

ANTOINE: When we're bored? I don't know what boredom is! (p. 255)

It is, therefore, appropriate that at the two points when Antoine is most distressed, his only recourse is the telephone. When he cannot find anyone to share in his excitement over becoming a father, he ends up in a phone booth. And when he is utterly "bored" with Kyoko, he calls Christine from a restaurant phone—three times. Antoine, like the others, needs the telephone, needs to make the connection. And to return to the courtyard image, it is significant that Truffaut establishes the interrelated texture of the residents' lives by having the communal phone in the cafe downstairs.

Literary Detachment

The urban and contemporary films that focus on the possibilities for interaction in man-made structures are but a part of the canvas shared by Renoir and Truffaut. Their best work includes exploration of human beings in the framework of nature. For example, Renoir shot *A Day in the Country* (1936) on location, and his camera celebrates nature by literally caressing the surfaces it encounters. As would be true of Truffaut's camera in *Les Mistons, Jules and Jim* and *Two English Girls*, it animates scenes which recall Impressionist tableaux. When our eyes are led over rain on leaves—Raymond Durgnat likens the effect to goosepimples in his study of the director[14]—we can understand Bazin's remark that Renoir makes the films his father would have made had Auguste exchanged his brush for a camera.[15] This pictorial sense is expressed through attention to light, motion, details, skin, and tactility.

Renoir's blending of sensuality and nostalgia, tenderness and irony, characterizes Truffaut's first short, *Les Mistons*. Like Renoir, Truffaut focuses on a young woman whose love is short-lived. His Bernadette is introduced on a bicycle, peddling through the lush and dappled landscape, the camera mirroring the joy of her movement with its own. Just as *A Day in the Country* establishes a young woman's youthful vitality in a shot of her swinging back and forth (the camera participating in her rhythm), Bernadette's appeal is that of a springtime creature in motion. The swing and the bicycle help the women to charge the air around them with a rhythmic presence. Like the glistening water that surrounds Renoir's boats, the sun seems to wink through the trees as Bernadette rides by. These images are not merely pretty landscape shots but part of a vision that affirms natural growth, flow, and expansion (terrestrial and human) while acknowledging loss and pain: Bernadette's fiancé dies in an accident; Renoir's film accommodates rain and the girl's tears, a storm and her desolation. (The storm is especially significant when we realize that it is neither in De Maupassant's story nor Renoir's original scenario. It is a fortuitous natural occurrence that Renoir chooses to build into the film, thus enacting his aesthetic of improvisation and his philosophy of openness.)

Renoir does not judge his characters: one pair is not condemned for indulgence in sensual appetite, nor is another for their languishing. The exuberant movements that express the formers' frolicking, and the poignant close-ups that capture the latters' deep emotion, fulfill a perception offered by Penelope Gilliatt: "Just as his father loved women for baring their bodies, Jean Renoir loves his characters for the immodesty of baring their souls."[16] He and Truffaut engage our sympathy for these characters by allowing us first to share in their freedom and sensuality via sweeping movements and then forcing us to confront their loss in more measured frames.

Jules and Jim and *Two English Girls* appropriate much of the thematic and stylistic texture of *A Day in the Country* and take it through both lighter and much darker shades. Truffaut's films are adapted from Henri-Pierre Roché's autobiographical novels, *Jules et Jim* (1953) and *Les Deux Anglaises et le Continent* (1956). Both films begin with a character's voice-over commentary and then yield to the voice of an impersonal narrator who will prove more intent on detaching us than were the intertitles of *A Day in the Country*. Over the dark screen of *Jules and Jim*, Catherine's voice recites, "You said to me: I love you. I said to you: wait. I was going to say: take me. You said to me: go away." The source of the lines is actually *Two English Girls*, but they crystallize the movement of both works. For the force that asserts itself like an omnipresent character is *time*. It is not gratuitous that one of the images in the credit sequence of *Jules and Jim* is an hourglass. In these triangular tales—one about two friends and the female they adore, the other about two English girls and the young Frenchman who introduces them to passion—a man and a woman can love each other, but rarely at the same time, or if at the same time, rarely for long. These are syncopated stories in that romantic love occurs on the off-beat. The telephones of *Bed and Board* are replaced by letters, or direct contact by the interference of time. Often unable to articulate their need to the other, except through the mediation of writing—which immediately removes the feeling from its temporal reality—the characters come together and separate in an emotional equivalent of musical chairs. As Catherine says to Jim, "It's your turn to suffer. When you stop, I'll begin."

Jules and Jim are two friends who become enamored of the smile on a statue. They meet Catherine, a beautiful woman who seems to incarnate the statue, and Jules marries her. The war separates Jules, the German, and Jim, the Frenchman, but they are reunited at the former's chalet. Jim stays with the couple and their daughter Sabine; after a while, roles shift and Jim becomes Catherine's lover while Jules remains her devoted friend. Catherine decides to live with Jim and have his children, but when she does not become pregnant, she returns to Jules. They lose touch with Jim and later find him again when he is about to marry his old girlfriend Gilberte. Catherine takes him for a ride and after telling Jules to watch them, she drives off a bridge, plunging them to their death.

Truffaut creates our interest in and affection for what might otherwise be unsympathetic characters through an active camera in the first half, and once again distances us from them through a more static presentation in the second part. In this manner, he neither condemns nor approves of them, leaving moral speculations to the audience. The camera participates in, rather than merely recording, the physical activity through which the relationships develop—from the cigarette trick performed by Jules' girlfriend Thérèse in a 360° pan to the excited pans and cuts that link the statue to Catherine. When the trio go bicycle-riding in the country, promenade in the woods, or frolic on the beach, the camera is as free as they are, constantly dollying, panning, and expanding focus. Especially in the race sequence on the bridge, the handheld camera tracks with Catherine so that we experience the exhilaration of her running.

In the latter half, this mobility yields to longer takes and more deliberate camera movements which depict more complex and painful situations. Most of the action now occurs within the confined space of a single house. Jim's perception that Catherine is more of an ant, less of a grasshopper, applies as well to the camera. There is less quick cutting, and increased emphasis on the way that the camera moves to unify characters and express their changing relationships. When Jim first has lunch with the married couple after the war, a sense of embarrassment is conveyed as the camera pans quickly from Jim to Jules to Catherine, suggesting that Jim can only speak to her through Jules. After Jim has installed himself at Catherine and Jules' chalet, Catherine decides to seduce Jules for a change: from a shot of Jim reading downstairs, the camera tilts up to Jules and Catherine in bed, and then back down to Jim. Unity and spatial tension are thus maintained. Later, she sings "Les Tourbillons de la vie"—written for her by another lover, Albert—which centers on the word *enlacé* (intertwined); the camera makes this concrete by panning from Catherine and Albert to Jules and Jim, reuniting them all in one frame. Likewise, when the basic triangle re-forms after a long interval, and they stop at a restaurant, the camera pans from the three to include Albert, for he has already become an integral part of their relationship. As in Renoir's films, the choice to reframe rather than cut suggests accommodation; the camera literally makes room for the entrance of a character.

Truffaut also makes effective use of speeded-up and slow-motion in *Jules and Jim*: war and death create their own temporality. Documentary footage of World War I which was shot at silent speed is cut into sound speed, resulting in a jerkiness that detaches us by making the war appear "unreal" compared to the "reality" of our story, particularly since the inset conveys how *movies* looked at the time. Moreover, the fact that *Jules and Jim* is shot in Franscope (a widescreen 2:1 ratio) whereas the battle sequence is not, distorts the soldiers' bodies to the point of dehumanization. On the other hand, Catherine's drive off the bridge is prolonged by slow motion as well as by a montage of different views of the car as it falls into the water. The emphasis given by slow motion balances the intensity created by abrupt stasis in the middle of the film: when Jules and Jim first greet each other after the war, a freeze-frame of their kiss takes the moment out of time, for it contains what is timeless—their friendship.

Emphasis is also established through the director's incorporation of a square inset when Catherine is introduced. This device not only intensifies her connection to the statue (here she is doubly "framed" like the slide) but self-consciously calls back to the tradition of silent cinema that feeds into Truffaut's work. The importance of art permeates both the relationship of Truffaut to his material and that of the characters to each other. Literature is presented as the core of the men's friendship: they translate each other's poetry and discuss Shakespeare. Most significantly, Jim is writing a novel about two friends named Jacques and Julien. The section that he reads to Jules from his manuscript refers to them as Don Quixote and Sancho Panza, which is precisely what the narrator calls Jules and Jim at the

close of the film. The intimate relationship that Truffaut suggests
here between art and experience takes its richest and most obvious
form in the statue that charms the young men. As will be shown in
Chapter Four, Catherine's characterization gives fuel to the theory
that one falls in love first with a work of art and later with the person
who resembles it.

The temporal changes of this film which spans twenty years are
signalled not through makeup, but art—through the works of
Picasso. The background of a number of shots contains paintings
which represent the different periods of Picasso's career; thus, our
measure of time becomes sensitivity to aesthetic context. In addition, the very structure and movement of *Jules and Jim* are indi-
cated through another art medium, music. Catherine's song is performed at the midpoint of the film, offering simultaneously a commentary on the action thus far, and a foreshadowing of the future.
The song is about meeting, then a short affair, a separation, then
reunion, in an eternal circle—the "geometry" of the film itself. The
structure is reminiscent of *La Ronde* (1950) which was directed by
Max Ophuls, one of the directors that Truffaut most revered. It
revolves around a carousel: lovers get on and off, change partners,
feel intensely but ephemerally, on a ride where nothing is permanent.

The vulnerability of those who try to ride with the flux (and the
underlying pessimism of Ophuls) can be seen in the last sequence of
Jules and Jim. Truffaut painstakingly shows us all the details that
follow the deaths of Catherine and Jim. We watch the coffins, the
flames that burn them, the ashes as they come out, and the urns in
which they are placed. This concentration on the remnants of their
bodies is a shocking corollary to the energy with which they lived.
Nothing remains of the passion and beauty but meaningless dust;
only Catherine's song continues her presence at the end, as the
melody swells on the soundtrack. The persistence of "Les Tourbillons" recalls Renoir, for, as Truffaut notes in *FV* (p. 66), the death of
Renoir's heroines is often counterpointed by music: "Nana, Mado,
Emma, the beautiful Mme Roubaud and many others had to be
killed, but in each case Renoir juxtaposed their death with that
which is most alive—songs."

A song and a statue are all that survive Catherine (actually one
should include her daughter Sabine, but during the last part of the
film, Truffaut ignores her existence); *Two English Girls* retains

sculpture as an operative metaphor—as will become clear in the
next chapter—but for an image of both immortality and self-
reflexivity, it replaces music with books. While it occasionally recalls Renoir, particularly through exterior shots of natural majesty,
Two English Girls reveals the fundamental differences between
Truffaut and his mentor. A young Frenchman, Claude Roc, meets
two English sisters, Anne and Muriel, whose mother invites him for
an extended visit. He falls in love with Muriel but his mother op-
poses the proposed marriage. Claude and Muriel agree to separate
for one year during which they will keep diaries for each other. He
becomes an art critic and man-about-town in Paris and ends the
relationship after a few months. Claude and Anne fall in love; his
mother dies; he sees Muriel again, and Anne urges them to go away
together. But when Anne confesses to her sister that she and Claude
were lovers, Muriel becomes violently ill and leaves. Claude writes
a novel, *Jérôme et Julien,* which is published after Anne dies.
Claude and Muriel finally consummate their love, but she leaves
him the next day and Claude remains alone.

When the film appeared in 1971, many were disappointed that it
lacked the vitality and engaging characters of *Jules and Jim.* But
reappraisal, particularly in the light of the film's deeper connections
to *The Story of Adèle H.* than to *Jules and Jim,* suggests that *Two
English Girls* may be Truffaut's richest and most complex film. It is
certainly one of his most pessimistic, but with passages of visual
beauty that rival the most sensuous images of Renoir (father and
son). Especially in and around the Brown home, Nestor Almendros'
photography skillfully moves through vibrant tones of brown. The
original version of the film—twenty minutes longer than the print in
current distribution—contained a "picnic on the grass" sequence
whose sunny texture invoked both Jean Renoir's 1959 film of the
same title and his father Auguste's rich colors. The most Renoirian
episode takes place on the island where Claude and Anne first become lovers. Accompanied by the tender music of Georges Delerue, the camera tracks along the water, following Anne as she walks
up the verdant bank. This fluid long take is interrupted only by the
voice-over commentary: "They arrived on the island with a program
that was summarized in one phrase: 'Live first, define it later.' "
However, it is precisely this narration—and its prevalence throughout *Two English Girls* and *Jules and Jim*—that marks a departure
from Renoir.

While it is true that Renoir distances us from his characters, the effect is generally unobtrusive, as when he literally presents individuals within frames (the doorways and windows of *Madame Bovary,* the puppet show frames around *La Chienne* and *Boudu Saved from Drowning,* and ultimately, theatrical stages as in *The Golden Coach*). Truffaut, however, creates an emotional counterpoint between sound and image—dispassionate narration over powerful visual material. The technique is evident in his first film: *Les Mistons* is recounted by a grown "miston" now looking back. Here, the voice serves both to explain the emotions of the boys and to add to the immediacy of the film another temporal layer: *Les Mistons* becomes a memoir. The image of presence coupled with the voice of the past results in a nostalgic flavor. (As Vladimir Nabokov writes in *Ada,* "Time is memory in the making.")

The Man Who Loved Women sheds light on this device as a sensitive editor retitles the protagonist's autobiographical novel: *Le Cavaleur (The Skirt-Chaser)* becomes *L'Homme qui aimait les femmes.* When the author asks, "why the imperfect tense?"—a question about the film as well—she responds that it sounds better and is more appropriate to the style of narration. But the center of this film is less the imperfect tense than the desire to present and thus perfect the past. The events are less important than the attempt of the character to come to terms with their passage. Therefore, one of the effects of voice-over narration is to emphasize continuity, the tension between memory and projection, rather than merely the present tense.

Les Mistons, too, is in the imperfect. When Truffaut returns to this device in *Jules and Jim,* the voice is drier and speaks more rapidly. The effect is now more a "cooling" of a "warm" image. He realized that it was a controversial story and did not want to alienate the majority of the audience. Whereas Renoir's stance had been, "the more emotional the material, the less emotional the treatment," Truffaut went a step farther and allowed the voice to reduce the visceral impact of the shot. The commentary is not less emotional, but virtually non-emotional. Truffaut's fear of emotional facility is also evidenced by his cutting away from a potentially sentimental moment; for example, Jim's farewell when he boards the train is presented in extreme long shot. And the insistence upon the details of the burial has an equally dislocating effect, inviting a clinical viewpoint rather than tears.

These distancing devices culminate in *Two English Girls* where the tension between visual lyricism and verbal commentary is most pronounced. We should be aware, however, that subtitles exaggerate this tension: the American version contains a *visual* interruption in addition to a verbal one. The most vivid examples are the potentially "erotic" scenes which are neutralized by the voice-over. When Claude first kisses Anne in her studio, we are told, "He had the crazy idea of touching Anne's breast: why not try? Claude said to himself, 'Will she scream, or slap me?' But no." The effect is comic through redundancy, and it seems that the action on the screen is illustrating the spoken text rather than being illuminated by it. More disengaging is the narration of the first sexual encounter between Claude and Muriel in Calais: "The ribbon burst, after a more vigorous resistance than Anne's. It was not a question of happiness, nor of tenderness. Claude had to arm Muriel-woman against herself. It was done . . . red stained her gold" (*TEG*, 63). As if the commentary were not enough to detach us, there is a zoom-in to the blood on the sheet, emphasized further by a freeze-frame of this intense red. The abstracted physicality of the stain is as dehumanizing as the ashes of *Jules and Jim*.[17]

If *Two English Girls* were merely a love story, these counterpoints could be seen as severe drawbacks. However, the film is more deeply concerned with the suffering of love—the obstacles, ruptures, and separations. As Truffaut explained, "I tried to make not a film on physical love, but a physical film on love" (*TEG*, 11). Despite this emphasis on the concrete, the attempts of the characters to invent love freely, and their failure, are inseparable from written text: their efforts are not only chronicled by words but constituted by them. Truffaut's narration is warranted by the literary self-definition and presentation of the lovers that it describes. The manner in which the text drains the image of emotion fulfills Truffaut's aim: "In this film, I wanted to squeeze love like a lemon" (*TEG*, 11). The characters do not permit their passion autonomy, just as the director will not permit the story to tell itself. Both require the mediation—or control—of language. For instance, when Claude first tries to kiss Anne, the commentary does to the audience what Anne does to Claude: "Anne detached herself from him in order to explain . . ." Truffaut's consistent overlapping of experience with the articulation of it reinforces the degree to which they feed upon each other. The proliferation of letters, diaries,

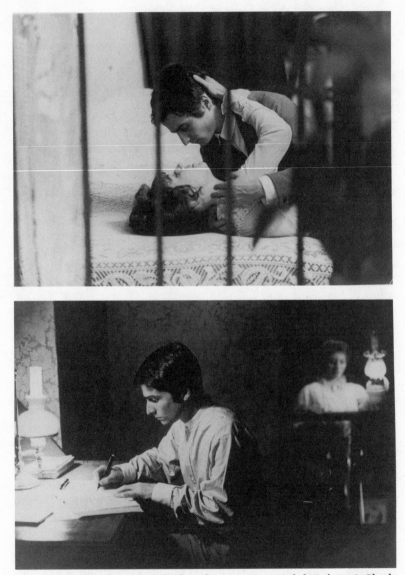

Imposing frames on emotions: Claude and Anne in *Two English Girls* (top); Claude embraces Muriel by writing to her (bottom.)

books, and memoirs attests to the fundamentally literary sensibility and expectations of the characters which the director (perhaps too faithfully) mirrors.

In *Jules and Jim*, the exchange of letters between Catherine and Jim is described as "a dialogue of the deaf." Even when the messages arrive at the right time, Catherine is displeased by insufficient attention. The notes from Jim seem to contain too little passion for her because, like Muriel, she puts a great deal of faith in the written word. It is significant that in the original version of *Two English Girls*, Muriel writes Claude the same letter that Catherine wrote Jim: "I am expecting your baby. Thank God, Claude: you are living in me. This paper is your skin. This ink is my blood. I press hard so that it will enter" (*TEG*, 64). A second letter follows, as in *Jules and Jim*, announcing that she is not pregnant. The letters are received only after the passage of time has invalidated them.

Of all the characters in both films, it may be Claude who emerges as the most dependent upon writing. His profession is that of art critic, and his profession of love to Muriel is in the form of a letter. Because we have not been shown any manifestation of his sentiment, he appears to be falling in love as he writes. The first words we hear him speak over the credits are, "Some day I will write our story." Then his diary is introduced at the beginning of the film. His emotions are revealed to us through the letters he writes his mother. We learn that he is breaking off from Muriel only when his mother reads aloud his farewell letter to the girl. The extent to which he seems to place text over individual is implied by his reaction to Muriel's painful diary (where she shatters his idea of her purity by confessing that she has been a compulsive masturbator since childhood). In a scene that does not appear in the re-cut version, the commentary states, "Muriel's confession provoked in Claude more curiosity than emotion. He thought mainly of its literary possibilities" (*TEG*, 52). He is then shown dictating to a secretary. The narrator informs us that he asked Muriel for permission to publish the confession anonymously, which she refused. We hear Claude repeating Muriel's words as the secretary types them.

Claude is the one who finally transmutes the experiences of *Two English Girls* into art. We are told that his suffering over losing Muriel is eased in writing his first novel, *Jérôme et Julien*: "Through the emotions of a woman who, throughout her life, loved two men simultaneously, it was easy to recognize, barely transposed, the story of his love for the two sisters" (*TEG*, 58). Claude thus masters his pain to the degree that he can declare, "I feel that the characters of the book have suffered in my place." Muriel had said that it is not love but the incertitude of love that disturbs life; Claude's response is the certitude of a text.

Neither Renoir nor his most representative characters demand such certitude. Even when their personalities are shaped by art, they are less concerned with security than stylization. If many of Truffaut's characters tend to be past-and/or future-oriented, seeking permanence through sculpture, literature, or film, Renoir's are firmly rooted in the present and seek out the *theater* as a model for self-presentation. We find the characters of both directors acting out roles, but those of Renoir seem to accept the short-term quality of a stage, whereas those of Truffaut project via more "stable" forms. If Jean-Pierre Léaud as Antoine, Claude, or Alphonse in *Day for Night* can be considered Truffaut's instrument for exploring certitude in love, then Michel Simon as Legrand in *La Chienne* or Boudu can be seen as Renoir's means of exploring incertitude in freedom (or vice versa). In *La Chienne*, whose very style wavers between naturalism (direct sound, authentic quality of courtyard and cafes) and stylization (Expressionist lighting, streets bathed with "underworld" shadows), Legrand moves through a number of roles that culminate in that of the happy bum. He can blithely ignore that his self-portrait has been sold for a large sum, whereas Antoine watches himself carefully during rushes. In effect, *Day for Night* seeks to create an image of permanence whereas Renoir's films, particularly *Rules of the Game*, undercut such a possibility.

Rules, Games, and Frames

Truffaut's work, particularly *Day for Night*, attests to the deep influence of *Rules of the Game*. His first critical article, published in 1950 in the *Bulletin du Ciné-Club du Quartier Latin*, concerned this film. About Renoir's masterpiece, he later claimed, "Personally, I cannot think of another film maker who has put more of himself— and the best of himself—into a film than Jean Renoir has into *Rules of the Game*."[18] And he quotes the central line that Renoir, in the role of Octave, speaks: "In this world there is one awful thing, and that is that everyone has his reasons"—a sentiment that permeates the work of both directors. While Hitchcock's voyeuristic composition—through peepholes, rear windows, and high-angle shots—seems to whisper that "everyone has his secrets," Renoir's position is reinforced by an eye-level camera—an "egalitarian" perspective—with a great deal of panning and tracking to reveal more sides of a character or situation.

Since *Rules of the Game* was so significant to Truffaut, further discussion of it can shed light on the nature and degree of Renoir's influence, especially in *Day for Night*. Both films are deeply personal documents in which we find many of their mutual concerns crystallized: the camera as narrator/participant; the role of art in the characters' lives and consequent intersections of actors and parts; the multiplicity of characters and relationships; the attitude of the director toward his characters; and the difficulties of loving. In addition, a cinematic self-consciousness is heightened by the fact that each director plays a major role in his film. *Day for Night* brings together for Truffaut, as *Rules of the Game* did for Renoir, the thematic and stylistic preoccupations that he had been developing through twelve years of filmmaking.

Rules of the Game opens with the unrequited love of aviator hero André Jurieu for Christine, wife of the Marquis de la Chesnaye; he tries, unsuccessfully, to kill himself in his car. Octave (played by Renoir), a mutual friend, arranges for the La Chesnayes to invite André to a hunting party at their estate, La Colinière. During the ensuing costume party, pandemonium breaks loose as André fights with another of Christine's admirers, then with La Chesnaye. La Chesnaye and André agree that Christine will leave with the latter. Octave confesses to Christine that he has always loved her and convinces her to go away with him. But another character, unaware that a double change of costume has taken place, shoots André. La Chesnaye and Christine reaffirm order by reassuming their roles: they tell the guests that there has been an accident, and they go back into the chateau.

Plot summary can convey a mere fraction of the density and richness of *Rules of the Game*, a film of interlacing triangles, multiple involvements, and inner harmonies, but without a linear plot. Numerous echoes and internal rhymes abound, such as the hunt of animals outside and the hunt of people inside—fatal parties that converge in Jurieu's dying "like a rabbit." The poaching of animals finds its chateau analogue in the poaching of women; one character is a lower-class parasite, as Octave is a higher-class one. The servants' relationships parallel and intersect with those of the masters.

This complex (though seemingly non-existent) structure of doubling and "triangling" can also be seen in *Day for Night* which is about the making of a film entitled *Meet Pamela*. The reflections, intersections, and divergences between the outer frame of *Day for Night* and the inner frame of *Meet Pamela*, between the actors and their roles, constitute the fabric, if not the plot, of Truffaut's film.

In *Rules of the Game*, the major tension is between theater and life, or artifice and nature. As in *Nana, Madame Bovary, Grand Illusion,* and *The Golden Coach,* Renoir explores the subtly interpenetrating relationship between the two. Like Nana, Boieldieu, Emma Bovary, or Camilla, Robert de La Chesnaye is a "theatrical" character, extremely stylized in his rather obvious eye makeup and in his attempt to orchestrate each situation as though it were a show. He is the "m.c." who literally tries to master the ceremonies of the weekend, but finds that the guests' human passions are flowing past rules, like the action of the film which spills out of doorways and frames. During the theatricals, the characters disguise themselves, which, as Truffaut points out, means they take off their masks.[19] In assuming a role, the characters find the license to express hidden impulses. Neither the guests nor the audience are certain where the stage begins and ends. The people in the chateau mistakenly assume that the spectacle of one man chasing another with a gun is part of the show. La Chesnaye orders his servant Corneille (an appropriate name in a work about rules in conflict with passion) to "stop this farce!" Corneille responds, "Which one?" And the visual composition at this point emphasizes how they are all pawns in a game: the large black and white tiles on the floor make the hall look like a giant chessboard. The subsequent sequences of mistaken identity will bear out this impression of cross-purposes and checked mates.

The composition and camera movement help reveal the ultimate inadequacy of theatrical frames to control the action. Bazin, to whom the revival of the film is dedicated (as *The 400 Blows* would be), is perceptive about what he calls the personification of the camera in *Rules of the Game*: "Throughout the entire last part . . . the camera acts like an invisible guest wandering about the salon and the corridors with a certain curiosity, but without any more advantage than its invisibility."[20] However, the camera offers a privileged perspective in shots of inclusivity and simultaneity that no single view *within* the action could capture. The image is layered, with activity filling the fore-, mid-, and background of the frame. The flow of the action among these planes represents the flux of experience as reality and illusion feed into each other.

Truffaut takes this personfication of the camera a step farther in *Day for Night* by beginning a shot in *Meet Pamela* and ending it in *Day for Night:* from a close-up of Stacey in the swimming pool, the camera pulls back as she gets out to take a letter, and rises to reveal the camera of the *Meet Pamela* crew filming the scene, and then cranes down to a close-up of the director Ferrand (Truffaut) who is watching the take. (And we know that just beyond what we saw, Truffaut must have been watching the take of the take of the take . . .) The provisional frame of both Renoir and Truffaut reflects the fluid nature of the relationships whether between men and women or between "art" and "life." The movement between the latter terms is signaled by the title: day for night refers to the filter by which night scenes can be filmed during the day, the artifice responsible for the illusion of reality. The first shot—a young man emerging from a subway onto a crowded street—looks "real" enough, but a cut to the director yelling "Cut!" reveals that it was a take from a film within the film. We are immediately alerted to the distinctions or overlap between the fabricated and the natural.

The extent to which experience and art feed upon each other is further illustrated when Ferrand gives Julie her lines and they turn out to be the same words that she had used about her own life. Or when the crew drives to a location, a street sign, "Rue Jean Vigo" (this street actually exists in Nice where Vigo created the first ciné-club), is followed by an arrow with the word *Pamela*, suggesting how the film creates its own world and that *Day for Night* is literally mapping how you arrive at *Pamela*. And when Séverine cannot remember her lines or positions in a take, she claims that it is because the makeup girl is playing the maid. Where mistaken identity proved fatal in *Rules of the Game*, it is a pretext in *Day for Night*—not only for Séverine, but for Truffaut: each retake of Séverine's scene gives him the opportunity to present it from a different angle. The perspective begins in *Meet Pamela*—we see what the camera within the film records—but moves into *Day for Night*—we see the interaction of actors and crew and equipment. Just as Renoir is attracted to the servants in the chateau (his camera crossing the horizontal boundary between upstairs and downstairs) Truffaut returns to the crew and machinery, crossing a vertical boundary to go behind the scenes. He negates the hierarchy of actors and technicians, as did Renoir with masters and servants, to affirm common bonds and interdependence.

Parallels can be drawn between the "leads" as well: the pivotal women of both films, Christine and Julie, are fed up with play-acting; the young and naive usurpers, André Jurieu and Alphonse, both ruin the situations by their insistence upon announcing their intentions to the woman's husband; and Octave and Ferrand, played by Renoir and Truffaut, are the real directors *within* the films as well. Octave engineers the actions before the camera like Renoir behind it, and it is noteworthy that when the audience in the chateau cries, "Auteur, Auteur!" after the show, the whole troupe comes out, but Octave emerges last, and is left on stage after the others exit.[21] His characteristic reply to all the guests, "J'en fais mon affaire" (I'll handle it), summarizes Ferrand's burden: throughout *Day for Night*, each actor and technician looks to him to take care of every problem. Just as Octave is associated with both levels of the chateau, Ferrand must "handle" things for performers and crew alike.

Both Octave and Ferrand are outsiders to the romantic situations, and the isolation of each is symbolically presented: for the theatricals, Octave wears a bear costume but cannot get it off afterwards, and everyone is too busy to help him remove it. He is a character stuck in his role, and his futile attempts reinforce his need for others. In a similar manner, Ferrand's hearing aid suggests the director's deafness to all that does not concern his film. These two props point to the different art forms from which the directors draw their inspiration. The bearsuit is a theatrical and visual image, as *Rules of the Game* takes its story from the dramatists Beaumarchais and Musset, and its cinematic style from Impressionist painting. Renoir uses the basic plot and structure of *Le Mariage de Figaro* and *Les Caprices de Marianne* and shapes them into flowing Impressionist tableaux. As in Auguste Renoir's *Moulin de la Galette* or Manet's *At the Cafe*, the action spills over the frame while the background assumes a vital presence. His compositions have an unfinished quality, reminiscent of the seemingly casual cropping of his father's paintings. *Rules of the Game* thus moves through a visual mode that invokes a proscenium or a frame.

Truffaut's hearing aid, on the other hand, implies a verbal self-definition and a fundamental connection to language. Truffaut's aesthetic roots are not in theater and painting, but in cinema and literature. The frame within the frame is not a proscenium but a viewfinder; rather than merely watching his performance, we hear Ferrand's voice-over commentary; and the hearing device again reinforces how communication (personal and cinematic) depends upon the mediation of technology.[22]

A most important difference between these self-characterizations is that Ferrand is successful where Octave is a failure. Ferrand is able to create the illusion of order out of a reality tantamount to chaos; he is, therefore, finally closer to the character of La Chesnaye than Octave. The Marquis and the director both orchestrate human passions in the attempt to accommodate them into one framework—the chateau and *Meet Pamela.* (Octave confesses that he wanted to be a conductor but never succeeded.) They use art as a principle of order, but both films acknowledge the ultimate inadequacy of art to control human experience. Ferrand confesses, "Films are more harmonious than life . . . there are no traffic jams in films, no dead waits. Films move forward like trains . . . like trains in the night" (*DN*, 135), an opinion which will subsequently be borne out when *Meet Pamela* moves beyond the artists' fear, disappointment in love, and death.

Renoir reveals the limitations of his camera frame in its attempt to capture all the human bustle in *Rules of the Game;* this constitutes an outer mirror of the difficulties of La Chesnaye's frames—literally his music box and theatricals, figuratively the chateau and its rules—in accommodating the exigencies and fluctuations of the guests. The film explores the tension between natural energy and the controlling effect of theater, flow and frame, outside and inside.

Ferrand's aesthetic enterprise will prove more viable than La Chesnaye's because the director recognizes limitations while the aristocrat does not. Both films take place on the edge of a major change: *Rules of the Game* is preceded by a title that situates the action on the eve of war; Ferrand explains that *Meet Pamela* signals the end of a film era that had been dominated by stars and studios. Despite the difference in scope between a social upheaval and a comparatively smaller aesthetic transition, one can contrast La Chesnaye's ignorance of the change with Ferrand's articulation of it. Whereas the aristocrat is not ready to face the future without his traditions, it is implicit in Ferrand's remark, "there will be no more films like *Meet Pamela*," that there *will* be films like *Day for Night*, or that traditional structures will yield to individual expression.

Ultimately, *Rules of the Game* reveals the void beneath the forms, the lack of values that might give meaning to the rules. We are presented with the refined brutality of the rabbit hunt, the ignorance of an aristocrat who lumps Negroes together with Indians and Buffalo Bill, and the final substitution of style for sensitivity when a young person is told to stop crying over another's death as everyone reenters the chateau. The group that follows La Chesnaye resembles a procession of shadows, lacking the substance of purpose to their lives. In *Day for Night*, however, the group of characters is engaged in the creation of a film. The fact that Truffaut chooses a banal script for *Meet Pamela* suggests that the final product matters less to the individuals involved than the process of fellowship in which it was made. *Meet Pamela* will become for its artists a record of their work together, an extension of the family portrait for which they pose before Séverine's departure.

The parallel situation of an accidental death toward the end of *Rules of the Game* and *Day for Night* adds to the distinction between them. At first, they seem similar: when Jurieu dies, La Chesnaye tries to smooth things over by announcing to the guests—on the porch which is presented like a stage—that an accident has occurred; when Alexandre dies, Ferrand must also put aside grief and find a stand-in to finish the film. But, on the other hand, if Jurieu's death betrays the futility of existence, Alexandre's crash is followed by the screening of rushes which attest to the fact that something remains of him or that film has robbed death of its finality. There may be as little inherent meaning in *Day for Night*'s world as that of *Rules of the Game*, but Truffaut ascribes significance to individuals who are unified in and committed to their work, especially when that work aspires to some permanence.

The emblems that best illustrate these distinctions are the calliope in *Rules of the Game* and the editing machine in *Day for Night*. Both are metaphors of artistic order, but as Leo Braudy has admirably pointed out, "the calliope recalls a society in which all the rules worked, but which is now accessible only as an artifact, an archaic reminder of a lost past enclosed within the frame of theater" (*Jean Renoir*, p. 90). The movieola to which Truffaut's camera returns can *create* meaning. It represents the triumph of incorporation, in the dual sense of materialization and inclusion. An instrument of continuity, it orders fragments of human action into a moving whole. Truffaut celebrates this fact in montage sequences of the celluloid's transformation, accompanied by joyous music. These sequences are among Truffaut's only directly emotional moments, unmediated by voice-over commentary; they constitute what are perhaps the truest "love" scenes of his work, such as when he permits the strips of celluloid to intertwine while the music soars. He no longer distances us from the passionate content via dispassionate form, but rather allows lyrical tracking, excited montage, and triumphant music to sweep us into the film's world.

These sequences exhibit the visceral qualities that Truffaut ascribed to *A Day in the Country:*

Without the assistance of commentary, Renoir offers us . . . poetic prose whose truth, at certain moments, gives us something like goosebumps. This film, the most physical of its author, will touch you physically. (*FV*, 56)

But it is characteristic that Renoir's physicality embraces nature and women while Truffaut's is most evident when embracing the cinematic medium and celluloid. His assessment that "women are the crux of all of Renoir's work" (*FV*, 65) can certainly be applied to his own films; nevertheless, even such a woman-centered film as *The Story of Adèle H.* is finally about the tension between chaotic experience and aesthetic control. Like Renoir's *Madame Bovary*, Truffaut's portrayal of a nineteenth-century woman will be shaped by the frames in which she sees and presents herself. Truffaut's Adèle inherits a legacy from ancestors such as Antoine Doinel, Dr. Itard in *The Wild Child*, and Muriel in *Two English Girls:* she *pens* her love, in the dual sense of writing and enclosing.

A distinction (of degree rather than kind) can be made in that Truffaut seems more concerned with aesthetic frames and Renoir more comfortable with natural flow. The latter can be seen in a superbly characteristic moment during *La Chienne*. As Dédé talks with his friend in a cafe, a waiter pours a drink. His attention wanders, the liquid overflows onto the table, he nonchalantly mops it up, and walks away. While this remains peripheral to the action, Renoir's attention to detail is not only amusingly realistic, but emphasizes how life is messy. The glass, like the frames of *Rules of the*

Game, assumes significance precisely because it does not contain its spirits.

In the context of overflow or the inadequacy of boundaries, one of Truffaut's most interesting films is *Mississippi Mermaid*, since it faces up to the messy, the provisional, and the imperfect—and is dedicated to Renoir. It begins with a clip from Renoir's *La Marseillaise* (1937); it closes on two figures receding amid a snowy landscape in a visual echo of the end of *Grand Illusion*. Whereas the central question in the 1937 classic was whether Maréchal and Rosenthal would cross a national boundary to freedom, the question for Louis and Marion is whether they will traverse an emotional one. Truffaut displays Renoir's influence, for it is as impossible to delineate the borders in his physical/psychological landscape as it was in *Grand Illusion;* the work of both directors finally insists that boundaries are arbitrary inventions to rationalize the complexity of experience. This includes the frontiers of genres in that *Mississippi Mermaid* moves back and forth between comedy and drama in the manner of most of Renoir's films, from *The Little Match Girl* (1928) to *The Little Theater of Jean Renoir* (1969).

In addition, Truffaut presents the simultaneous existence of Marion's love for Louis and her attempt to poison him: how can we draw the line between these emotions? The book that Louis reads during the last sequence intensifies this question, for Balzac's *La Peau de Chagrin* contains the following perception: "Who can determine the point where ecstasy becomes an evil, and where evil is still an ecstasy? . . . And what is madness if not an excess of a desire or a power?" *Mississippi Mermaid* ends with the inseparability of love and suffering: Louis claims that it is joy and pain to look at her, Marion confesses that "love hurts."

Even the borders of ordinary verbal communication do not hold, for Truffaut plays with the space shared by *vous* and *tu*, or distance and intimacy. After they are married and sleep together, the characters still address one another in the formal *vous*. This implies that nothing can be taken for granted and that they do not yet know each other completely; there is still the intimacy of the *tu* to look forward to. Later, Marion complains that he was nicer to her when he used the polite form—"Tu étais plus gentil quand tu me disais 'Vous' "— to which Louis responds, "Ah, vous croyez?" As their relationship becomes more complex, the use of the *vous* suggests that they need to create some distance because they are too close; it becomes another frame for emotional material that is too strong. The fluidity of this verbal boundary returns in the last words of *Mississippi Mermaid,*

MARION: Je vous aime.

LOUIS: Je te crois.

In a film that seems to belong to his Hitchcockian period, Truffaut rejoins the heart of Renoir's work by focusing on the unexpected, undefinable, and uncertain aspects of love.

In conclusion, there is a sequence from *Shoot the Piano Player* that most eloquently illustrates Renoir's influence since it dissolves boundaries in space, time, and emotion. The lovemaking of Charlie and Lena is presented with a fluidity, simultaneity, and complexity which are characteristic of Renoir's vision—and Truffaut's. A closeup of Charlie and Lena kissing is superimposed on a slow 360° pan around her room. This spatial overlap dissolves into a temporal overlap: when Charlie and Lena are in bed, Truffaut fades in and out of brief shots of the lovers stirring at different moments, suggesting gently fragmented time in which emotions are overflowing the frames. Lena's voice unifies these stopped images as she confesses that she longed for him, "aching for you to touch my hand"; Charlie, however, is asleep. The effect is a haunting one of separateness as well as intimacy; Truffaut's camera and montage thus acknowledge distance and transience. Nevertheless, in the next scene, Lena tells Charlie he must resume his musical career and live again. He asks why, and she responds, "Pas pourquoi, pour qui" (not why, *for whom*). This can be interpreted as the fundamental stance of Renoir and Truffaut, for their films consistently offer the "for whom" as the frame and substance of human experience.

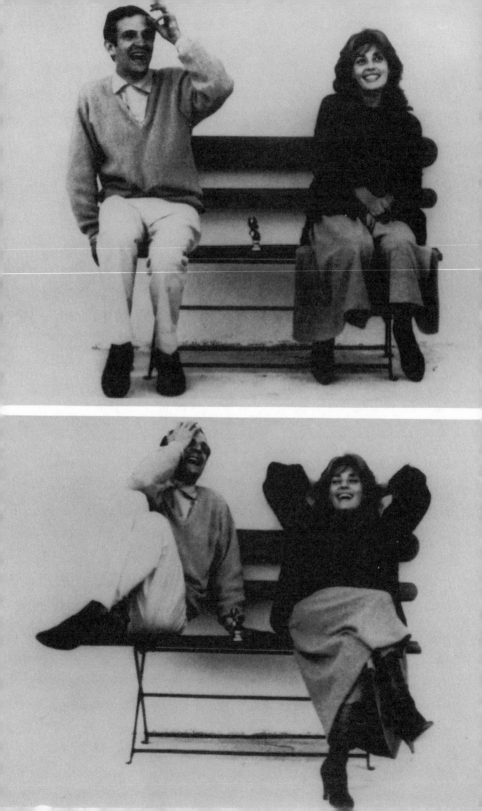

4

"Are Women Magic?"

Beautiful Lies

TO THE QUESTION posed by numerous males in Truffaut's films, we can add, "are women mad?", "are women vulnerable?", "are women more complex than the men assume?" The answer to all of these is yes, for Truffaut has created a rather bizarre gallery of rich female portraits. It is impossible to generalize about the women from *Les Mistons* through *Confidentially Yours*, for they can be as repellent as attractive, as destructive as warm, as absolutist as adaptable, and as inclined toward madness as love. Truffaut's awareness that a multiplicity of selves inhabits even one woman is evident in the "doubling" that is characteristic of his work. There are films that center on a male protagonist, whose own needs lead him to embrace two complementary female figures: Theresa/Lena in *Shoot the Piano Player*, Franca/Nicole in *The Soft Skin*, Linda/Clarisse (played by the same actress) in *Fahrenheit 451*, Christine/Fabienne in *Stolen Kisses*, Christine/Kyoko in *Bed and Board*, and Anne/Muriel in *Two English Girls*. And there are films that devote more attention to one female psyche with (at least) two manifestations: Catherine in *Jules and Jim*, Julie/Marion in *Mississippi Mermaid*, Julie/Pamela in *Day for Night*, Adèle/"Madame Pinson" in *The Story of Adèle H.*

Moreover, if we see Truffaut's work as a whole, another pair is formed by Julie Kohler (Jeanne Moreau) in *The Bride Wore Black* (1968) and Camille Bliss (Bernadette Lafont) in *Such a Gorgeous Kid Like Me* (1972), both of whom display no less than five personalities—one for each of their admirers. Despite the fact that the films are adapted from different novels (William Irish's *The Bride Wore Black* and Henry Farrell's *Such a Gorgeous Kid Like Me*) Julie and Camille can be seen as two faces of the literal *femme fatale* that Truffaut often presents: Kohler (colère-anger) killing for revenge and Bliss killing for pleasure. Whereas the former is intensely moral, the latter is amoral (calling her murderous activities "fate-bets"), for Camille takes about as much responsibility for her actions as a "kid"—gorgeous or otherwise. In fact, "kid" is an important term to keep in mind, for the resonances within Truffaut's cinema bring us inevitably to his first film, *Les Mistons*, which can be seen as the foundation for both *The Bride Wore Black* and *Such a Gorgeous Kid Like Me*. All three films explore the adoration of one woman by five males.

Les Mistons introduces Bernadette (Lafont) as the first of Truffaut's beautiful and inaccessible "apparitions" for the male. A group of young boys are smitten with her as she rides around Nimes on her bicycle, her skirt billowing in the summer wind. The narrator who is looking back at this chapter from his past states that she was "the wondrous incarnation of our secret dreams." We see the boys worship even her "pedestal," the bicycle whose seat they sniff reverently while she is in the water. They follow Bernadette and her lover Gérard, spying upon them, and their communally thwarted love is rechanneled into hostility. These little voyeurs annoy the pair (experiencing "the vicarious thrill of the interrupted kisses of the lovers") until they learn of Gérard's death in a climbing accident. When Bernadette walks past them in black at the end, they are able to observe her without yearning. Too young to comprehend, they have glimpsed the mysteries of love and death.

The voice-over narration places the emphasis on the boys, and we see the woman uniquely from their eyes. She is the *object* of affection, especially when she plays tennis and the camera participates in the infatuation by whirling around her little skirt and supple breasts. *The Bride Wore Black* picks up where the plot of *Les Mistons* leaves off: what happens to the woman after the death of the man she loved. Julie becomes the *subject* of the film, the active principle, the one whose thwarted love is rechanneled into hostility. The focus shifts to her response to her older (but no less naive) admirers. By the time of *Such a Gorgeous Kid Like Me*, Truffaut permits the woman to tell her own story—as the title makes clear—and she controls all the characters and events. (To take the doubling a step further, Bernadette Lafont gets her revenge on the *mistons* who tormented her in his first film.)

Truffaut's work revolves around the relationship between the adolescent and the goddess, and his treatment of his own female characters in a sense resembles that of the *mistons*. One way of studying his films is in the movement from adoration (Bernadette) to resentment (*Shoot the Piano Player* and *Jules and Jim* kill off the women—Theresa, Lena, Catherine—and even *The 400 Blows* includes Antoine's lie—and perhaps subconscious wish—that his mother died), to witnessing the death of the hero/rival (in *The Soft Skin, Fahrenheit 451, The Bride Wore Black*, and *Mississippi Mermaid*, the wives destroy the men, although Linda less directly so), to detachment (from the extremes of Camille and Adèle).[1] *The Man Who Loved Women* (1977), however, suggests that Truffaut has come to terms with the opposite sex: the adolescent male is still the focus (Bertrand is "a wolf who has remained a child") but the goddess is redefined into a group of women, each autonomous, warm, and articulate. And *The Last Metro* as well as *Confidentially Yours* offer heroines of new strength and maturity: both Marion and Barbara are as resourceful as they are beautiful to behold.

Shoot the Piano Player can be interpreted as a continuation of *Les Mistons* since Truffaut's second feature presents five older adolescents who are preoccupied with women: the two gangsters Ernest and Momo; Plyne; Edouard Saroyan and his second self, Charlie Kohler. These males constitute a spectrum of distorted perceptions of women, from the gangsters' coarse remarks to Plyne's "purity of womanhood" speech. Truffaut stated that the real theme of the film is love and the relations between men and women.[2] This is evident from the very first scene in which the stranger tells Chico about his marriage and the number of virgins in Paris—and this theme is developed during the subsequent scene in the bar. The perspective is predominantly that of male fascination: one dancing couple consists of a man peering intently down a woman's dress, which he justifies by declaring "I'm a doctor"; Clarisse is dancing with a short man, repeatedly enticing and pushing him away till he slaps her; two awkward young men watch Clarisse, their eyes practically popping out of their heads. Even the song performed by Bobby Lapointe, "Vanille et Framboise," deals with sex, in the spirit and actions of the first half of the film. (The song we hear on the car radio in the second half is rather about emotional commitment and love, and is more in keeping with the developments of this part.)

The "kidnapping" scene is primarily a pretext to talk about females. One of the gangsters tells how his father was killed in a car crash because he was looking at a woman; they discuss how women torment men with makeup, brassieres, and stockings; the other thug recounts how he tried on his sister's silk panties; and they elicit from Charlie those famous last words, "when you've seen one, you've seen them all." At the other extreme is the cafe boss Plyne whose conception of woman belongs in a medieval court rather than a cafe: "la femme" is "pure, delicate, fragile, supreme, magical." While his position is a bit excessive, it is not totally removed from Edouard's own behavior. Plyne dies because Lena cannot conform to his expectations; Theresa dies because Edouard expected the fidelity of an idealized love rather than imperfect experience. In his inability to accept his wife's altruistic adultery (she slept with the impresario in order for Edouard to get his break) and to comfort her, he resembles Plyne (as well as Catherine and Adèle) in their demand for an absolute—and therefore doomed—form of love. And like the *mistons*, he destroys what he cannot comprehend, namely the woman he loves. From this perspective, Truffaut seems to be establishing a context of male culpability to which his future heroines will address themselves.

A case in point is *The Bride Wore Black*. Julie Kohler is as sharp as the razor with which she slices the painting of her face—an eloquent image of the self-destruction that characterizes numerous Truffaut heroines. A parody of the woman who believes she can win a man's love by adapting to his predetermined ideal, she insinuates herself into each of her five victims' lives by incarnating their respective dream women. Truffaut said that the five men provided him with an opportunity to portray five ways of looking at women,[3] but they also permit five ways a woman can manipulate those views of women to her own ends. Although the men are quite different from one another (we are told that their sole link is a preoccupation with hunting and women), each will be punished for a fault that seems to obsess Truffaut: belief in the ideal over the immediate, the eternal over the ephemeral, the dream goddess over the woman.

The playboy Bliss, about to be married, sees Julie as a potential conquest. She appears mysteriously, dressed in white; she remains elusive, while appealing to his vanity. He assumes she has fallen for him and, therefore, falls for her (off the balcony). The sentimental bachelor Coral has existed alone in his timidity (not unlike Charlie Kohler); she becomes the romantic stuff his dreams are made of, the image of a perfect woman he believes destined for him. She feeds poison to his body only after nourishing a fantasy that is fatal to free affective experience. The stuck-up political aspirant Morane is locked within his complacency and pretensions, unable to see beyond his petty aims. Julie appears to fulfill his need for a subservient wife—a domestic of a higher order—and then locks him up where his pleas will prove as hollow and useless as his speeches.

Fergus the artist (and playboy) casts her in his own deifying mold. In eternizing her as a work of art (a theme to which we will return via *Jules and Jim*) and altering her appearance to fit a preexisting image, he prepares the canvas for his own death. By seeing her as Diane the Huntress, he becomes himself the hunted, even drawing the arrow for his own shooting. At one poignant moment when he is behind her, Fergus begs Julie to stay still because he can say "I love you" only when her back is turned. It is therefore appropriate that after her "frontal" attacks, she shoots Fergus in the back. Finally, for Delvaux, the brutal crook, the best woman is a whore. Julie meets him on his own terms and turf—prison—and stabs him with an instrument as common and blunt as himself. In this context, Gavin Millar's remark about the film is instructive: "Beyond the mediocre murder mystery lies a parable about affronted virginity in conflict with five types of guilty male sexuality."[4]

Camille Bliss in *Such a Gorgeous Kid Like Me*, on the other hand, is no virgin. As is true of her namesake—Julie's first victim in *The Bride Wore Black*—Camille's association with death is more comic than terrifying: Truffaut's touch with Camille is as light as the scarf that lures Bliss off the balcony. She is one of Truffaut's most liberated heroines, vulgar and vital, a gambler with life and death. We get to know her through a series of interviews taped by a sociologist, Stanislas Prévine, in the jail where she is imprisoned for murder. She is the material of his dissertation, *Criminal Women*, but as she describes her experiences—and her innocence—he becomes increasingly enamored of her. We learn that she did not actually commit the murder for which she is serving time, and Stanislas manages to get her released: he finds Michou, the child who filmed the scene of the crime at the moment Camille's victim killed himself. Camille's notoriety enables her to embark on a singing career. Stanislas comes to see her after a show, and she shoots her husband Clovis when he finds them together. Camille places the gun in Stanislas' hand: the sociologist "takes the rap."

As in *The Bride Wore Black*, Truffaut creates a context of male limitation through five adult adolescents. Arthur, played by Charles Denner, who also played Fergus, loves the heroine best and places her on the most impossible pedestal. He is representative of the way the later film is a comically inverted mirror, or even parody, of the earlier: where Fergus was an artist, Arthur is an exterminator; where the former was a playboy, the latter is a prude. He can make love only when an "accident" precedes the act and a sermon follows.

Camille's other men include her husband who cares only about two things (sex and booze) and is scared of his mother; the singer Sam Golden, a parody of the "macho" performer: his addiction to Americana leads him to put on a record of Indianapolis Speedway noises whenever he has sex (which is quite often); the attorney Murène, a con man (also sex-crazed) who hooks Camille with a line about not being able to relax with a woman. And finally Stanislas represents the timid adoration of the intellectual, and it is upon his blind love that her freedom comes to depend. To one degree or another, all of these men exploit Camille, so that if they seem to be her "victims" they are no less her victimizers.

In all but the last case, the exploitation is of a sexual nature: Camille eventually learns that this is the seat of her power, the only weapon by which she can enjoy, and succeed in, a man's world. Murène takes money from her, so she takes money from Arthur. She is accused and imprisoned for a murder she did not actually commit (Arthur jumps from the cathedral tower without her touching him); therefore, when she is released, she does commit murder as she shoots Clovis. At the end of the film, she has acquired a sixth man—Stanislas' former lawyer whose previous last words about Camille had been, "I'd like to see that creature crushed." We can imagine that he will soon be the one under her foot.

Stanislas begins interviewing her for his sociology thesis; intending at first to use her as data, he ends up being used by her. The only male character who does not get to enjoy her sexual favors, Stanislas is perhaps the most important figure in the film since it is his professional and increasingly personal concern with Camille that frames her own account. Her experiences come to us through the mediation of his tape recorder and later through his statement written in jail. His appraisal of Camille supports Truffaut's characterization of her—"Il ne s'agit pas de juger mais de comprendre" (one should not judge but understand)—particularly when we note that their interviews take place in a courtroom. In this locale of judgment, we are not the jury but the audience.

Numerous distancing devices are employed throughout *Such A Gorgeous Kid Like Me;* as we will see in Chapter 5, but the overall impression of the murderess is one of spunky retribution. It is significant that we never see her kill anyone—her responsibility for the deaths of her father, Arthur, and her mother-in-law is indirect, her attempt to murder Murène and Clovis with rat poison fails, and her shooting of Clovis takes place offscreen—and that each of her victims is more a comic type than an individual. We cringe more when she holds a microphone than a gun, for there is less evidence of her being a criminal woman than a dreadful singer.

Ultimately, *Such a Gorgeous Kid Like Me* is a farce where *The Bride Wore Black* is compelling and disturbing, for the bounty bitch lacks the depth and resonance of Julie's character. This is partially attributable to the qualities that only Jeanne Moreau could bring to the role and to the inescapable connections that one is led to make between her Julie and her Catherine in *Jules and Jim* seven years earlier. Moreau endows both characters with her own qualities of intelligence, sensuality, and mystery. Her face eloquently attests to experiences of love and pain and suggests in both films a personal but resolute moral code. Julie and Catherine defy conventional morality but with an acute sense of self-imposed justice to which they remain faithful. They seem to use and destroy the men around them without any thought for the consequences of their acts; however, Moreau's face reveals a deeper awareness. The drooping mouth suggests the cost of freedom and power; the dark and deeply shadowed eyes betray the knowledge that in destroying others, she cannot but destroy herself.[5]

Graham Petrie is right to find in *The Bride Wore Black* that "her ability to provide so many facets of the ideal gives her an almost supernatural or at least super-human quality that links her to the figure of Catherine," since the latter also provides a version of the ideal for Jules, Jim, Albert, and others.[6] *Jules and Jim* communicates this in uniquely cinematic terms. The two friends are shown slides of a statue, presented in quick cuts from different angles. They are enchanted by the beautiful face, and they follow it to the island of its origin. The camera participates in the search, hesitating, moving nervously from one statue to another and leading us to share their excitement. As they find the object of their quest, the camera triumphantly circles around it. When Catherine appears, she is visually linked to the statue since the camera makes the same excited movements around her. The men see her as the incarnation of their prized objet d'art, particularly because she shares with the sculpture a mysterious smile. Later her face is explored and then captured for an instant, then released and captured again in a series of freeze-frame close-ups. The camera attempts to make an immobile and immortal figure of her, representing the way Jules and Jim will try to "keep" her.

A similar relationship involving art, love, and possession exists between Fergus and Julie in *The Bride Wore Black*. As the model for his paintings, the image made flesh, Julie occupies a position like Catherine's vis-à-vis the statue. Jules, Jim, and Fergus place the woman on a pedestal for reasons outside of her own character; and, in worshipping the mythic at the expense of the human, they ensure their own demise. Julie fulfills the role in which Fergus casts her: Diane the Huntress. Likewise, Catherine becomes the goddess who is, by definition, a destroyer of men. But *The Bride Wore Black* presents an interesting reversal: Fergus falls in love with her because she resembles his art; he ends by loving the canvas because it resembles the woman. In painting her on the wall beside his bed, he completes the process from art-into-woman to woman-into-art. He permits himself the delusion that in capturing her form he can possess her spirit.

Jules and Jim will be no more successful than the artist in their desire to hold Catherine, for she is more complex than a statue, more mysterious than a model. If the world of art provides her lovers with a vision to be realized, it does no less for her. In the scene where she jumps into the Seine (because Jules and Jim are not paying enough attention to her), she says that she likes the heroine of the Swedish play they have just seen because "She wants to be free. She invents her own life." This is precisely Catherine's intent, to make of her own experience a fluid work of art, improvised, spontaneous, and rich in characters. She insists on being her own director, is willing to be their star, but only on her own terms. Her attempt at self-determination may recall that of the bride, but if the active principle of Julie was revenge, Catherine's is freedom in love. Both women are admirable in their strength and energy, but they are repellent in a fundamentally similar way: the principles become more important than the men who love them, and they lose the capacity to taste experience in their hunger for the absolute. In this sense, they are finally as guilty of choosing the cold ideal over the warm immediate as the bride's victims.

But where Julie is basically a one-note character who goes to the extreme of self-control, Catherine is a veritable orchestra who changes tones impulsively and unpredictably. Anything one can say about her has its contrary. She is absolute with respect to her sense of freedom and to the adoration she inspires and insists upon, but relative in her relationships. One day Jules is out of favor; the next day, Jim. She is creative and destructive, the source and embodiment of both life and death, open and mysterious, calm and passionate; she had aristocratic parents but enjoys peasant pursuits; resisting all labels, she is friend and lover, mother ("allons-y, mes enfants") and spoiled child. Ultimately, she suggests an androgynous figure, as masculine as feminine. For example, she is the one who sings "Les Tourbillons de la vie," which Albert wrote about her; since the song is from the male point of view, she becomes both the subject and object. When she appropriates a cap, moustache, and cigar and pretends to be "Thomas," we are told that the men were touched "as if by a symbol they could not quite understand." Perhaps the symbol is hermaphroditic, for it recalls Jules' frustration over the inversion of genders between German and French, with "life" being neuter.[7] There is something of this ambiguity in Catherine, for she does represent "life"—but life that contains the seeds of its own violation.

The images associated with her throughout the film, fire and water, contribute to the all-embracing impression of her character. She joins water when she jumps into the Seine; touches fire when she burns her old love letters. (When she sets fire to the letters, the flames jump onto her robe, perhaps foreshadowing how her destruction of others will spread to herself. In this scene, Jim puts out the fire; in the last scene, she will drag him down with her.) The rain makes her decide they will go to the beach; later the rain leads her to return to Paris. Water is the death she chooses when she drives off the bridge; fire is added when their coffins are burned. Her most personal symbol is therefore the vitriol that she carries with her— liquid fire—a blend of elements as contradictory as herself.

Despite the title of the film, it is Catherine who dominates. Stanley Kauffmann's inspired point that *Jules and Jim* is about an isosceles triangle that becomes equilateral[8] is well-taken, but the film is also a triangle that becomes a circle with Catherine at its center, pulling the other characters in or radiating out. More than an individual, she is the incarnation of a timeless force. Jules sees her as "la

Femme," made for all men rather than just one, and she is also called "an irresistible force that can't be shaken," "a queen," "a real woman," "a vision for all men." If we compare her to the other females in the film, she becomes all the more remarkable. Her predecessor Thérèse is also a liberated and energetic woman, but she has spunk without depth. Her rival Gilberte's best attribute seems to be fidelity; she has depth without spunk. And finally Denise in the cafe is presented as a stupid "bel objet . . . sex in its pure state." In such a context, it is no wonder that Catherine is worshipped as Queen.

She *is* superhuman, but a great deal of the film's tension derives from the fact that she is also human. In other words, she is the definitive Truffaut goddess—all things to all men—but inherent in such a "reflected" identity is the ravenous need for the attention to which she has been accustomed. Whereas Julie's sense of self was enclosed by an idea that left her blind to the way men saw her (namely as a woman to be loved), Catherine's is a function of the eyes of others. To a question that the film provokes—what is the self that remains when there are no lovers to define her?—the answer might be that she never allows the lonely opportunity for the question to articulate itself. When one lover momentarily dares look elsewhere, she must punish him with another lover to "even the score." With a sense of retribution like Julie's, she tells Jim that "Gilberte equals Albert" in order to justify her affair with the latter. She needs the admirers as much as they need her, demanding their absolute fidelity as much as they insist on serving her. No one is to blame, for the way the men see her coincides with and fulfills the way she perceives herself.

What Catherine finally is to herself remains a mystery for, paradoxically, her self-absorption precludes self-knowledge. Truffaut's deletion of a line from the novel is instructive: Catherine says, "I am a mother above all," but the film undercuts this sentiment by emphasizing her more vivid and consistent identity as a lover. In fact, her wish to be a mother might be connected to her need for permanent adoration: procreation confers upon lovemaking the potential of the absolute. Her relationship with Jim is totally based on her desire for a child by him; when she does not become pregnant, they separate ("I think of this child we will not have . . . I love you less"). When she subsequently becomes pregnant, she passionately declares to Jim that he is alive in her. Her sudden miscarriage results in her leaving him.

In demanding a freedom for herself that she will not permit in others, she displays a lack of both responsibility and lucidity, which are prerequisites for selfhood. At one point she even tells Jim, "I don't want to be understood." Unable to accept her own vulnerability or to comprehend that of her lovers, she proves she really is a goddess rather than a complete woman. Like the queens of mythology, her human emotions conflict with her superhuman identity: she is vain, petty, jealous, and selfish—an implacable destroyer when she feels insufficiently worshipped. The triangle that originated in such affection and solidarity falls apart through her frustrated needs, especially when she brings in Albert to punish them. Jim had told her, "You wanted to invent love from the beginning . . . but pioneers should be humble, without egoism," and she responds to Jim's awareness of her selfishness by trying to shoot him. Having seen through the smile, he must be destroyed. Catherine's delusion that freedom and openness can thrive without obligations and pain, and that she could create herself beyond human limitations, resulted in a goddess who would die rather than give up her throne.

The source of tension for Catherine (and one which recurs in Truffaut's films) is the possibility for identity—apart from how we think others see us. (Or, as Kierkegaard so perfectly puts it in *Either/Or*, "What is the self that remains when you have lost everything but yourself?") Roger Greenspun is right to say that "Catherine seems compelled to act out the contradictory impulses implicit in such a confusion of roles,"[9] but neither Jules nor Truffaut nor Roché can finally penetrate the roles in which they have cast her. Truffaut's females are often portrayed as existing less in, of, and for themselves than as realizations of male visions. The men, and the audience, perceive first the image and subsequently the woman who embodies it. (Here we might recall a *Cahiers* favorite, Otto Preminger's *Laura*, in which the detective falls in love with a portrait of a woman long before meeting her.)

Jim's remark that Catherine is an apparition to be appreciated by all men will be echoed, for instance, in *Stolen Kisses* when Antoine finds Fabienne Tabard. A less dazzling but more wise Truffaut goddess, she too will be introduced and worshipped from the perspective of the enraptured male. Like Jules, Jim, and Fergus, Antoine will become enamored of a woman because she corresponds to the romantic expectations fostered in him by art. We meet Antoine as he reads Balzac's *Le Lys dans la vallée*, the story of the impossible

love of Felix for the older Madame de Mortsauf. His image of the
perfect woman is tied in with nineteenth-century romanticism/
sublimation/absolutism, and his anachronistic sensibility is emphasized by the place in which he is reading the novel: a military
prison where the sergeant-major lectures on mine detection by
means of crude sexual imagery. The gap between "dismantling the
mine is just like handling a girl—you've got to go easy" and Felix's
ideal (and therefore unconsummated) love is developed in the next
scene when Antoine is with a prostitute; he tries to kiss her and
stroke her hair while she insists on impersonal efficiency.

By contrast, Fabienne "materializes" one evening in the shoestore where Antoine works—a literal apparition. First, we hear the
song of the siren, and the subjective camera tracks with Antoine's
mesmerized movement, leading us slowly toward the sound. We
share in Antoine's first glimpse of this beautiful and sophisticated
woman, glowing in the darkness, a presence both mysterious and
friendly. The screenplay notes, "Antoine is enthralled by this apparition" (AD, 175), and his awe is evident in the report he phones in
to the detective agency:

IDA: What shape face?

ANTOINE (waxing lyrical): It's a perfect oval shape . . . I mean a
slightly triangular oval. And her complexion is radiant . . . as if illuminated from within!

IDA: Look, Antoine, what we want is a report, not a declaration of love!
(AD, 177)

Imprisoned by the dichotomy between the absolute and the accessible, he is blind to her as a living human being, but fortunately
Fabienne is warm, generous, and lucid enough to emerge from his
romantic plaster. Antoine's naive contention that she is "far above"
such a thing as adultery is ironically juxtaposed with her visit to his
apartment after he has mailed her a declaration of hopeless love.
With infinite grace, she establishes that they are not characters in a
nineteenth-century novel but a man and a woman in a bedroom, a
situation which certainly has its own magic. She finds Le Lys dans la
vallée "a pathetic tale . . . because in the end what caused her
death was that she couldn't share that love with him." The goddess
steps off her pedestal and into his arms, humanized, proposing a
contract as definitive as it is provisional: "I'll come there, by your
side, now. We will spend a few hours together and then, no matter

what happens, we will never see each other again. All right?" A compromise, yes, but one which permits the richness of experience to triumph over fantasy, even if for a few hours. Dominique Fanne expresses this well when she finds that Fabienne "disrupts his dream, she leads him to stop looking in order to start living."[10] Given their situation, Fabienne's offer is a necessary and affectionate compromise between the coarse and the unconsummated.

After this demystifying encounter, Antoine is able to appreciate the "exceptional" qualities of his girl friend Christine, one of the first modern and well-adjusted women in Truffaut's universe. The penultimate scene in which they share breakfast and hopes for a future implies that they will learn and grow together for, beyond being lovers, they are friends. The romance of buttering dry toast without breaking it ("you take two pieces, you put them on top of each other, like this, then you spread the butter on . . . and thanks to the piece underneath, the one on top will never break") or the ceremony of his placing a bottle opener on her ring finger render the common things around (and inside) them miraculous.

What remains slightly unsettling, however, is Fabienne's fate. Antoine—and Truffaut—have used her in that noble French tradition of the older woman who leads the young man to love and maturity and then conveniently disappears. Truffaut gets comic mileage out of her insufferable husband but then leaves her to him. Her staying with such a man is inexplicable, and it is problematic that her sole purpose in life seems to be the "éducation sentimentale" of shopboys. In a film that struggles to overcome nineteenth-century images, Fabienne Tabard is paradoxically used in a nineteenth-century role. It is only in *The Man Who Loved Women* that Truffaut penetrates this image through the character played by Geneviève Fontanel. A maturely sensual beauty reminiscent of Jeanne Moreau, Hélène is the 41-year old owner of a lingerie shop. When Bertrand invites her to his apartment, she gently refuses because

I am attracted only to boys younger than myself. . . . The passage of time gives us some harsh blows; our faces are not ruined as fast as those of boxers but it's the same thing . . . I do not accept the degradation of life, or rather I don't accept that love accommodate it. (*HAF*, 33)

The fact that she says this against the background of a shoestore links her visually to Fabienne. The implication is that Hélène, like her predecessor, is not simply an object but a subject—a woman who does not so much "initiate" young men as enjoy them.

In the sequel to *Stolen Kisses, Bed and Board*, we suspect that Antoine has not changed all that much, particularly when he says that the aim of his flower-dyeing experiment is "Absolute Red." (Significantly, the flowers burn, in what may be a comic echo of how the absolute consumes itself.) Our suspicion is borne out by his attraction to Kyoko, a Japanese woman who represents the ultimate in mystery and exoticism. Christine mocks his infatuation by making herself up as a Japanese lady one night, but a close-up reveals the tears that express her true emotions. She subsequently displays a certain strength in the face of Antoine's painful egotism by making a life for herself without him. Christine proves to be one of the few wives in Truffaut's work who is not a killer. Catherine, Franca (*The Soft Skin*), and Linda (*Fahrenheit 451*) must have the husbands on their own terms or not at all. Marion (*Mississippi Mermaid*) tries to murder Louis for his money; Theresa (*Shoot the Piano Player*) kills herself; Julie Kohler and Camille Bliss are pros; Mathilde (*The Woman Next Door*) shoots her love and herself.

Antoine finds that Kyoko is no more than an "object" of his affection, unable to communicate with him beyond a few perfunctory remarks. When he is at a restaurant with her, he phones Christine three times, attempting to wangle his way back into her life. Although she takes him back, the dominant impression at the end is that of the tension they expressed in a previous scene. Antoine declares, "You are my kid sister, my daughter, my mother"; Christine answers, "I'd hoped to be your wife."

This sentiment will be echoed by the girl friend of Alphonse (Antoine's reincarnation—and the name of his son in *Bed and Board*—played again by Jean-Pierre Léaud) in *Day for Night*. Liliane finds him a moody and spoiled child "who will never be a man. What he needs is a wife, mistress, nurse and little sister all at once." Liliane appears as a rather cute and coarse woman (vaguely reminiscent of Camille Bliss), but Alphonse romanticizes her as his wife-to-be. Like so many of his "ancestors," he asks everyone on the set if women are magic (receiving some delightful answers such as Bernard's "No, but their legs are"). The "correct" answer (in other words, the only one that makes living possible and desirable)—that women are no more magical than men, therefore, we are all magical—is offered by Julie Baker. The complex characterization of this actress has great resonance in Truffaut's gallery of women. A goddess to others, a vulnerable and confused woman to herself, she provides echoes of both the warm and disturbed heroines who preceded her.[11] An English actress who has suffered a nervous breakdown, Julie is to play the star of *Meet Pamela*, the film within the film of *Day for Night*. Her name links her to Julie Kohler who at one point took the name of the schoolteacher Miss Becker. Perhaps "Julie Baker," therefore, brings together the apparition, the obsessive, and the teacher—as *Day for Night's* character will succeed in doing—and Julie/Marion, whom she resembles physically and psychologically. All three women are in some sense actresses who perform for the sake of their husbands.

In the three films, the Julie character is presented first as a photograph, a fixed surface which conceals the complexities of the woman/model. The tension between icon and individual emerges when Ferrand holds up pictures of Julie while discussing her psychological fragility. Before she appears in *Day for Night*, some confusion already exists about her identity. The three other stars of the film within the film retain their own names (Alphonse, Alexandre, Séverine). Only Julie takes on a second, and in the screenplay, she actually has three names: "Julie Baker (Nelson)—Pamela." Séverine's blunder in one of the takes is to call her Julie instead of Pamela. When the woman in question finally arrives, we learn that her "real" life is not all that distant from the role she will play: Pamela marries Alphonse and falls in love with his father; Julie's husband, Dr. Nelson, is twice her age. There is a sense in which Julie still considers her marriage a forbidden relationship, for she furtively pulls Dr. Nelson into an alley, glancing nervously around her, to kiss him. (We subsequently learn that he abandoned his wife and children for her.)

The concept of doubling is developed as Pamela tells her new mother-in-law how she met Alphonse: he was supposed to take a walk with her cousin Dorothy, but she got sick, so Pamela "took her place." Moreover, it turns out that the stuntman will be "doubling" for Julie. Later, Ferrand reads approvingly her version of *Meet Pamela*: "A girl realizes that the boy she married is only the reflection of his father . . ." The theme of identity is still being explored through actors and their roles, characters and their reflections, and individuals and their former selves or reputations, such as Séverine and Alexandre. In addition, Truffaut employs echoes of his earlier creations in his concern with reflected identities.

In the bungalow scene between Alexandre, Julie, and the cat, Truffaut "quotes" the sequence from *The Soft Skin* in which Pierre and Nicole, another "ma petite fille" couple, have escaped to the country. Nicole placed the breakfast tray outside the door and a cat came along to drink the milk on a plate. *Day for Night* presents this scene from the point of view of the crew who must reshoot until the cat finally licks the milk. Julie's repetition of and resemblance to Nicole (and how suggestive that in French, *répétition* also means rehearsal) extends to her "real" situation with respect to Alphonse. Both he and Pierre yearn for permanence in their relationships and deny the women their right to freedom. Pierre tries to "capture" Nicole in a photograph with himself; the same impulse is visible when Alphonse refuses to be in the group photo because Liliane is not there. He takes his absolutist needs to an extreme with Julie, fixating upon her only hours after Liliane's departure. In order to keep Alphonse from leaving the film before its completion (behavior that would have echoed her own while shooting a previous film), Julie spends the night in his bed. Mature and maternal, she resembles Fabienne in both her comment about magical people and her gesture of generous sensuality.

In typically childish fashion, Alphonse mistakes the warm gesture for the right to possession and, assuming they will leave together when shooting terminates, telephones Dr. Nelson: "I love your wife. We made love. Set her free!" He enacts an inversion of *Meet Pamela*—the young man taking the wife from the "father"—and in reversing the roles, throws Julie back into her former hysterical state. But through her husband's understanding, and her own professional commitment, she proves more responsible than Alphonse, able to forgive and forge a stronger identity for herself. She can grow only because her husband accepts her, not idealistically but in all her fallibility.

Marion of *Mississippi Mermaid* also needs to be accepted by Louis as her actual—and therefore troubled—self rather than in the deified role of Julie Roussel. All that Louis and the audience know of Julie at the outset is the raw material of an imagined ideal: letters and a photograph, beautiful and deceptive postures. His term for Julie is revealing: he calls her "un mensonge adorable" (a beautiful lie) and, like his Truffautesque predecessors, he prefers this fantasy to the complex truths which render her merely human. His kinship to Antoine and Pierre is evident from what he reads, namely Balzac.

Jacqueline Bisset as Julie: She detains her husband for a furtive kiss (top); Alphonse pleads, "stay." (bottom)

Whereas Antoine read *La Recherche de l'absolu* in *The 400 Blows* and *Le Lys dans la vallée* in *Stolen Kisses*, and Pierre wrote his own study of the author, Louis reads *La Peau de Chagrin* in the cabin. Each of the protagonists is a bit nostalgic and awkward, or as Louis acknowledges, "the people who use want ads are idealists." In placing his destiny in the impersonal hands of a "personal" column, he betrays the need to have someone conform to his image, rather than the ability to respond to the unique and often inarticulatable personalities one meets. As he says to Marion, "The letters of Julie Roussel were very beautiful . . . we tried to establish something definitive, and then you came, bringing me the provisional . . . "

Nevertheless, in the course of the film Louis learns to accept the irrational woman over the myth, to embrace the liar rather than the lie. The goddess is exposed and loved in her ugliness as well as beauty (the tormented Queen as well as Snow White). After the sunny island of La Réunion (the Julie realm) and the whirlpools of her nightmares (the Marion realm), the film ends in a cloudy image in the snow; it combines ground and water, light and dark, the elemental and the transient. On one level, this shot connotes a "re-union" of the woman's personality: in her black feather coat, she is both image and individual, moving toward an undefined destiny in the snow.

A relatively naive young man with expectations and two women who undergo various "exchanges" continue to be the basis for Truffaut's next film, *Two English Girls*. While *Les Deux Anglaises et le Continent* is a companion piece to the other triangular story he adapted from Roché, *Jules and Jim*, it resumes and illuminates a number of his earlier efforts, and looks forward to *The Story of Adèle H.* Don Allen in *Truffaut* remarks that

the film's atmosphere is very reminiscent of André Gide's *La Porte étroite* (one man loved by two sisters; self-sacrifice; self-deception and repressed sexuality all round; the frustration of any sexual consummation in the Gide and its postponement until too late in the Truffaut). (p. 144)

Amid the literary resonances of *Two English Girls*, from Roché and Gide we must again return to Balzac.

Although we do not observe Claude Roc reading *Le Lys dans la vallée*, he manifests his connection to the author by visiting Rodin's statue of Balzac. For one of the underlying tensions of *Two English*

Girls is literature versus sculpture, or language versus flesh and clay, or Muriel versus Anne—with Claude caught between all of them. Léaud plays a role markedly different from his Doinel or Alphonse characterizations. Still something of an outsider in the world of women (as we see in the magnificent shot of the sisters and mother singing joyfully in harmony while ironing, Claude watching outside the door, book in hand), he lacks the engaging energy, humor, and resourcefulness of Truffaut's original protagonists. He is acted upon rather than active, constantly manipulated by no less than four women: Anne, Muriel, Mrs. Brown, and his own mother.[12]

This is eloquently expressed when he and the three ladies Brown take shelter in a cave from the rain. To keep warm, Mrs. Brown seats herself between her two daughters who rock her back and forth. She then invites Claude to take her place, and he is playfully pushed from one sister to the other. His voice-over reveals that he felt "like a pawn in a strange game," a sentiment that will be borne out by the film's fluctuating movements. He is always checked as he gets closer to a mate: first, his mother sets up his meeting with Anne; then Anne sets up his relationship with Muriel; Mrs. Brown echoes that "Anne has pledged Claude to Muriel," and intensifies this possibility for Claude; Mrs. Roc prevents his marriage to Muriel; when he is involved with Anne, she guards against their growing overly attached by taking on other lovers; she (inadvertently) keeps Muriel from going away with Claude by confessing to her that they had an affair; Muriel will not permit a "sequel" to her long-awaited night with Claude. To this emotional *va-et-vient* in which nothing is certain, Claude and the sisters will respond with the order of art, confronting solitude and death with printed selves and clay forms.

Claude's voice frames the film: pictures of the text of *Les Deux Anglaises et le Continent* flood the screen as he says, "Some day I will write our story." It is *his* tale, but as is true of *Such a Gorgeous Kid Like Me*, he can control events only insofar as he transcribes them; like the sociologist Prévine, Claude often seems like male innocence maneuvered by female power. The scene that best captures his situation is that of Claude playing "statues" with the two sisters. He whirls each woman around, and she is to "freeze" in the pose in which he leaves her (a game with a good deal of symbolism!). After turning both into temporary statues, Claude is then spun

Claude and Anne (*Two English Girls*).

round by them as the commentary informs us that "Claude always lost." He is not sufficiently in control of himself to be still.

The statue metaphor, rich in Truffautesque connotations of posing and permanence, weaves through the relationships and sheds light on the women as well as on Claude. The first "sculptress" is Claude's mother: she tells him she built him by herself, "like a monument, stone by stone." Subsequently, and on a literal level, Anne becomes a sculptress. However, it is finally Muriel to whom the imagery is most relevant. Once again, the presence of the central female character is anticipated by the male and the audience: Muriel exists first as a photograph (Anne shows Claude a picture of her sister at the age of ten) and as a recurring topic of conversation. Anne verbally presents Muriel to Claude, but she will appear only when she is ready. She is expected at dinner, but the subjective camera returns with Claude to an empty chair, the presence of her absence. When Muriel finally comes down, her mysterious quality is heightened by Anne's admonition "not to look at her yet." Claude is confronted by a woman blindfolded due to eye strain, peeking out of her bandage to eat her soup; as he watches her, we hear the

letter he is writing his mother about her. He will endow Muriel
with the attributes familiar to us from Truffaut's work: "Muriel is
purity," he thinks of her as "unapproachable," he does not allow
himself to believe she will return his feelings.

The power of suggestion provided by Anne—her predicting that
Claude and Muriel "love each other but don't know it yet"—leads
him to write to Muriel, confessing how he is absorbed by the "image" of her with the child they will have. He is enamored of the idea
of their union (which is above all Anne's creation). When Muriel
rejects him, his response is that he aimed too high. (She, at this
moment, is marching outdoors by herself, shouting "I adore you,
Claude . . .") Several years later, Claude comes to see her in Anne's
studio and finds her standing immobile in the middle of the room, a
veritable statue in dark glasses. Anne has in a sense molded her for
Claude's vision, animating her with possibilities of sensuality, but
he can see only the form and not the woman. She kisses him passionately, but he is unable to respond, or to let her come down from
her pedestal. He leaves her amid Anne's other work, visibly troubled by the discrepancy between his image and his desires. For
Claude, Muriel represents something absolute and untouchable,
categorized and self-contained. In viewing her from this perspective, he reinforces that part of her that views herself in a similar way.
And in defining her through letters and diaries rather than embraces, he intensifies her own impulse to do the same.

Muriel's relationship to words is much like Claude's; one could
say that they are perfectly matched in their fundamental reliance
upon language. Their most intimate communications are the letters
that Anne carries between them, and the diaries that they write for
each other (as opposed to the diaries—and even letters—of Adèle
H.,which are ultimately self-addressed). Claude begins writing the
day he meets Anne; his diary is therefore bound up with the first
stage of his relation to women and permits the intimacy that would
be out of place in actual conversation. As Anne raises her veil, the
voice-over establishes, "I had the impression of a modest and
aggreeable nudity." Writing then becomes a means of connection
between Claude and Muriel; when their letters are forbidden for a
year, she suggests they keep diaries which they will send each
other. The result is a kind of verbalization/objectification whereby
they become the sum of their words, spirit removed from flesh, as
abstract in their identities as their print is palpable.

Human pedestals and statues: Henri Serre, Jeanne Moreau, and Oscar Werner in *Jules and Jim* (top). Kika Markham, Jean-Pierre Léaud, and Stacy Tendeter in *Two English Girls*.

Anne's medium, on the other hand, is form without spirit, or only so much soul as body can suggest. The active principle of the film, she carries the messages between Claude and Muriel—and the burden of that communication. Anne and Claude do *not* touch via letters, with the glorious exception when she writes to him, "You are more real than my sculpture." Claude had said something similar to Muriel when he wrote that their life together would be more important than the books he wants to write. Muriel, however, never expresses such a sentiment, for her self is, to a great extent, enclosed by mirrors and pages; her eyesight is weak because her inner sight is the stronger. In fact, the difference between Anne and Muriel is brought out in their response to words, particularly those that classify. Anne is able to go away with Claude, living first and "putting the label on afterwards." Muriel needs precision of terms and becomes hysterical because she cannot understand what Claude means by "women-friends." The term is too relative, too open. She must have words that limit, define, and ultimately control, while her sister can express—and therefore create—herself physically. Anne works with her hands and respects the body, aesthetically and sexually, in a manner reminiscent of D. H. Lawrence's heroines. (An interesting comparison could be made between *Two English Girls* and Lawrence's *Women In Love*, particularly in light of the concern with female sexuality/art/love/freedom/identity shared by Lawrence, Roché, and Truffaut.)

Like Catherine in *Jules and Jim*, Anne learns that a woman is capable of loving more than one man and attempts to live by this felt knowledge. Catherine's shift from Jules to Jim was marked by a kiss "that lasted all night"; when Anne says goodbye to Claude before leaving with her other lover Diurka, "their farewell lasted all night." The result is much like that of *Jules and Jim*: "Anne had regular lovers. The lovers suffered; Anne thrived," says the commentary. Nevertheless, Anne displays only the noble aspect of Catherine, devoid of jealousy and destructiveness. She encourages a relationship with Claude only after it is clear that he and Muriel have no future. And even then, as they begin their first kiss in her studio, she detaches herself to place a wet cloth over the head of one of her creations. This "blindfolding" is like a visual echo of Muriel, and Anne's action can be interpreted as sparing her sister the sight of their embrace.

Anne does not play her lovers off against each other, and if she "directs" the relationships, she does so with generosity. It is noteworthy that early in the film, she recounts to Claude the story she has just heard about a robbery. Someone stole a boat, and the owner's response was to drop the case because the thief probably needed it more than he did. To a certain extent, Anne lets Muriel take Claude because she believes her sister's need for him is greater than her own. This ability to sacrifice her own pleasure for the peace of others is also evident from the facts surrounding her death: unlike Catherine, she refuses to let others "go down with her." When she learns that she has tuberculosis, she breaks her engagement but does not tell the fiancé that it is because of her illness. Her last words, "my mouth is full of earth," return her to the element with which she can be associated. While Catherine's elements were water and fire, Anne's mode of work and love is rooted in earth, in solid affections.

Muriel, by contrast, connects herself to water and reveals her ties to the more problematic side of Catherine's personality. She describes herself as "a river that rises and falls," with the waves rolling behind her, reinforcing the fluctuations of the speaker. Whereas Claude meets Anne in a garden, he waits for Muriel by the ocean; behind him, the boat conspicuously reflects a shimmering play of water, even after they leave the frame. Like Catherine, she wants to be all things to Claude, and where the women loved by Antoine or Alphonse complained of the number of roles expected of them, Muriel claims, "I am your wife. I was your sister, your friend, everything." Truffaut implies that both the man who expects all and the woman who tries to be all are on shaky ground and bound for disappointment. Muriel takes this position to its extreme when she declares, "I want all of Claude or nothing. If not, let it be like death." This demanding nature even extends to her visual presentation: if Anne tends to share her space, seen usually in two-shots and interacting with people around her, Muriel's personality insists upon the close-up. The only other face she allows into the frame is her reflection in the mirror.

The first time we see her after the introductory dinner, she is seated before her mirror, writing "resolutions." The camera moves into a close-up of reflections inside reflections, since the surface of her glasses compounds that of the mirror. Her self-imposed rules for conduct tell us that this is the face of a woman trying to master unruly parts of herself, splitting into subject and object, transgressor and authority, blind emotion and lucid control. We learn much later that this "doubling" has a literal foundation, namely that she has been a compulsive masturbator since childhood. She sends her diary to Claude (or rather asks Anne to send it), and her confession is calculated to punish him in the same way that Catherine's lovers punished Jules: "We're even." The main difference is that Claude's rival is absolute, being herself.

She demolishes his myth of her purity by chronicling the obsession to which she was "a slave." It began when she was a child and her girl friend taught her how to touch herself. Truffaut presents this sequence through a powerful juxtaposition of the past (grainy scenes of two little girls, her friend displaying a knowing and almost lecherous smile) and present (Muriel in extreme close-up, her eyes attracting and repelling us in their intensity). She admits to her anger at being "driven by an unknown force" and quotes the advice she received from an organization in America; their letter suggested that she split herself in two so that, after an act of weakness, "say it was not you"—which the montage supports by literally showing us two different people.

Muriel's excessive attachment to and recoiling from her own body (and self) lead her to an internal turbulence in which repression and release are all the more intense. To a certain extent, there is really no room for Claude in her world since the passion is so self-contained. As Muriel declares when Claude breaks their engagement, "I won't write my diary for Claude any more, only for myself." (And Claude's response seems to be a rather detached numbness.) Muriel is like another Victorian heroine, Tennyson's "Mariana" whose lonely and monotonous refrain,

> She only said, 'The night is dreary,
> He cometh not,' she said;
> She said, 'I am aweary, aweary,
> I would that I were dead!'

punctuates a poem of amorous aching. Waiting for a lover who she knows will not come, Mariana luxuriates in her own despair, with a repression that takes on its own sensuality. The aching, more familiar and certain than a lover, is the raison d'être of these women. When Anne confesses that Claude was one of her lovers, Muriel becomes ill, manifesting what the commentary calls "the violence of her suppressed love." Perhaps the violence refers more to the suppression than the love since pain, and the perverse purity of loneliness, become precious to Muriel, being all that she (and Mariana) can possess completely.

Muriel's passionate night with Claude supports this notion, as we are told that Claude unintentionally "provides Muriel with a weapon to use against himself." That weapon is, in a sense, joy, an emotion for which Muriel has little desire or capacity. She admits, "I can live without you as I can live without eyes or legs" and leaves him the next day. In their consummation (rendered violently concrete by the red stains on the sheet) is her release: for Muriel, Claude is no longer the unknown or the object of an intensity nourished by hopeless longing. Like the self-destructive Catherine, she departs, but lingers on in the lover's imagination.

Fifteen years later, Claude, alone and free, is still thinking of her. His mother's death freed him from "the most demanding of his women"; this phrase should remind us that a letter to her stated, "I love Muriel. She resembles you" (a provocative but less-than-conclusive sentiment); and Anne's untimely end deprived him of the most sympathetic. Nevertheless, the scene that follows Anne's death presents his book, *Jérôme et Julien*, in a store window, suggesting how art compensates for death. If Antoine was told in *Stolen Kisses* that making love after a funeral is a way of proving you exist, Claude learns that making a book answers death with permanence—and life with order and self-creation. By the epilogue, the three characters have become his book, objectified but immortalized, as frozen and living as the lovers of Rodin's "Kiss" which we see at the end of the film. Claude has lost much, but has spun the women into fluid statues.

From the perspective of studying the women in Truffaut's work, the film remains problematic. Roché's Anne married and had four children; why, then, did Truffaut kill her off? One would have liked to see this warm and beautiful girl ripen into womanhood, perhaps motherhood, and become one of Truffaut's only fully and happily developed females. Does he punish her for being too free, too strong, too healthy? Does she have to die so that Muriel can live? One is reminded here of the question asked by Marsha Kinder and Beverle Houston in their article, "Truffaut's Gorgeous Killers,"

is it possible in Truffaut's vision for a woman to exercise seductive power and break out of conventional limitations without becoming a wild killer? If a basically 'nice girl' transgresses sexual lines, either through self-sacrifice (like the wife in *Shoot the Piano Player* who goes to bed with a man to help her husband's career), or through a deliberate attempt to gain freedom (like the artistic sister in *Two English Girls*), she may have to pay with her life.[13]

One response offered by Truffaut in conversation is that he was inspired by the Brontë sisters when making the film, and that Anne's death from tuberculosis was borrowed from Emily Brontë's own life. One is permitted to relegate to the background the sister who has a beginning, middle, and end in order to focus on the complex woman who haunts the hero. Truffaut's alteration of the novel, therefore, places the emphasis on Muriel rather than Anne, which is to say on language and madness rather than the sensuality and openness to experience that demanded Roché's attention. What seems to interest the director most is Muriel's search for identity, a process that is ultimately self-contained, obsessive, and inseparable from the written word.

Adèle H. and Beyond

Truffaut's concerns with absolutism and madness, or art and identity, culminate in *The Story of Adèle H.* (1975). The French title is richer for *L'Histoire d'Adèle H.* is not only a tale but a *history*, and Truffaut takes great pains to reinforce the historical dimension of the film. He uses still footage, sepia-toned photographs and maps; he frames the narrative with a statement of its authenticity at the outset, and the printed declaration "C'était l'histoire d'Adèle H." at the close. The fact that the source of the film is a real journal invites comparison with Truffaut's other adaptation from an actual record of events, *The Wild Child* (1970). The comparison is instructive, for if the story of Dr. Itard and the child Victor traces the growth of an individual from savagery into civilization and from an encapsulated self to one aware of the existence of others, the chronicle of Adèle (the "wild child" of Victor Hugo) consists of a gradual movement *away* from humanity. This retreat assumes geographical form in the film's shift from Nova Scotia to Barbados and spiritual form in Adèle's disintegration. The crucial point that the films have in common is that both processes are enacted through language. Itard's Journal notes Victor's increasing capacity for communication, while that of Adèle reveals her descent into solipsism.

In 1863, a young Frenchwoman arrives in Halifax in search of Lt. Pinson, a British officer stationed there. Though he once courted

Adèle, her love for him proves unrequited, irrational, and obsessive. The cold and arrogant lieutenant will have nothing to do with
her as she begs, threatens, bribes, and embarrasses him, spying
upon his nocturnal encounters with rich women and offering to
sacrifice her entire existence for him. We learn that she is the
younger daughter of Victor Hugo, sister of Léopoldine who
drowned at the age of nineteen. Concurrent with her desperate
encounters with Pinson, she writes letters filled with lies to her
parents, and her "memoirs," incessantly weaving a verbal web about
herself. Through her feverish transmutation of life into literature,
increasingly less connected to reality, she finally lives only to write,
a woman become a book (and here, we can recall the book-people at
the end of *Fahrenheit 451*). By the time she follows Pinson to Barbados with her torn dress, wild hair, and glazed expression, she has
become her own work of art. This may link her to Catherine but,
unlike the heroine of *Jules and Jim*, her creation acknowledges no
consciousness outside of her own. She is cared for by a native
woman who then takes her back to France. The epilogue informs us
that she spent her next forty years in an asylum.

From the outset of the film, Adèle lies about who she is, splitting
herself into a number of identities, each one appropriate for an
occasion. Her first action is a resourceful evasion of the law as she
sneaks into the country by joining the line of returning residents.
She later tells the notary that she is looking for Pinson for her *niece*
who is in love with him; her kind landlady is told that he is a cousin
enamored of her; she goes under the name of Miss Lewly, and later
Madame Pinson. When a little boy asks her name, she answers
Léopoldine; however, upon receiving her parents' letter of consent
to marry Pinson—accepting her on her own terms—she returns to
tell him her name is really Adèle. Then she disguises herself as a
man, in a momentary transfer of identity reminiscent of Catherine's
"Thomas." For she truly is both the male and female of the relationship, the subject and object, the queen of and slave to her own
obsession.

She attends a performance of a hypnotist and, fired by the
thought that he can make people commit acts against their will, she
goes to his dressing room after the show. To the possibility of his
mesmerizing Pinson into marrying her, his response is that it is a
question of money. Prepared to pay all he desires, Adèle then
realizes he is a fake when someone who had been an "innocent
audience participant" turns out to be his assistant. The split be-

tween her passion for Pinson and her internalized romantic quest is then made evident, for instead of acting upon the lieutenant, she proceeds to hypnotize herself. Her repetition of a few words puts her in a kind of trance, as she writes and says aloud, "je suis née de père inconnu" ("I am born of an unknown father"). She feverishly convinces herself that she is *not* the unwanted child of the most celebrated writer in the world and, negating genetic determinism, becomes her own parent.

The Adèle of the memoirs is in fact autonomous, an intensified and permanent reflection of the woman before our eyes. The first letter she writes to her parents establishes her doubling (and repeats the shot of Muriel in *Two English Girls* in a similar stance, stressing the connection between the two women): Truffaut presents her face in the mirror, a square surface that visually encloses and "reproduces" her, while the rectangular sheet of paper in her hand does the same on a verbal level. The camera moves in to a close-up of her reflection as, fabricating a different Adèle, she lies about her relationship to Pinson. The mirror makes clear that although the letter is addressed to her parents, she is speaking to herself. We are hearing more of a soliloquy than a monologue, and this theatrical terminology is supported by Adèle's actions and the way they are presented. She is consciously adopting a persona in a one-woman show; and on the other side of the footlights the audience is constantly reminded of the stage. We are distanced from Adèle by the numerous frames around her.

If the dominant form of *Jules and Jim* is a circle, the controlling image here is the square or rectangle. Truffaut often frames the characters and events via windows (our first sustained view of Adèle is her face peering out of the carriage), doorways (the multiple framing when Pinson's superior chastises him over the wedding announcement: the camera remains outside the half-open door, and takes in the window inside the room with the activity beyond it), mirrors, photographs, newspaper clippings (such as the one announcing her mother's death), books, and letters. After showing portraits from her family album to the landlady, Adèle "poses" for the camera implicit in her mirror: at the end of two scenes, she tilts her head slightly to the angle of nineteenth-century portraiture, midway between frontal and profile. Later, she even creates her own frame/stage in constructing a shrine to her love. Flanked by flowers and two lit candles, a photograph of Pinson makes literal her claim, "Love is my religion." This altar—a miniature stage with

doors for a curtain—serves to distance us further from her as she
kneels in excessive adoration. And if we have seen *The 400 Blows*,
how can we not recall Antoine's altar to Balzac?

The impulse for both Antoine and Adèle can be summed up in the
title of the Balzac story that led the boy to worship the author: *La
Recherche de l'absolu* (the search for the absolute). The curtains
around Antoine's altar caught fire, and it consumed itself; Adèle's
model will consume her. That desire for the absolute which is evident in the line she writes to Pinson, "I am your wife definitively,"
cannot be sustained in the arena of daily experience; the only stages
on which it can exist are art and death. Therefore, to the finality of
the printed title, *"Les Misérables*—Victor Hugo," which throws her
into a fit of anger, or of Léopoldine's drowning, which leaves her
with recurrent nightmares, she responds with her own amalgam of
their terms: she drowns in words.

Truffaut creates this impression through the image of the ocean
with its potential for "going under." Her first nightmare is a vivid
whirlpool which we experience with her: superimposed on her tossing, turning, and choking body is a sepia-toned shot of a woman
drowning. Truffaut's conjunction of the sea and language begins
when she subsequently writes, "That a girl shall walk over the sea
and into a New World to be with her lover—this I shall accomplish."
The declaration is accompanied by an image of her standing by the
waves, establishing the ocean as the realm of the absolute and impossible.

By the second dream sequence (the same nightmare), we can
sense how the sea is no less a metaphor for madness, which a part of
her still resists. When she writes the letter to her parents that falsely
declares her marriage to Pinson, her face and voice are superimposed on a swift tracking shot of the ocean and we understand that
she is literally skimming the surfaces of madness. She tells her
parents to write to her as Madame Pinson; Adèle is about to sink,
the fictitious bride is born in the water. Truffaut literalizes the final
image of her "going under" when she is sleeping in the shelter for
beggars. A woman in the neighboring bed tries to open Adèle's
suitcase which is on the floor between them; she awakens and
slithers to the *other* edge of the bed and then under it, crawling to
the valise and wrapping her body around it, as she warns the woman
to leave her book alone. She pulls it beneath the bed with her and
goes back to sleep.

By the third nightmare, now in Barbados, we see only the out-
ward manifestation of her turmoil. Truffaut does not permit us to
participate in this one for she has slipped farther away from us. We
are increasingly distanced from her in this final episode; from the
close-ups of the early sequences, she is now seen in long shot, a dark
figure drifting through narrow streets. We are cut off from her
consciousness since the only letter we hear is the one that Madame
Baa sends to Hugo; and this one is doubly distanced since, unable to
write, she asks a learned man to compose it. Adèle has become an
object as incomprehensible, obsessed, and dead to those around her
as Catherine or Julie Kohler. She finally appears as the more extreme double, and true sister, of Muriel. The fact that the maternal
figure in both films is played by Sylvia Marriott (Mrs. Brown and
Mrs. Saunders) contributes to the impression that Adèle is deeply
related to Muriel. The latter had declared, "I am like a river that
rises and falls," while the waves rolled behind her. Adèle addresses
us from the ocean in a reprise of the earlier shot of her vision. It is
the dream self made real, triumphantly claiming that she will walk
on the water into the New Land.

The New Land is finally an inner space, sublime and impossible,
whose roads are paved with words. If Catherine's letter to Jim
stated, "This paper is your skin, this ink is my blood, I press hard so
that it will enter, answer me quickly," Adèle's version would simply
delete the last three words. She expects no answer. Significantly,
her first gesture when she meets Pinson is to cover his mouth with
her hand. Later, when she spies on his amorous activities with the
woman in the glass house, a mysterious smile forms on her lips, as
though she had already separated the man she observes from the
image she idolizes. Both Adèle and Muriel transmute experience
into a diary which expresses their yearning for the permanent (the
word) over the "provisoire," the spiritual over the physical, and
sustained suffering over temporary pleasure. Out of their loneliness
and anguish, they create a self which is finally impervious to the
men they love (and perhaps even to the director since it is the
women's voices we hear).

Truffaut never comments upon his heroine, and succeeds in making us care *about* Adèle without necessarily caring *for* her. His
statement that "the idea was to make a film about love involving
only one person" points to the ultimate isolation—the refusal of
empathy—that Adèle demands. He adds, "the second idea was to

Isabelle Adjani as Adèle H.

Adèle's journal, and her journey to Barbados.

make a film that had a maximum of inner violence. Emotional violence,"[14] and given these two intentions, we should realize that
Pinson is merely a pretext for Adèle's story. Her relationship to her
father, on the other hand, is more complex and emotionally troubling. In refusing his repeated offers of love, for which she hungered
when she was younger, she asserts her freedom from his powerful
presence and her own need for it. But at the same time, she tears
herself in two, denying what she most desires. In the context of
emotional violence, perhaps Hitchcock's influence on Truffaut
should be recalled, for Adèle's neurotic behavior could be partially
rooted in guilt. Her bitter retort to the landlady about how lucky she
was to have been an only child reveals the deep resentment of
Léopoldine. Like so many of Hitchcock's characters, Adèle may
have willed the death of her sister, her father's favorite, before it
occurred, and her sense of culpability may be one of the reasons for
her creating a new identity.

Molly Haskell's superb review of the film substitutes cinematic
ancestry for Adèle's father; she places the heroine's turmoil in the
context of the "women's films" such as Max Ophuls' *Letter from an
Unknown Woman* and *Madame de:*

In all of these, a woman in love defies social decorum and propriety, rejects
the normal woman's destiny in marriage and family, lives as an outcast—in
sin or in violation of duty—and finally goes beyond even the beloved himself in embracing an emotion that is religious, total, self-defining, based on
denial rather than fulfillment, and, by communing with no mortal being,
can end only in martyrdom and death. What the world (and most feminists)
see as a woman 'throwing her love away' on an unworthy man is in fact a
woman throwing away the world and all dependencies for a love radically
created by her, preparing herself, kamikaze-style, for immolation on its
altar.[15]

Haskell's mention of *Vertigo* is also illuminating: Hitchcock's film
presents the male obsessed with the idealized *image* of a woman, a
more Truffautesque situation, whereas the obsession of *Madame de*
and *The Story of Adèle H.* is finally in the emotion itself. Haskell
helps us appreciate Truffaut's sensitive but detached handling of
both types of passion by pointing out how he understands "that such
an obsession is not only magnificent but terrible, not only sublime,
but selfish and cruel."

Despite the emotionally charged material, Truffaut forces us to
observe his heroine with a dry, cool eye. Whatever sympathy we

feel for her is won rather than thoughtlessly given, for we must overcome the distances that the director builds into the film. In addition to the visual framing devices, the detached tone of the narration at the beginning and end of the film cools the story. And if *Fahrenheit 451* celebrated books, bringing us closer to the graphic feeling of the words on screen, Truffaut keeps us at arm's length in *The Story of Adèle H.* by not permitting us to see the print. Adèle's use of language is oral, incantatory, and a means of self-expression whereas language in *Fahrenheit 451* was visual, tactile, sensuous, and a channel of communication. That her words are *not* conceived as contact with readers is evident from the methods employed by the real Adèle: the diary was written in code which has only recently been deciphered.[16]

Her characterization is also calculated for tension rather than tears. As Frank Rich puts it in his article, "The Passionate Liberation of Adèle H,"

If Truffaut had wanted to tear our hearts out, he could have provided a soft-featured, soft-spoken goddess, a latter-day Lillian Gish, but . . . Adjani's face tells us more about her burning soul than is comfortable—she's so intense it's intimidating—and, rather than identifying or sympathizing with her, we recoil in vague annoyance.[17]

Interestingly, this male critic's interpretation of the film is most "feminist," rooted in a perspective of "passionate liberation" for women. Rich offers an intelligent analysis of how Adèle forges a "lucid spiritual intensity that takes her beyond herself, her era and her obsession and up to the frontier of a new and revolutionary age." For the part of Adèle that yearns for marriage coexists with the consciousness that marriage is "degrading"; she suggests an "open marriage" beyond monogamy; she realizes her ties to "sisters [who] suffer in bordellos and marriage." Her self-determination takes her from the dark tones of her room in Halifax to the white light that bathes her as she stands by the waves and proclaims her victory. This last shot leads Rich to connect the heroine to Catherine, "Adèle's rightful heir—and you half-feel that Adèle lived on . . . to 1915 so that the torch between her and Catherine might be literally passed."[18]

We might add that we last see Catherine in the water—with her own measure of defiance and victory—but the reality of her demise is brought home to us. And it is rather Léopoldine that she echoes, for Catherine drowns, dragging her lover down with her, as Adèle's sister had unwittingly done, ever to haunt those who remain on earth. Rich's interpretation is seductive, but the exultation he perceives is too often cancelled by the despair and loss at the heart of the film. The light and the stance of the ending seem more troubling than triumphant, for in destroying those who loved her, and herself, Adèle is more an emblem of absolutism and death than liberation and life. Like a seagull, Adèle rises majestically by the waves but makes a fearful sound. And if we remember the last shot of *The 400 Blows*, we can link Adèle to another character who yearns for the sea, but must stop, frozen, at the shore.

The tension between idolatry and love, inviolate principles and active process, informs almost all of Truffaut's work. Those characters who can overcome romantic ideals and respond to imperfect individuals are the real heroes; those incapable of compromise are more often tragic figures. As Kinder and Houston point out, "in the earlier films dominated by the *femmes fatales*, these lethal women seem to represent not womankind but a romantic individualism that is both seductive and dangerous."[19] Truffaut seems to suggest that to learn to live is to learn to accept limitations, and perhaps the most difficult one to accept is that daily experience is neither a book nor a film. It is both less and more than art in the same way that a woman is less and more than a beautiful statue. Art and life feed upon each other, but the fluidity of the latter cannot fully accommodate the finality of the former. Truffaut articulates this sentiment in *Day for Night*, one of his few films to portray women outside romantic (self) definition. As the director Ferrand, he tells Alphonse that films are more harmonious than life, "there are no traffic jams in films, no dead waits."

His assistant Joelle is most cognizant of the discrepancy between cinema and reality; an equally efficient "conductor" in both dimensions, she emerges as one of Truffaut's strongest female figures. Although a secondary character, Joelle embodies those attributes of lucidity and loyalty which are so desirable on screen and off. One assumes that she is modelled on Suzanne Schiffman, a behind-the-scenes presence who has assisted Truffaut on almost all his films. She can also be linked to Clarisse in *Shoot the Piano Player* and Thérèse in *Jules and Jim* in that these secondary characters are friends to the males; posing no romantic threat, they neither destroy nor are destroyed. Joelle diverges from these early characterizations in that her personality is less a function of a string of lovers/clients than of her solidarity in a non-sexual sense. In this respect she is reminiscent of another strong "comrade" in Truffaut's universe— Clarisse in *Fahrenheit 451;* but where the latter was totally de-sexualized (a fact that Truffaut makes explicit in his Journal), Joelle can enjoy physical pleasures as well.

After Bernard helps her with a flat tire, she begins to change into a cleaner sweater. He assumes the pose of a "séducteur malgré lui-même" until Joelle's casual acceptance shocks him out of his blubbering:

BERNARD: What?

JOELLE: Just as I thought! When it comes to handing out a line, there's no one better at it than you. But when it comes to the real thing, there's nobody at home down there!

BERNARD: Then you—you really want to? (*DN*, 117)

Joelle slips off her pants and responds with a phrase which is reso-nant with applicability to every character in Truffaut's universe: "Sure—but let's not drag it out forever, huh?" Her reply is richer in the French, "Oui, mais il ne s'agit pas de s'éterniser" ("Yes, but let's not eternize ourselves"). Later, when she accidentally finds Bernard in bed with Odile, her reaction is a healthy laugh.

Her strength, like that of the director, derives from her love of work; and she is actually the first of Truffaut's women to define herself, happily, through her profession. He seems to be moving toward a deeper understanding of the modern (rather than nineteenth-century) woman, for in *Day for Night* and *The Man Who Loved Women,* females have identities that are not necessarily di-rected by or toward desired males. Stacey, for example, is proudly pregnant, with no signs of a father in sight; the physician who con-ducts all the medical examinations in *Small Change* is a woman. Truffant's description of Joelle in the introduction to the screenplay underlines her human as opposed to merely feminine qualities:

This young woman would not surrender her job of script girl even at gun-point. . . . Joelle receives the confidences of nearly every other crew member . . . she arranges all the necessary little things the director has no time for, she pulls all the strings. . . . Joelle's complete lucidity could be very irritating were it not complemented by her great discretion. Her idea of love can be summed up in a single sentence: "I'd leave a guy for a film, but I'd never leave a film for a guy!" (*DN*, 12–13)

Even her name fulfills this picture with its blend of the masculine "Jo" and feminine "elle." An antidote to Catherine, Julie Kohler, Muriel, Adèle, and company, Joelle is generous and responsible and lives in and for her immediate world.

Nathalie Baye, who plays Joelle, brings the same directness and charm to her role as Martine in *The Man Who Loved Women*. Here, she is the first of a number of attractive women who cross the path of Bertrand, a solitary, nervous, and obsessive seducer. Like her successors, Bernadette and Fabienne, Martine is forthright rather than coquettish, and can generously take or lucidly leave love.

The Man Who Loved Women is an affectionate truce with the world of the opposite sex, just as *Small Change* makes peace with the world of childhood that was painfully depicted in Truffaut's earlier work. While Bertrand's fickle behavior at the beginning of the film might lead to the assumption that his women are interchangeable (as his typist will lament), it turns out that they are all "unique and irreplaceable" (as his editor will realize).[20] The point of his departures and transports is legs; Truffaut makes this graphically clear by shapely superimpositions from Bertrand's imagination. Nevertheless, these women manage to overcome mere physical charm, as well as the roles in which Bertrand casts them; each assumes individual personality, with an openness that contrasts with the absolutism of Truffaut's previous heroines.

For example, Delphine is introduced as a neurotic adulteress who enjoys making love only in dangerous situations. Impulsive, contradictory, and jealous, she undergoes a transformation which represents Truffaut's growing appreciation for "sane" women. Delphine is imprisoned for attempting to shoot her husband; upon her release, she confesses her new awareness:

I changed a lot in prison . . . I really learned how to love life. When you are locked up all day, then you know what is important and what isn't. You want only one thing—to be outside, free to roam about. . . . It's wonderful not to be jealous any more (*HAF*, 85–86)

To prove her point, she proceeds to share Bertrand in a cozy menage-à-trois with Bernadette.

Amid these kaleidoscopic fragments of Bertrand's amorous universe, one woman does emerge as the most significant—as well as Truffaut's most intelligently engaging female characterization. Geneviève Bigey is an editor who convinces her publishing house to accept Bertrand's autobiographical novel, *The Man Who Loved Women*. Her structural importance is evident from the film's opening scene, as she is the first (and last) narrator; her voice-over is the frame and the vehicle for his story. Even before we know who is speaking, Geneviève is visually set apart from the crowd of women at Bertrand's funeral: she stands above the rest, and is occasionally given her own frame in close-up. Like Joelle, she is a professional and, therefore, liberated woman; both are devoted to their work, which is in each case "behind-the scenes business" that permits an art object to emerge. Geneviève is in a sense an even more hopeful character than Joelle since romance is integrated into her work: after being close to a text, she grows closer to its author.

Geneviève's dialogue contains some of the most profound remarks of the film. She provides a key to Bertrand's fickleness when she tells him he must learn to like himself better: "It's very simple. When you don't love yourself, you are incapable of loving others" (*HAF*, 110). In addition, she articulates the liberated vision of relationships between the sexes. While sharing Bertrand's appreciation of the game that is a part of love, she is aware that "the rules of the game" are in the process of changing: "And what will disappear first is power. The game will always be played, but equally" (*HAF*, 113). She fulfills her theory by her action, which is to "play" tenderly with Bertrand.

Geneviève's fundamentally joyful and productive personality is evidenced not only by what she says and does, but by how she looks: her smile is perhaps less mysterious than Catherine's but certainly more constant, vital, and expansive. Bertrand expresses this well in the following exchange:

(She laughs) I don't know if I'm being very clear.
(Bertrand returns her smile) Oh yes, you are very clear; it's luminous.
(*HAF*, 115)

Geneviève thus goes beyond clarity to rich glow, and beyond words to warm actions. (Truffaut, who often restrains performers from smiling, acknowledged in conversation that he had her smile a good deal to balance the seriousness of what she is saying.) At the end of the film, a close-up of her face dissolves into the book, *The Man Who Loved Women*. A female character becomes a text, not in the destructive manner of Adèle H., but in the creative—and therefore magical—manner of a whole and modern woman.

5

"Les Enfants Terribles"

Small Change (1976) marks a return to the territory of Truffaut's first films, *Les Mistons* (1957) and *The 400 Blows* (1959). Together with *The Wild Child* (1969), these films constitute a vision of childhood, unequalled in the history of the cinema for sensitivity, humor, poignancy, and respect for children themselves. With neither sentimentality nor condescension, Truffaut captures the need for freedom and tenderness, the spontaneity and the frustrations of being a child in a society made by and for adults. His praise of Jean Vigo— the only other director to have rendered childhood with such poetic realism—can now be applied to his own efforts:

In one sense, *Zéro de Conduite* represents something more rare than *L'Atalante* because the masterpieces consecrated to childhood in literature or cinema can be counted on the fingers of one hand. They move us doubly since the esthetic emotion is compounded by a biographical, personal and intimate emotion. . . . They bring us back to our short pants, to school, to the blackboard, to vacations, to our beginnings in life. (*FV*, 37–38)

The resonances in *Small Change* lead us to Truffaut's earlier films, to his own experience, and to a collective emotional truth about childhood. As Jacques Rivette said of *The 400 Blows*, "in speaking of himself, he seems to be speaking of us."[1]

In the light of Truffaut's attachment to spontaneity and improvisation, it is no surprise that children have figured so prominently throughout his work. In the introduction to the "cinéroman" of *Small Change*, he explains, "I never tire of filming with children. All that a child does on screen, he seems to do for the first time" (*SC*, 12). Even in the films that are not about children, his little girls and boys are memorable, such as Sabine in *Jules and Jim,* Sabine in *The Soft Skin,* Cookie in *The Bride Wore Black,* Michou in *Such a*

145

Truffaut with the boys of Small Change.

Gorgeous Kid Like Me, and George in *The Green Room.* And he often adds kids to his adaptations: in *Shoot the Piano Player,* he created Fido, Charlie's younger brother; to *Fahrenheit 451,* he added the children who run away in fear from Clarisse; in *The Bride Wore Black,* he included a shot of children welcoming back Mlle Becker; even in *The Wild Child,* he incorporated children of the neighbor Lémeri, neither of whom are mentioned in Itard's original journal.

As a critic, Truffaut had detested the way children are generally depicted on screen, such as the idealized distortions of René Clément (*Forbidden Games*) or Jean Delannoy (*Chien perdu sans collier*—whose poster the boys tear in *Les Mistons*). His search for authenticity led him, at least initially, to present children from the inside: in his first film, the story proceeds from the point of view of the *miston*; this strategy is developed in *The 400 Blows* (which made Antoine Doinel and François Truffaut virtually synonymous for audiences); by the time of *The Wild Child,* he takes the role of Dr. Itard, the father-figure; and by *Small Change,* his cameo appearance as the father of Martine, the first child we meet, suggests that he is no longer to be identified with the Antoine Doinel of 1959. When he nods his approval to Martine to mail a postcard, he gives her the go-ahead to begin the action of the film. Seated in a car, he is both involved with and detached from the action—close enough for sympathetic direction, far enough for (gentle) mockery.

Truffaut claims that he needed to make this film as a response or contrast to the oppressive qualities of his previous film, *The Story of Adèle H.* [2] The latter had been a study of one person in one situation, linear, intense, and enclosed. Desiring a complete change of tone, he decided to make a film that is incidental and anecdotal rather than strictly plotted, weaving together many characters rather than focusing on one. Structurally, *Small Change* resembles *Day for Night* in its leisurely following of a group of characters and interlocking events; it is unified by place, the French town of Thiers; by time, the last month of the school year; and by communal activity, children moving between classes and summer vacation. As in *Day for Night,* Truffaut's love for his subject—here children rather than cinema—results in the overwhelming authenticity of what is presented. *Small Change* is not a documentary, but heightened reality.

Truffaut had already been thinking about this film at the time of *The 400 Blows:*

When we had five days of shooting in a classroom, I said to myself that I would have liked to stay there for an entire film, without being the prisoner of a linear scenario. Later, when I spent three days at the Institute for Deaf Mutes for *The Wild Child*, the desire returned to make a film about a group of children. This was *Small Change*: to install myself and a crew in a town in the provinces, during two months, to play on the unity of place and time, with an entire school at my disposal, and the whole town in the background.[3]

He began screentesting a variety of children—all amateurs—with the speech of Molière's Harpagon that we hear in the film's first sequence; as individual personalities began to make their impressions, he and Suzanne Schiffman reworked the story. As usual, the film's construction and flow emerged from improvisation.

Small Change follows approximately a dozen children, ranging in age from infancy to twelve years. The film's movement is from the first drink of milk at a mother's breast to the first kiss of romance; in between are the small events ("although nothing is small when it comes to childhood," adds Truffaut [*SC*, 11]), comic, tragic, and in-between—that constitute growing up. As in *The 400 Blows*, the tone is established and the characters introduced in a classroom sequence. The teacher, Monsieur Richet (Jean-Francois Stévenin, formerly Truffaut's Assistant Director), demands to see the card that is distracting his student Raoul. This scene attests to the symmetry of Truffaut's filmic universe and points up the difference between the stifling atmosphere of his first feature film and the expansive one of his later work. *The 400 Blows* opens with the picture of a nude that has circulated among the boys, but the overbearing teacher catches it in the hands of Antoine. It has been shared but he becomes the recipient of the punishment. In *Small Change*, Raoul is the recipient of the card, but Richet shares it with the class, able to open his course to discuss the geographical origin of the card.

Richet is a warm and sympathetic instructor who is about to become a father. The joy and comedy of his paternity are balanced by the dismal home situations of the film's main characters, Julien and Patrick. The former is a shabbily-dressed, taciturn student who mysteriously shows up toward the end of the term. His "home" seems to be a dilapidated shack, and he wanders through the film alone, bruised, secretive, occasionally stealing objects or sleeping in the back of the classroom. We learn that he lives with a crazed mother and grandmother who have abused him physically and emotionally. Patrick is a far happier child, but his only family is a paralyzed father who is dependent upon him. We follow Patrick's gradual initiation into romance: he becomes enamored of his friend's mother; later he picks up a girl at the movies, but, unlike his friend, Patrick can't bring himself to kiss her; finally he meets Martine at a summer camp and exchanges with her his first kiss.

Truffaut explains how the roles of Patrick and Julien evolved:

They represent two types of children who contrast well, the blond and the dark, one very open, the other more somber. . . . I knew from the beginning that I wanted to speak of an abused child, since a few million exist in France; we hear about them in the newspapers but never in films.[4]

He realized that both of these boys could have been more fully developed characters, but he did not want to sacrifice the younger children that we meet in the film. There is Sylvie who cares for her goldfish, Plick and Plock, and shrewdly captures the attention of all her neighbors by broadcasting that she is hungry. There are the DeLuca brothers who hustle their way through the film, delightfully conning everyone in sight. And there is little Gregory, two and a half years of age, who is left alone in his ninth-floor apartment for a few minutes after his mother realizes that she has lost her wallet. He follows a cat to the window ledge and, in a moment of horror for all but the baby, falls to the ground. "Gregory go boom," he laughs, and picks himself up from the grass as though nothing had happened. Shock turns to laughter as Truffaut cuts to the mother fainting; Gregory walks away, gurgling happily. The sequence ends with Lydie Richet recounting the incident to her husband at dinner. He finds it terrifying that children are so vulnerable to danger all the time. But the confident mother-to-be responds, "That's not altogether true because . . . children are very solid, they knock themselves against life, but they are in a state of grace, and then they have tough skin too!" (SC, 49).

Truffaut has repeated this sentiment in numerous interviews, always marvelling at the way children bounce back from bodily and psychological wounds. One does not have to look very far to appreciate the autobiographical source of this perception: as the next chapter will make clear, Truffaut's unhappy childhood toughened his own skin and provided the raw material of his art. The abuse encountered in prison, reform schools, and his own home, was the fuel of a compensatory aesthetic. It is difficult not to hear Truffaut in the moving speech that Richet offers to his students at the end of the term:

> . . . it is because I have bad memories of my youth and I don't like the way children are treated that I chose to be what I am: a teacher. Life isn't easy, it's hard, and you have to learn to toughen yourself to face it . . . not to harden but to toughen yourself. By a strange sort of balance, those who had a difficult childhood are often better equipped to deal with adult life than those who were very protected and loved; it's a kind of law of compensation. (*SC*, 130)

Small Change offers a comic version of art as compensation during a newsreel within the film: Oscar le Siffleur (the Whistler) is a mime who whistles instead of speaking. A result of the presence of American soldiers in France, Oscar was a war baby whose father spoke no French and his mother no English. Because his parents did not have a common language, he could communicate with both only by whistling. Now grown up, Oscar is a renowned whistler who turned deprivation into art. Truffaut distances us by means of the newsreel narration, the outrageously funny scenes of Oscar's development, and the intercutting of an attempted "make-out scene" between two young couples in the balcony. Nevertheless, the fact that Oscar's mother is named Madeleine Doinel (Oscar as brother to Antoine?) and is played by Truffaut's daughter Laura strengthens the connection between director and whistler. Truffaut admits that what he liked about the story (which he made up) was that Oscar succeeds so well that he becomes a professional whistler: "I always loved this transformation from weak points to strong points."[5]

The weak point is often one of communication, the inability to express and receive, to act and respond. Oscar's on-screen transformation is juxtaposed with the levels of communication within the movie theater (just as Richet's growth is intertwined with that of his students). While one of Truffaut's daughters is getting pregnant in the newsreel, his other daughter Eva is watching and waiting in vain to be kissed by Patrick. His aggressive friend Bruno has picked up the two young ladies for them, and he is quite successful on his side. (At one point, his well-endowed conquest peers into her sweater

Small Change: A book links Patrick with Julien (top); Baby Gregory's bedlam (bottom).

and looks up with satisfaction!) But Patrick—perhaps through timidity and lack of experience—just sits there with wide eyes. Eva tries to put him at ease by whispering that their friends are idiots, but when Bruno changes seats and kisses her, she seems to enjoy the idiocy. The scene ends with Bruno in between the two girls, one arm around each; Patrick seems as comfortable with kisses as Oscar might be with words.

Nevertheless, encompassing these two difficulties of expression is the movie theater itself. Truffaut presents the movie house as the town's *lieu de rencontre*, the focal point where everyone comes together: children, parents, teachers with boyfriends, and—significantly—those who are never seen anywhere else. The theater is the only place in which we see Julien succeed at something, namely getting inside without paying. Here, he controls the situation by making a place for himself; finally Julien becomes part of a shared experience, no longer outside.

The child in relation to society is, for Truffaut, the outsider par excellence, a mischief maker (*Les Mistons*), a hell-raiser (*The 400 Blows*), or a savage (*The Wild Child*). Even eight years before making *The Wild Child*, Truffaut proposed, "Morally, the child is like a wolf—outside society. In the early life of a child there is no notion of accident—merely of *délits*—while in the world of the adult, everything is allowed."[6] And in a recent interview, he proposes that, on one level, all children are on the periphery of social experience: "Adults are derisive, inauthentic, and their unhappiness does not touch me like that of a child, deprived of the power of decision."[7] But Antoine Doinel, Victor (the wild child), and Julien in *Small Change* are doubly distanced because they are outsiders even to the "mini-society" that children create for themselves in classrooms or playgrounds.

For example, the five boys in *Les Mistons* are literally always outside, following and spying upon the woman of their dreams, spectators of an experience they do not yet understand. It is noteworthy that the only time we see them "inside" is at the movies. Because they cannot participate in the activity, because love itself is something foreign to them, they band together into an organism that confers upon them an antisocial identity: they send a lewd postcard to Bernadette and sign it "with the one name that avenged us all: the *mistons*." But Truffaut's subsequent child heroes are defined by their exclusion from peer groups: the wild child is

treated cruelly by the young patients at the Institute for Deaf
Mutes; Julien's classmates jeer at him when he doesn't remove his
clothes for a medical examination; and, most poignantly, in *The 400
Blows* Antoine's separation from innocent childhood is heightened
by the background against which he plans to steal a typewriter: he is
juxtaposed with dozens of children laughing at a marionette show.

Antoine Doinel, neglected by parents and mistreated by
teachers, is cut off—and therefore cuts himself off—from the two
"insides" where most children's identities are formed: home and
classroom. His progression from a potential insider to an exile is
gradually established in school as he is ordered first to stand in the
corner, then to leave the classroom; he completes the pattern by
taking to the street. Interiors are seen as enclosures of loveless
authority, conveyed by a relatively static camera. Exterior shots
contain panning, tracking, and the visual lightness that corresponds
to the character's mobility in the setting. The suggestion is that
children, like cameras, need to move, and that the kinds of treatment Antoine receives under four roofs—home, school, jail, reform
school—are not terribly different from one another. Once again, the
only interior space that offers joy rather than callousness is the
movie theater, from which Antoine and his parents emerge in high
spirits.

When Antoine plays hooky, he finds in the amusement park a
kind of mediating space that accommodates movement and stasis.
His ride on the revolving drum is not only an exhilarating event
(visceral for Antoine, visual for us), but perhaps a metaphor for the
best way to live. When Antoine is inside the drum, he is both in and
out, both still and in motion, both removed from his surroundings
and whirling with them. The ride is transient but intense, frighten-
ing but ultimately safe. It is difficult to ignore that the ride resembles a zoetrope, the forerunner of the movie camera, and that Antoine's perception of it, which we share, calls to mind the fluid
frames of a film. (Is the spectator of a film not both inside the theater
and outside the screen—suspended in the flow of moving pictures—ideally partaking of the best of both worlds?)

Through the course of the film, Antoine learns that inside may be
safe but stifling, and that outside may be free but lonely. In class he
is wedged into a corner; at home he sleeps in between two rooms so
that every passage of his parents intrudes on him, and he is constantly in the way. Both in school and apartment, Antoine has "no

room." Even in jail, he is removed from a spacious cell to a cramped one in order to make room for the freshly arrested prostitutes. Nevertheless, his escape into freedom at the end, breathlessly conveyed by a tracking camera, leads him to an exterior dead end—the edge of the sea. In his flight from *la mère* (mother) to *la mer* (sea), he remains on the periphery of things, with no living room to give shape to his freedom.

Similar inside/outside tension informs *The Wild Child*, which deals directly with the movement from natural expanse to civilized enclosure. The film opens on a sunny natural setting, and the swift movements of the beastlike child are once again mirrored by sweeping camera movements. His essential harmony with nature is expressed as he climbs a tall tree, sits in its branches, and rocks back and forth while the camera slowly moves back to an extreme long shot. We see him as the center of the landscape, his gently rocking body an extension of the abundant tree. He is subsequently able to flee from his pursuers, but is then captured precisely because he hides *inside*, scurrying into a hole. The men smoke him out, tie him up, and take him away. He is thrust into a dark room, where he yearns so much for the outdoors that he smashes a window with his head. We then see him huddled in the corner of a jail cell.

The wild child's next encounter with an enclosure is at the Institue for Deaf Mutes where he is inspected and catalogued like an object (reminiscent of Antoine being fingerprinted and photographed by the police), tormented by other children, and exhibited to curious Parisians. Dr. Itard, played by Truffaut, decides to remove him to his own home on the outskirts of Paris, displaying both a scientific and humanistic desire to educate the savage. Our first glimpse of his place links it more to nature than to the city, since the house is surrounded by lush vegetation, pierced by sunlight and singing birds—like the landscape in the first scene of the film. And if the operative frame of *The Story of Adèle H.* is the mirror, that of *The Wild Child* is the window, simultaneously enclosing and leading out. The child's favorite spot seems to be at the open window, boundary between inside and outside, constriction and mobility, affection and freedom. When the boy successfully completes an exercise, Itard rewards him with a glass of water which he drinks by the window. His teacher realizes that "this child of nature was trying to reunite the only things that survived his loss of liberty: a drink of fresh water, and the view of the sun and the country."

At key moments in his development, the window, permitting a view of the nature beyond it, figures prominently in the shot. It is a constant reminder of the boy's background, both for him and the audience. For instance, when Itard and Madame Guérin give him the name of Victor (because he responds to the sound of O), he turns from the window to look at them. The window is no less an omnipresent temptation, to which he finally succumbs in the penultimate scene: when Mme Guérin asks him to fetch water, he jumps out of the kitchen window and runs away into the forest. And it is through the window that Itard sees Victor's return; the camera does not move from its position inside the room, but waits for Victor to enter its territory, now identified with the house.

Like Itard himself, the locale suggests breathing space, with the recurring windows providing a visual echo of the questions he asks himself about the worth of his undertaking. Through the glass, he sees Victor outside, swaying with the full moon, responding to an instinctive rhythm. On another occasion, Victor is seen crawling happily in the rain, his entire body drinking in a familiar element as he returns temporarily to his animal posture. In this context, the window allows for ambiguity about where Victor really belongs. The dynamic rather than ornamental presence of these windows, as well as the setting of Itard's home, suggests that this is a mediating landscape between nature and society, accommodating both but dominated by neither. It is a privileged space in which the boy can learn while he looks outside and run in the fields with his home in sight. It is crucial that Itard repeats to him, "This is your room . . . you are home . . . this is your place." Located between the civilized savagery of Parisian society and the brutal rules of the natural state, it represents structure with openness.

The fact that this home conveys both expansion and isolation for the child is reinforced by Truffaut's extensive use of the iris shot. The only self-conscious cinematic device in the film, it generally centers on Victor at significant moments; the iris presents both a gradual revelation from darkness to Victor's relation to his surroundings (mirroring Victor's own development), and a gradual shrinking of possibility, particularly in the last shot. The end of the film appears more ambiguous than optimistic since the camera "closes in" on Victor's seemingly somber face, caught by the frame in a manner reminiscent of the last shot of *The 400 Blows*. A pessimistic interpretation could also find support in the fact that the film begins with an iris out from darkness and ends on an iris into darkness. This use of the camera eye also induces a certain nostalgia since it was prevalent during the silent era, and helps us realize that *The Wild Child* is almost a silent film. Apart from Itard's voice-over narration, most of the action is visual rather than oral. As a self-conscious touch, the iris shot distances us from Victor at the same time that it brings us close to him (mirroring Itard's relationship to the boy), thereby reinforcing that this is not a documentary but a "true story." And like the window, the iris comments on the child's possibilities in space; it can be opened or closed, freeing or isolating the character.

Another element of *The Wild Child* that contributes to the image of the outsider is the music. Antoine Duhamel gave form to Truffaut's concerns by alternating the solitary and slow voice of a recorder with the lively tempo of Vivaldi. The former is introduced when the wild boy finally allows an old man to wash his face; this is also the first time the camera moves into a close-up. The conjunction of this sight and sound endows the boy with the beginning of a human identity, while the flute-like music creates a plaintive and nostalgic feeling. It will be used to convey not only Victor's isolation but that of Itard: the tune overlaps the scene where Victor grabs an apple from Itard by grasping the concept of the mirror, and the subsequent shot of the doctor holding a candle before his diagram of the human skull. The music returns in two memorable episodes which also revolve around candles: the brief iris in and out of Victor in the darkness, observing a candle, and the scene in which Itard sees Victor outside, swaying to the moon. He stands by the window with his symbol of light, the candle, while the boy remains outside with his own symbol, the moon. The recorder reinforces the isolation of each, the fact that the moon cannot shine indoors nor a candle give light outdoors.

The mandolin music, on the other hand, accompanies scenes of progress and communication, such as Victor's fetching of the objects requested by the doctor, or their walk in the countryside during which the child wears Itard's top hat. It is, therefore, slightly jarring when Truffaut uses the music as Victor crawls happily in the rain; could this be a subtle acknowledgment that he belongs to the elements and is ultimately more "in tune" with the rain than with people? Even if this is the case, the escape sequence reveals that the boy is no longer at home in nature: he cannot climb the tree, he

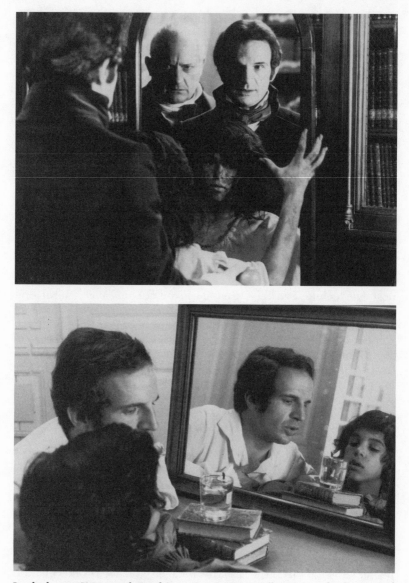

Itard educates Victor: with Piñel (Jean Dasté) (top); candles mirrors, books—central images in *The Wild Child* (bottom).

cannot obtain food. Itard has brought out in him not only the desirable potentials for sensitivity, expression and communication, but the boy's dependency upon him and his walls.

Victor can be seen as the extreme case of both Antoine and Julien since these boys share the absence of parental affecton. Unwanted and neglected, they are outsiders to love and, through the lack of love, are strangers to their environments. We learn from Antoine's interview with the psychologist that he was an illegitimate child and that his mother wanted an abortion rather than his life. When Itard discovers the scar on the wild child's throat, he hypothesizes that the boy was abandoned by parents who also slit his throat. When his colleague Pinel responds that this might have been because he was abnormal, Itard chooses to believe that it was rather because "he was illegitimate, in the way."

In *Small Change,* the term of *outsider* applies most poignantly to Julien, who is also spatially uprooted. He materializes at school one day in mid-term, mysterious, dirty, and silent. The camera adds to his mysteriousness by tilting from the ragged feet to his face, gradually revealing the person. A connection with Victor is invited when the porter, exasperated by his continued silence, asks if he is deaf. When we later see the boy entering an isolated and run-down shack, we recall how Itard attributes Victor's dumbness to the isolation in which he lived. A stranger to the class, Julien sits in the last row and, like Antoine, is ordered out into the hallway. He is locked out of his "home," roams the streets, and finally ends up in an amusement park. But where Antoine was permitted the joy of going on the ride, and—more significantly—of having a companion with him, Julien's more miserable state is expressed through his solitary actions in this particular setting. He waits until everyone has left the park and then picks up the trifles that have fallen out of riders' pockets.

Like Victor, Julien is physically scarred; however, Truffaut exercises the same modesty or refusal of explicit violence as in *The Wild Child.* Julien is taunted by the children because he doesn't want to remove his clothes for the school medical examination. He is therefore brought in separately, with the camera poised outside the window. As he is undressed, the camera slowly moves in, actively investigating and revealing. But before it gets close to Julien, there is a cut to a nurse running hysterically for the principal, her urgency underscored by a handheld camera. By not permitting us to see the abused body of Julien, Truffaut achieves three effects: he makes the horror more powerful because nebulous and left to our imaginations; he respects the character's wish for privacy; and he places the emphasis on the psychological rather than physical toll of the violence. To have shown the scars might have invited a rather cheap sentimentality; by keeping us distanced, he allows more integrity for his character, implying that Julien would not let us see his pain.

Similarly, the camera never enters the forlorn house where the boy lives. In a climactic sequence, we learn that Julien has been brought up by two crazy recluses, his mother and grandmother. They are dragged out of their shack—an enclosure of savagery— and led away to prison amid the jeering of indignant spectators. His mother keeps mumbling, "My son is happy, he goes to school," as though the act of letting him out were a gift, while the renewed use of the handheld camera gives a newsreel quality to this particular "exposé." Here, the civilizing process is a question of getting out, and of exposure in a multiple sense of the term. It is also significant that there is no father, a fact that provides another link between Julien and Antoine, who did not know his father (but at least had a stepfather).

The other side of the coin in *Small Change* is Patrick, who has a paralyzed father but no mother. It is worth noting that his first appearance (a shot that is later repeated) is a visual echo of "the stranger" in *Stolen Kisses* who peers in at the gate of his beloved, Christine. Like so many of Truffaut's characters, Patrick is a stranger to maternal love and, therefore, develops a crush on a woman who represents both a mother and an idealized romantic figure. The object of his affections is his friend's mother, Madame Riffle, who bestows kisses on her son Laurent as Patrick looks on hungrily. His infatuation is nurtured in her beauty shop, where he meets Laurent for school every day.

There he sees a poster which has tremendous resonance for *habitués* of Truffaut's universe. It is the Wagon-Lit poster—also seen in *The Bride Wore Black* and *Stolen Kisses*—"Travel-Confort sur les rails," in which a man and a woman get ready for bed in a train compartment. (An indication of its significance to Truffaut is the length to which he went to obtain it for *Small Change:* after a vain search to locate the poster, it was blown up from a photograph.)[8] As Patrick stares at it, a series of quick cuts into the poster animates it. Mme Riffle enters, and the crosscutting between her face and the poster establishes the connection between the two in Patrick's eyes. Subjective camera presents Patrick's image of her: in soft-focus, she is romantic and idealized. This poster has functioned before as the stuff dreams are made of, the popular image that feeds individual imaginations. In *The Bride Wore Black*, it hangs in the room of Coral, the lonely and pathetic bachelor; when Julie Kohler sees it, she intuits that he has been seeking, hopelessly, the perfect woman all his life.

We first see the poster in *Stolen Kisses* when Antoine is a concierge in a small Parisian hotel. In the cold and dull lobby, it hangs as a reminder of motion and passion, escape and love, trains and sleep. The couchette is another privileged space, both inside and outside, or "comfort on the rails." The poster further links Patrick to the world of *Stolen Kisses* in which Antoine's idealization of Fabienne Tabard echoes the younger boy's crush on Mme Riffle. Antoine was seeking parental affection no less than passion (he first likes Christine "because she has nice parents") and Patrick is likewise seeking the warmth of a home in addition to the romance of a woman. The episode in which Mme Riffle invites him to stay for dinner is presented with loving detail: close-ups of the meat, vegetables, potatoes, salad, cheese, fruit, and cake as Patrick devours them. For this is probably one of the most important meals he will ever have—a moment *inside*, in which stomach and spirit are being filled. Rather than indulging us in a sentimental response, Truffaut has the scene end with the magnificently out-of-place line of etiquette that Patrick must have been taught: "Thank you for this frugal repast."

Part of the interconnected quality of *Small Change* comes from the way that food and "being inside" also figure in the character of Sylvie. When she shouts, "I'm hungry, I'm hungry," through her father's megaphone, the neighbors prepare another "frugal repast" and pass it into her window. The movement of the basket from inside to outside to inside converts imprisonment into spectacle; as she brings her goodies in, Sylvie's motivation becomes apparent: "Everybody looked at me," she murmurs, "everybody looked at me."

It is this desire for attention that activates so many of Truffaut's—and everyone's—children. In a comment about *Small Change*, he particularizes the nature of this attention: "The point that all the children in this film have in common is their desire for autonomy with, between the lines, their need for tenderness of which they are not yet conscious."[9] One can see these as parallel drives—simultaneous yet unable to ever come together—or as contraries: in the words of Richet to his class, "By a strange sort of balance, those who had a difficult childhood [lack of tenderness] are often better equipped to deal with adult life [autonomy] than those who were very protected and loved; it's a kind of law of compensation." In the extreme sense, the wild child who has been totally unprotected is, therefore, able to kill animals and stay alive. When he is brought in and cared for, he can no longer survive outdoors. Children develop trust and/or resilience (soft skin and tough skin), the degree of either texture depending upon their relationship to parents. (*Small Change* was originally entitled *La Peau dure*.) When Lydie Richet is nursing her infant, the excited father reads aloud from Bruno Bettelheim about how the baby's relationship with his mother will determine his future interactions with women.

It is significant that Richet presents this argument while his wife is nursing their child, for milk has been a central image in Truffaut's work about children. In *The 400 Blows*, Antoine had to steal a bottle of it the night that he ran away from home, wolfing it down furtively; in *The Wild Child*, Victor had to beg for it by squeaking out the sound or spelling the word with his wooden letters. It is indicative of Truffaut's growing mellowness that by the time of *Small Change*, the milk is freely, naturally, and lovingly given. And how important that the Richets have been moving into a new apartment—to "make room" for the child!

Richet's reading from Bettelheim can shed light on Antoine Doinel as well: we can see how his behavior in *Antoine and Colette*, *Stolen Kisses*, and *Bed and Board* is rooted in *The 400 Blows*, or how Colette, Christine, and Fabienne have to deal with the ghost of the mother that he mentally killed off in the first film. Nevertheless, Antoine does not fit so easily into Richet's picture of compensation. While it is true that he learns how to make it on his own, he is scarred by his need for an absolute and all-defining love. Emotionally he remains an adolescent until—and to some extent, after—Fabienne Tabard's visit to his apartment in *Stolen Kisses*. In an older woman who offers him both the warmth and intensity which he was always denied, he seems to find the strength to then assume responsibility for Christine.

Antoine's situation is more complex than that of Julien, for as

Truffaut has pointed out, Antoine was less *mis*treated than simply not treated at all. In an *Arts* interview of 1959, the director refers to the experiment that Emperor Frédéric II tried with children. Permitted contact only with their nurses, the infants were to be treated without brutality, but could be neither spoken to nor touched. They all died very young. Truffaut concludes, "It is of this experiment by Emperor Frédéric that we were thinking in writing the scenario of *The 400 Blows.* We tried to imagine what would be the behavior of a child who survived such a treatment, on the brink of his thirteenth year. On the verge of revolt" (*Arts* 725, 1959). Although Antoine was spoken to in his formative years, one can imagine from his confession to the psychologist how much contact he actually enjoyed:

ANTOINE: Because at first I had a nurse; then when they had no more money they sent me to my grandmother . . . but she got too old and couldn't look after me, so I went back to my parents when I was eight . . . and I noticed my mother didn't like me much . . . She yelled at me for nothing . . . So . . . also I . . . when there were fights at home . . . (He keeps his eyes lowered and fidgets with his hands.) . . . I heard that my mother had me when she . . . when she . . . well, when she wasn't married yet . . . and once she had a fight with my grandmother and I found out she wanted to have an abortion. (He finally looks up at the Psychologist.) I was born only thanks to my grandmother. (*400 Blows*, 140–41)

To be deprived of both language and physical affection is for Truffaut the imprisonment of human expression, the nadir of human experience. And where could this be more poignant than in childhood, where the power and magic of words are first discovered?

Language is in fact one of Truffaut's deepest preoccupations, subtly but undeniably prominent in the actions of all his kids. This can be traced from *Les Mistons* in which they take their revenge on the lovers by scribbling their names in public places or by writing a lewd postcard to Bernadette, to *Small Change* whose action begins with a more wholesome postcard that Martine sends to her cousin. It is addressed to

> Raoul Briquet
> H.L.M. Béranger
> Thiers
> Puy-de-Dôme
> France

Europe
Univers,

with the world literally expanding through words.

For Antoine, the printed word is a key to freedom, as he forges an absence note from his mother. His relationship to the written word becomes an all-consuming one when he discovers Balzac. The last sentence of the story to which he becomes attached, *La Recherche de l'absolu*, could serve to characterize his sentiment: "Eureka, I've found it!" He turns in an assignment that attests all too strongly to his reading of Balzac; the teacher punishes him for plagiarism. Antoine's mistake here is like that of an explorer in a strange land: what he has found (the words), he assumes is his. The boy carries his adoration of the writer to the extreme of building an altar to him, replete with photograph and a lit candle, which starts a fire in his room. The search for the absolute consumes the real—and therefore relative—things around it.

An interesting reversal of this image is explored in *Fahrenheit 451* where another newcomer to imaginative texts causes fires. The flames of Antoine's altar spread to the libraries of *Fahrenheit 451*; however, the cause shifts from a devotional candle to a deliberate destruction. The book is the badge of the outsider, the unruly child. By the end of *Fahrenheit 451*, Montag undergoes a transformation and *does* in a sense fulfill Antoine's impulse: he makes the words he reads his own, as he becomes a living altar to a text. This connection between Antoine and Montag is noted by Truffaut in his introduction to the screenplay of *The Wild Child:*

> I realize that *L'Enfant sauvage* is bound up with both *Les Quatre Cents Coups* and *Fahrenheit 451*. In *Les Quatre Cents Coups* I showed a child who missed being loved, who grows up without tenderness; in *Fahrenheit 451* it was a man who longed for books, that is, culture. With Victor of Aveyron, what is missing is something more essential—language.[10]

In fact, *The Wild Child* often seems to be more concerned with the origin, development, and use of language than with the story of Victor himself. When Itard says to Victor, "But language is also music"—hoping that someday the child will experience its rhythms, tones, and expressive power, he reveals one of his deepest impulses in "taming" Victor. He wants to open Victor's world with words—

notes that connect things to ideas, chords that vibrate into thought, and phrases that communicate emotions. It seems more than arbitrary that at the climactic moment when he tests Victor's sense of morality by unjustly punishing him, of all his cards he chooses the combination, "book" and "key." Like the conjunction of book and man at the end of *Fahrenheit 451*, this compound yokes the human and the verbal into a noble purpose.

Although Truffaut was basically faithful to the records of Dr. Itard, the manner in which he swerves from the account points to his profound concern with language itself. His lapse of fidelity is constituted by omission, such as ending on an open (and in Truffaut's opinion, optimistic[11]) note which neglects to mention that Victor's next twenty years showed almost no improvement. This implies that the portion he did choose to dramatize—the child's introduction to language and affection—was sufficient reason to warrant removing the child from the natural state. Truffaut also omits all mention of Victor's sexual awakening.

In *Fahrenheit 451*, he also insisted upon the absence of sexual contact. If we recall from Chapter 2 that the sexual/romantic tension that usually permeates his work is displaced in the connection between Montag and books, we might be able to find a similar displacement in Itard's relation to the written word. *The Wild Child* is the story of a scientist who writes up his experiment, recording for posterity a case study. Truffaut's introduction of a voice-over narration and shots of Itard as he writes does more than give the film the flavor of a chronicle; it creates a second layer of drama between Itard's relation to Victor as person, and to Victor as persona in his literary creation. He immediately goes to his desk after Victor's achievements or failures, transmuting rather inconclusive incidents into solid text.

For example, when Victor first manifests creativity by making a chalk holder, Itard's exultation is conveyed by his voice-over. Visually, however, it is not Victor who truly receives his approval; Itard takes the chalk holder over to his writing desk and a close-up that unites this instrument with his recording of it underlines the primacy of his writing. The *re*-creation (verbal) is as important as the creation (human). In this sense, *The Story of Adèle H.* can be seen as a complex companion piece to *The Wild Child:* not only does Adèle inherit aspects of the savage boy (she is the daughter of more than one Victor) but of Itard as well. Both of these highly civilized characters are "book people" in the sense of *Fahreneheit 451*: Adèle is her diary, Itard is his journal.

Another perspective is afforded by the presence of Jean Dasté (originally the sympathetic teacher in Vigo's *Zéro de Conduite*) as a doctor in both *The Wild Child* and *The Man Who Loved Women*: his remark in the latter film illuminates the former. He tells Bertrand that "nothing is more wonderful than seeing the appearance of a book you have written . . . except of course the birth of a baby that you have carried for nine months, but of that we are not capable, at least not yet!" (*HAF*, 89) Itard's journal is thus his *child* in an even deeper sense than Victor might be.

There is often a tension shown in the film between the wild child as raw material and Victor as person—since Itard *is* a scientist as opposed to a father—which is supported by the very nature of cinema. In reminding us, through the use of the iris, that we are watching a reenactment of an authentic experience, Truffaut reinforces that the child we actually see is *not* the truth (Victor is not Victor but an actor) while the doctor's *words* have remained real. Itard's interest is therefore in the eternal persona that Truffaut literally re-creates in the film. It is as though Itard captures and develops each "good take" of Victor's exercises: one can almost feel in the doctor's actions the director shouting, "Cut! Print it!" Truffaut provides some support for this connection when he states that he "directed the film from in front of the camera instead of behind it."[12] For the man on and off screen, the crucial relationship is ultimately that of his artifact (both art and fact) and audience, within which Victor is means rather than end.

Truffaut invites inclusion of *Such A Gorgeous Kid Like Me* in this context when he admits about its heroine, "For me, she's . . . the female replica of *The Wild Child* where you have somebody who is wild and somebody who is trying to educate her."[13] Like Itard, the sociologist Stanislas Prévine is attracted to an "antisocial" creature for the purposes of his written document; like Victor, Camille Bliss enters the scientist's life as the data for an experiment. She is literally the raw material of *Criminal Women*, his sociology thesis. This relationship is symbolized by the fact that, like a spectator in a zoo, he brings peanuts to this caged woman. However, in the course of the film, he is overpowered by her human reality as she transforms herself from means to end.

The narrative structure of *Such A Gorgeous Kid Like Me* begins with elaborate framing which, like that of *The Wild Child*, makes the audience aware not merely of the story but of the way the story is being told. Stanislas' manuscript constitutes the outer frame: the film opens in a bookstore where a woman who is looking for *Criminal Women* is told by the owner that it was never published. His face and voice dissolve into a flashback to a year before, as Stanislas comes to the prison to begin interviewing Camille Bliss. Within this new temporal level, his tape recorder becomes the frame that encloses and presents Camille's narrative; Truffaut's camera repeatedly records Stanislas' recorder, so that the "talking box" punctuates the film as Itard's journal did *The Wild Child*. The effect of these close-ups of reels as they capture or reproduce Camille's voice is to make us aware that *Such A Gorgeous Kid Like Me* is not merely about the heroine, but rejoins Truffaut's ongoing concern with the attempt to record experience.

As Camille tells her story, we see flashbacks to her past and, by the time she describes how Arthur found the men she had left to die of rat poison, we have a flashback within a flashback within a flashback. If this were not sufficiently dislocating, we also come to realize that Camille's voice-over narration is less than trustworthy. The comic counterpoint between what she says and what we see arises on two memorable occasions: she tells Stanislas that she was released from the Delinquent Center for good behavior, whereas the camera reveals that she ran away; and she claims that her attitude after Clovis shot the television set was quiet and dignified, while we see her cursing and screaming hysterically. Apart from the humor, these juxtapositions create the awareness that the camera is a more faithful recorder than Stanislas' machine.

As the sociologist gets to know Camille, there is an increasing tension between what is taped (Camille as victim and data) and what remains untaped (Camille as victimizer and manipulator). Stanislas brings her nuts, cigarettes, and then her beloved banjo; Camille gives him gloves and later touches his face while confessing that she would never again be good to anyone, except him. None of these interchanges is recorded, and each is a step in Stanislas' downfall. Without the mediation of his machine, he loses control; by not maintaining distance from his subject, he becomes her object. An educator who thinks he can tame this wild child, Stanislas is instead locked into her cage, as becomes literally true when he is arrested for her crime. Truffaut's multiple framing keeps us detached so that

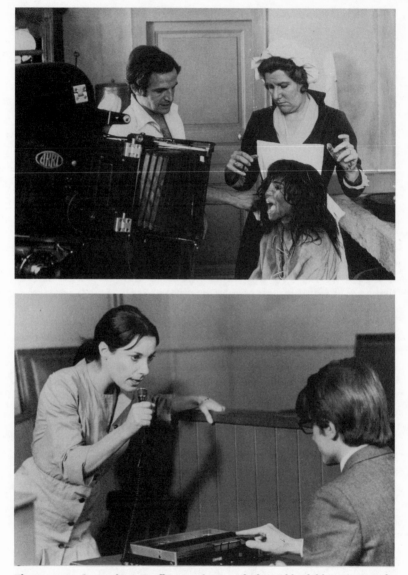

The process of recording: Truffaut on the set of *The Wild Child* (top); Stanislas
Prévine records Camille Bliss (bottom).

Martine chronicles events at the end of *Small Change.*

we do not fall into the same trap as the sociologist.

We are reminded that we are observers rather than participants (something that Stanislas should have remembered but did not) by aspects of the film's humor. For example, the farcical tone of *Such a Gorgeous Kid Like Me* is established in an early shot from Camille's childhood: when her drunken father kicks her, she flies through the air and lands on top of a haystack. Immediately following is a square insert of her face in the upper left corner of an otherwise dark screen. This conjunction can be interpreted as an acknowledgment of "movie magic," first within the frame and second in the editing room. We are later detached through laughter after Camille ends an interview with a display of affectionate interest in Stanislas. As they wave farewell through the bars, we hear a gush of the most sentimental strains from a 1930s filmic romance rising to a crescendo as the gates clang shut between them. And the culmination of the film's self-consciousness can be found in the episode with the child director Michou. He won't permit Stanislas to see his film because "it's still in rushes." When he is finally persuaded to project it, his remarks like "See the zoom!" constitute a parody of serious cinemania. While someone is jumping from a tower in his film, he calls attention to the form. In a less blatant manner, of course, Truffaut does much the same thing when he cuts from one of Camille's outbursts to a close-up of the tape recorder and then a shot of the transcription.

The director takes the sociologist's undoing a step further by focusing on the woman who is transcribing his tapes into the book. Hélène (Anne Kreis) loves Stanislas and is therefore jealous of Camille. There are repeated close-ups of her taking shorthand and typing conclusions; at one point, she turns off the tape recorder in disgust at Camille's cursing. "You're not going to print that vulgarity, are you?" she asks Stanislas. He refuses to change her terms and states, "Language is a major vehicle of the personality." The last shot of the film returns to the question posed in the outer frame— what happened to *Criminal Women?*—by resting on Hélène as she types furiously. The implication at the end is that Stanislas has lost control even of his own tapes since Hélène, too, lacks objectivity: the story is inseparable from the way it is being presented. Hélène's point of view and language will become the terms, and therefore the determinants, of the story itself.

To return to Truffaut's analogy between his two films, Stanislas' failure stems from his assumption that there is a one-to-one relationship between language and fact, or that Camille's words are the truth. This naïveté extends into the belief that his own written statement will get him out of jail, simply because he is telling the truth. But *Such a Gorgeous Kid Like Me* is about the debasement of language where *The Wild Child* was about its nobility. Whereas Truffaut presented oral communication as the goal that Itard sets for the child, the later film explores its potential for deceit. It is through verbal facility—through both premeditated and spontaneous lies— that Camille ensnares her men, especially Stanislas. Truffaut's comedy is a dark one, for the spoken word proves to be as much a cage as a key. Camille's first impulse when she sees the tape recorder is to sing her raunchy number, "Connais-tu la fille au banjo?" The microphone is less an invitation to truth than performance, and voice is the medium of spectacle rather than sincerity.

Why spend so much time on language in a chapter ostensibly about children? Precisely because one of the reasons why Truffaut is so continually drawn to childhood is that it constitutes the origin of language acquisition. Inseparable from Truffaut's older characters, who define and/or create themselves through written words, are those who discover words. One subtly magnificent shot in *The Wild Child* conveys the process for both kinds of characters: after Victor has been punished for trying to smash his wooden letters, he returns to arrange his alphabet, in the left foreground of the frame. In the right mid-ground, Itard is writing in his journal. And behind him is the window, through which we glimpse a sunny expanse. We see both the beginning of language and the consummate use of it. At least four relationships are balanced in the shot: Victor and his alphabet, Itard and his own, Victor and Itard, the window (freedom) and Victor. Despite the multiple connections, the tone is one of harmony. It supports the fact that Itard/Truffaut is teacher no less than scientist and therefore deeply linked to the figure of Richet in *Small Change*.

We have already seen how, in *Small Change*, both Julien the abused child and Patrick the infatuated child are Truffautesque characters. Although Martine has a comparatively smaller role, she is in a sense the most important character, for it is her writing that frames *Small Change*. Her postcard to her cousin opens the film, and her letter closes it. In the last episode, we see her writing about her attraction to Patrick in the darkness illumined by her flashlight pen. By contrast to earlier letter writers like Muriel in *Two English Girls* and Adèle H., Martine is not associated with a candle, the image of difficult romance and eventual self-enclosure. Rather, the flashlight pen is a perfect emblem for Truffaut's heroine: it offers light and ink, but is of the terms and texture of contemporary experience. It can be used indoors and outdoors, and affords mobility. In addition, we hear her voice-over narration, describing the gradual development of their awkward but happy romance. Love and language go together for Martine, so that she emerges as the central Truffaut figure: her written words activate the film, for it is her card from the center of France that carries us to Thiers.

She can be our mediator, guide, and narrator because she is the symbol of both communication and consummation. Martine fulfills not only *our* expectations by revealing the connecting details, but those of Patrick as well. Frank Rich has pointed out how the boy's first encounter with her "is visually tailored to match an image on a Wagon-Lit poster that had fueled his fantasies of love in the first place,"[14] for they meet on a moving train. And when the kids in the dining hall play a trick on Patrick (Martine goes to the bathroom whereupon they tell him she went out to kiss him) he finds in Martine a willing partner for a first embrace. When they return to lunch together, the kids scream in "an explosion of vitality" (SC, 137); they are the audience to the spectacle of the new couple, and their response is contagious.

It is difficult to ignore that Truffaut appears briefly as Martine's father in the first scene. His presence is suggestive for it affirms his paternity—not merely with regard to the character, but to the film itself. Despite the validity of his remark about *Small Change*, "I believe that in directing *The 400 Blows* I was Antoine Doinel's brother; in *The Wild Child*, I was Victor's father; now, I'm a grandfather,"[15] we should be aware that he is in a profound sense the father in all three cases. The latest film includes both of Truffaut's children—Eva (14) at the movies, Laura (17) in the film within the film as Madeleine Doinel, a fairly obvious illustration of "like father, like daughters." His paternity to *The Wild Child* is a bit more complex. Truffaut compressed Itard's records of 1801 and 1806 into a period of nine months: Itard's labor results in a kind of birth—that of a child who now realizes his need for the father. Truffaut has gone so far as to call Itard the "père adoptif," perhaps because he is the one who confers an *identity* upon the boy.

From Antoine Doinel, whose parents never addressed him by name in *The 400 Blows*, Truffaut moves to Victor, who is given a name by Itard. One can find a certain symmetry in Truffaut's filmic universe: to compensate for the mother who repressed her hostility for the unwanted Antoine, Itard seems to repress his affection for the wild child. The austerity and scientific detachment that characterize both Itard's attitude and the tone of the film have led spectators to find a lack of emotion. But Truffaut's restrained performance—on screen and off—can also be interpreted as a strenuous battle to keep overpowering feelings under control. Like Charlie in *Shoot the Piano Player*, Itard neither smiles nor shows much emotion—not because the characters are devoid of such sentiments but precisely from a fear of being dominated by them. Itard's act of putting Victor into the closet can be likened to Truffaut's act of putting Victor in an iris shot; these frames or distancing devices are meant to keep the boy at arm's length for the sake of the experiment: we, like Itard, require objectivity. In other words, Victor as object cannot be eclipsed by Victor as subject, for that would constitute a betrayal of Itard's records and purpose.

The depth of Itard's feelings are revealed, as one might expect, through the words. For example, when he tries to elicit Victor's sense of injustice by putting him in the closet after a successful exercise, the voice-over explains, "How sweet it would have been, at this moment, to be able to make myself understood by my pupil, to tell him how much the very pain of his bite filled my soul with satisfaction. . . ."[16] And visually, in the left foreground, Itard holds Victor in his arms, stroking his hair; his display of tenderness is balanced, tempered, and commented upon by the drawing of the skull hanging on the right side of the screen. This tableau suggests that the humanist and the scientist are simultaneously unified and held apart by the child. Itard is gentle but rigorous, always anxious about the long-term effects of his actions.

A story that Truffaut recounted in a 1976 interview sheds light on his characterization of Itard:

A Jewish man during the Occupation lived in fear of being deported—it was for him the greatest danger. He suddenly became very strict with his children, hiding all his feelings, so that if he was taken from them, they would be less sad, it would be less terrible.[17]

In the light of transience, loss, and separation, Itard—like so many of Truffaut's characters—withholds love because he is so vulnerable to its potentially painful consequences. By the time Victor runs away, we realize that Itard needs Victor as much as the boy needs him.

The Wild Child contains a dedication that renders the film even more personal for Truffaut. The fact that it is dedicated to Jean-Pierre Léaud, the boy that he discovered and kneaded into Antoine Doinel through *The 400 Blows*, suggests that the Itard/Victor relationship has an analogue in the Truffaut/Léaud experience. However, *The 400 Blows* is dedicated to André Bazin, whom Truffaut termed his "père adoptif." When Truffaut refers to Itard as Victor's "père adoptif," we can see how both characters are projections of what may be the most resonant identities of Truffaut: the son and the father. In *The Wild Child*, he plays the father in order to fulfill his role of son; as he admitted in 1970, "I think that Itard is André Bazin and the child Truffaut."[18]

6

"Cinema in the First Person Singular"

The Boy Who Loved Films

The Man Who Loved Women (1977) affirms the continuities and the autobiographical nature of Truffaut's cinema. It centers on a male protagonist whose self-definition implicitly builds upon the first actions performed by Antoine Doinel in *The 400 Blows*: Bertrand Morane (Charles Denner) decides to write his memoirs after looking at a drawerful of photographs of pretty conquests. Antoine had been caught looking at a picture of a pin-up girl, and his teacher isolated him in a corner where the boy scribbled on the wall,

> Here suffered poor Antoine Doinel
> Unjustly punished by Little Quiz
> For a pin-up that fell from heaven . . .
> Between us it'll be an eye for an eye, a tooth for a tooth.
>
> *(400 Blows*, 17)

The conjunction of looking at a woman and writing a personal declaration—recording the consequences, justifying oneself, and passing on one's experience—begins with Truffaut's first feature and is developed in his sixteenth one. Bertrand takes his place as an extension of Antoine; however, the evolution and implications of this connection can be fully understood only when we realize that Antoine as well as many other characters, themes, techniques, and structures are intimate reflections of François Truffaut.

The 400 Blows (whose French title comes from the idiom, "faire les quatre cents coups"—"to raise hell") is a chronicle of emotions and events that the director experienced at first hand.[1] John Russell

Top: The director's dream in Day for Night. *Bottom: Truffaut's reception in Japan.*

173

Taylor is right to compare Truffaut with another revolutionary and lyrical poet, William Wordsworth, claiming that the film ". . . may very reasonably be seen as a cinematic equivalent of *The Prelude*, vividly chronicling the 'growth of a poet's mind' . . ."² Born in Paris on February 6, 1932, Truffaut spent his first years under singularly loveless circumstances: his parents (an architect and a secretary) had little to do with him, turning the infant over to a wet nurse and then leaving his upbringing to his grandmother. He returned home at the age of eight, when his grandmother died. An only child whose mother insisted that he make himself silent and invisible, he took refuge in reading (his maternal grandmother had introduced him to a love of books) and later in the cinema.

Like Antoine, and Julien in *Small Change*, Truffaut found a substitute home in the movie theater: he would either sneak in through the exit doors and lavatory windows or steal money to pay for a seat. He explains that sometimes, "I had lunch money for school, but I'd skip lunch and school as well to go to the cinema."³ Antoine and René in *The 400 Blows* reenact the hooky-playing, the cinemania, and the concoction of outrageous excuses of the young Truffaut and Robert Lachenay (who was an assistant on *The 400 Blows*); they also display the touching friendship exemplified by René's unsuccessful attempt to visit Antoine at reform school. For example, as soon as René's father goes out to his club, the boys run to the movies; when Truffaut's parents would leave for the theater, he would wait ten minutes and dash out to a film, in a horrible anxiety over the starting times because he was afraid that his parents would come home before him.

The young Truffaut wrote down the title of every film he saw—perhaps an early manifestation of his, and subsequently his characters', need to record or hold on to an experience. Even as a child, he noted the director's name, particularly when the film was badly received: "I was always for the artist, the misunderstood artist who provokes sneers. . . ."⁴ Film and writing therefore went hand in hand, for he compiled his lists into approximately three hundred files, in alphabetical order, one for each director from Marc Allegret to Fred Zinneman. The emotion in the dark was inevitably followed by recollection and recognition of the personal contact, the artist in the art.

Like his young protagonist, Truffaut ran away from home at the age of eleven after inventing an outlandish excuse for his hooky-playing. Instead of Antoine's lie about his mother's death, Truffaut told the teacher that his father had been arrested by the Germans: "This was in 1943, and my uncle had been arrested the week before. There is always some element of truth in children's lies. But my father came to school to get me. This caused another scene, and I didn't dare go home" (*400 Blows*, 217). Nevertheless, his father found him and put him back in the classroom. The school authorities watched him so carefully that he chose to "devour Balzac in the municipal library" rather than attend classes. His subsequent flight from home and school led to a series of odd jobs, minor robberies (a typewriter and copper doorknobs), and the creation of his film club. Truffaut's father again tracked him down and finally turned him over to the police. He spent two nights in the central police station, as does Antoine, and was then locked up in the Observation Center for Delinquent Minors at Villejuif. At that time (1948) Villejuif was "half an insane asylum and half a house of correction." Here the similarities end since we leave Antoine "frozen" at the edge of the sea, whereas Truffaut's departure was arranged when Bazin assumed responsibility for him and enabled the boy to begin writing film criticism.

To return to the centrality of Antoine's writing, we subsequently see him wiping a foggy mirror that reflects his face, while a voice-over repeats the line he must conjugate as punishment for marking up the wall. His erasing action is another "defacing" in the service of better seeing/revealing his image, or a kind of self-affirmation. On a larger scale, *The 400 Blows* can be seen as Truffaut's poetic mark on the wall, or his attempt to even the score; nevertheless, by the last scene, the sea washes away Antoine's footprints as the film "cleans the slate." And in the context of the erasable (or dissolving) nature of these incidents and of cinematic continuity itself, it is significant that the last shot of *The 400 Blows* cannot be erased: Antoine's face is indelibly frozen because it becomes a still. Truffaut's zoom-in to freeze-frame (more arresting in 1959 before this technique became a stock-in-trade of television commercials) provides a mirror image of an earlier shot in the police station. When Antoine is arrested for stealing a typewriter, he is fingerprinted and photographed for the files. The mug shot is in fact a freeze-frame which conveys the definitive and permanent way in which he has been caught.

The still of Antoine's face can be seen as the first example of the sculpture metaphor that Truffaut would develop in *Jules and Jim* and *Two English Girls:* he turns Antoine into a living statue whose entrapment is expressed by the immobility of the frame. The Truffautesque impulse to both capture and animate, as the camera freezes or tracks, recalls the texture of another great Romantic poet, John Keats. The Keatsian desire for flight—to fade away with the song of the nightingale—is visible in the whirling of Antoine's ride in the amusement park. He enters a large wooden cylindrical drum which picks up speed till its riders are flattened against the side walls by centrifugal force. Truffaut crosscuts between objective shots of the boy whizzing by and Antoine's point of view of the spectators' faces which appear to be spinning. Like the speaker of "Ode to a Nightingale," Antoine flies "in an ecstasy of weightlessness" (*400 Blows*, 41).

Moreover, both Keats and Truffaut present the soaring in terms of their respective art forms. For the former, poetry is the vehicle of transport,

> Away! Away! for I will fly to thee,
>   Not charioted by Bacchus and his pards,
> But on the viewless wings of Poesy,
>   Though the dull brain perplexes and retards. . . .

And the structure of Truffaut's rotor is that of the zoetrope, the forerunner of cinema. Antoine's ride is thus a celebration of moving images, which can be contrasted with the stasis of the freeze-frames when he is photographed. In both cases, Antoine is pinned against the wall by forces beyond his control, but the very movement and transience of the ride render it an image of exhilaration rather than limitation. As in the last shot of the film, there is nowhere to go but in the same circle—only faster; however, Antoine can get off to rejoin his friend René. It makes all the difference in the world to have a point of reference during the flight, and someone to come back to when it is over. (And it is a characteristic personal touch that Truffaut himself can be glimpsed on the ride, the director experiencing the event along with his character!)

The avowedly autobiographical material of the Antoine Doinel cycle is then resumed in "Antoine and Colette," one of the five episodes that comprise *Love at Twenty* (1962—the other parts were directed by Renzo Rossellini, Marcel Ophuls, Andrzej Wajda, and Shintaro Ishihara). Antoine falls in love with Colette at the "Jeunesses Musicales," and moves across the street from her house in order to be near her, but succeeds only in getting closer to her parents. The musical get-togethers were really the Cinémathèque screenings; Antoine's hopelessly leech-like attachment to Colette is a chapter of

Truffaut in military prison (1951).

Truffaut's own past which upset him to the extent that he enlisted in the army. He was only eighteen at the time and accepted the three-year minimum enlistment occasioned by the Indochina war. He ended up in an artillery regiment in northern Germany prior to what should have been his departure for Indochina. But after finding himself on leave in Paris, "with new films to see and no desire to go back,"[5] he became a deserter.

Repeating the escape/capture/escape pattern that we saw in terms of school and home, Truffaut was taken back to Germany, again a prisoner in handcuffs, his head shaven. As might be expected, he was not a typical convict: "They interlocked two pairs of handcuffs on me so that I could turn pages as I read. That made the soldiers laugh. I remember that I was reading the third issue of *Cahiers du Cinéma*, a great number on Bresson" (*400 Blows*, 220). Twice he was locked up in the mental asylum at Andernach, and, through the help of Bazin, was finally discharged for "instability of character." Those who have seen *Stolen Kisses* will recognize that this is Antoine's situation as the film begins.

ADJUTANT (reading off): Private Doinel, enlisted for a three-year term, is hereby discharged from the Army as temperamentally unfit for service.

(To Antoine.) I can't figure you out. Some boys simply don't like the
Army. They're drafted, they serve their term and that's it. In any case,
they never volunteer. Can you tell me why you enlisted?
ANTOINE: Well . . . it was . . . you see, I had personal reasons.
ADJUTANT: Because of some girl. Of course. It's a disgrace! The Army is
not a refuge . . . You're always AWOL . . . Well, good luck and here's
hoping we never set eyes on you again. Now beat it!
   Trying to conceal his laughter, Antoine clicks his heels, turns around
and leaves. (AD, 121-22)

Through *Stolen Kisses* and its sequel, *Bed and Board*, Antoine
undergoes some rites of passage that occasionally invoke the director's life; Christine attacks Antoine's novel, "I don't like the idea
of telling all about your youth, of blaming your parents, of washing
dirty linen in public. . . . I'm not an intellectual, but I know this:
writing a book to settle old scores isn't art!" (AD, 209). But Antoine
evolves into a more automonous figure. This is partially attributable to the emphasis upon improvisation discussed in Chapter 3.
While Antoine and Christine remain an essentially French couple,
Truffaut wanted *Bed and Board* to be in the spirit of the American
comedies of Leo McCarey, George Cukor, "and, of course,
Lubitsch, who excels at injecting laughter into the events of everyday life" (AD, 12). The result is therefore an increased distance
between director and persona, as Truffaut realized in his Introduction to the Doinel screenplays:

I looked at him with the same critical eye I had for Pierre Lachenay in *The
Soft Skin*. This is probably because in *Bed and Board* we are no longer
dealing with an adolescent, but with an adult, and even though Antoine
Doinel and Pierre Lachenay resemble me like two brothers, I am never as
gentle with adults as I am with adolescents. (AD, 12)

Truffaut recognized that this may be one of the reasons that audiences tend to feel coldly toward his films that do not center on
women or children, for these heroes are often over-aged adolescents. His male characters from Charlie Kohler to Louis Mahé to
Bertrand Morane tend to be awkward in their excessive adoration,
and antiromantic in their very romanticism. We are perhaps more
inclined to accept this in Antoine for, having seen *The 400 Blows*,
we can understand how such a background would create an insecure
lover.

Beginning with *Stolen Kisses*, it becomes difficult—and ultimately unimportant—to ascertain the romantic conjunctions between Doinel and Truffaut. All that we know of the latter is that in 1957 he married the daughter of Ignace Morgenstern, a major film producer. Madeleine Morgenstern "represented for me the ideal woman, the one I was waiting for."[6] They subsequently divorced (but remained close friends) and the two central women in Truffaut's life became Laura and Eva, his daughters. He was deeply attached to them, perhaps fulfilling as a father the affective needs denied him as a son. This is not surprising, given that one of the dominant although subtle motifs throughout Truffaut's work is paternity. Even in his criticism, he passionately denounced the traditional "cinéma de papa" while embracing Renoir and Hitchcock with a kind of filial fidelity.

Within the context of fatherhood, Truffaut reveals more of himself through the so-called fictional characters than through the persona of Antoine. Protagonists as outwardly dissimilar as the wild child, Marion in *Mississippi Mermaid*, Camille Bliss, and Adèle H. share a deprived and/or problematic relationship to their fathers. As early as *The 400 Blows*, the class in English pronunciation revolved around a question that could only be articulated with difficulty, "Where is the father?" Apart from the humorous aspect of the French inability to pronounce the "th" sound, this phrase has resonances both within the film (Antoine has never known his real father) and outside it; for instance, in *Two English Girls*, a film which contains two powerful mothers but no fathers, the commentary informs us that Claude, "like David Copperfield, never knew his father." For those who are familiar with Truffaut's literary allusions, this description then leads us to *Fahrenheit 451*, in which Montag, another character deprived of affective roots, begins his quest for a past by reading *David Copperfield;* among the first words are the radically appropriate "I record that I was born."

A revealing story in this regard is that, prior to *Stolen Kisses*, Truffaut wanted to buy the rights to a French novel whose protagonist had not known his father; like Antoine, this young man is "a bastard." He goes to a private detective and manages to track down his father. The film was to star Jean-Pierre Léaud, but then the author would not sell his story. Truffaut made *Stolen Kisses* instead, retaining only the detective agency through which unhappy characters search essentially for lost love. In the same interview,

Truffaut confessed that through the films that are adaptations of novels, "I can protect myself behind the book."[7] For example, through the borrowed character of *Mississippi Mermaid's* Marion, he finds an outlet for his painful memories: she tells Louis of how she was denied affection as a child, growing up as an orphan in public institutions. And Louis later attributes part of her behavior to the fact that Marion "never knew her father." Her ties to the director are strengthened further through her admission that she attempted numerous escapes and finally ended up in reform school after committing crimes. Likewise, Camille Bliss of *Such a Gorgeous Kid Like Me* begins her criminal life by moving a ladder and thus killing her father; the result is that she is locked up in the same Observation Center for Delinquent Minors that enclosed Truffaut and Antoine. Like the latter, she runs away, only to end up in a real prison.

Camille's first action becomes the last one performed by Alphonse in *Day for Night*. In the film within the film, the young man shoots his father in the back for having run off with his wife. This provides a symmetrical close since *Day for Night's* first shot ended with Alphonse slapping his father's face. Truffaut's subsequent film, *The Story of Adèle H.*, can be interpreted as a neglected child's sustained cry for and slap at a father, in this case the formidable Victor Hugo. Although we never see the man ("where is the father?"), his presence permeates the film in the same subtle way that it permeates Adèle's consciousness.[8] She believes that he always preferred her sister Léopoldine and tortures herself with this belief now that Léopoldine is dead. When the bookseller, Mr. Whistler, presents her with a gift, she opens the package that reveals the title *Les Misérables* and the author's name (a scene that Truffaut now defines as quintessentially Hitchcockian). Her passionately angry response is a refusal to be his daughter, which is heightened when she hypnotizes herself into believing that she is "born of an unknown father." There is also the hint that Lt. Pinson is for Adèle merely a projection of her father, since the more he ignores her, the more violently she embraces him. And by the end of the film, when she walks past him blindly in Barbados, it is apparent that Pinson himself is not really the object of her obsession. As we saw in Chapter 4, the object is rather to deny her father and become autonomous—her own parent—by creating an identity in the same way that her father did, through the written word.

Literature and paternity are also interwoven through *Fahrenheit 451*. French critic Jean Collet points out in *Le Cinéma en question* (p. 93) that the Captain of the Firemen is "a rather revealing image of the father, a chief image in Truffaut's universe. Conciliation with him is impossible. Montag will escape by killing him." The last lines recited in the film also recall Adèle's situation. An old man who knows he will soon die is teaching a child how to memorize the following text from Robert Louis Stevenson's *Weir of Hermiston:*

I do not love my father, I wonder sometimes if I don't hate him. That is my shame, perhaps my sin, at least and in the sight of God not my fault. How was I to love him, he never spoke to me, he never smiled upon me, and I do not think he ever touched me . . . .

This sentiment is not found in Bradbury's original novel, but does manifest itself throughout Truffaut's work. While its recurrence does not permit us to make any assertions about the director's own relationship to his father, it becomes apparent that this is one of his deepest preoccupations.

It extends into other familial tensions, most notably the two-sister pattern that links Adèle not only to Muriel Brown but to Marion— through Catherine Deneuve, the actress who plays her in *Mississippi Mermaid*. Pauline Kael's sensitive review of *The Story of Adèle H.* recalls how in *Two English Girls*, Muriel refused the man she loved because he had been the lover of her older sister, who had died:

But Truffaut couldn't seem to express what engaged him in the material, which may have been an unworked-out allusion to the deceased Françoise Dorléac, who had appeared in a Truffaut film, and her younger sister Catherine Deneuve, who subsequently starred for him.[9]

However, the aspect of *Two English Girls* that Kael presents is not in Roché's novel: Truffaut is the one who introduced the death of the older sister. Perhaps one of the reasons he was drawn to Adèle's story was that her older sister drowned. And whereas Claude had been the artist/lover who immortalized the dead sister through his art, the figure in the case of Adèle H. is Victor Hugo himself, the more powerful conjunction of artist/father.

If so many of these characters are engaged in a quest for a father, then it becomes even more crucial that Truffaut played the father

figure in *The Wild Child*. For this film is less a child's search for
paternity than the attempt of a father to make the encapsulated child
aware of his need for a father. Truffaut realized the significance of
choosing this story only after the film was completed:

> The decision to play Dr. Itard myself is a more complex choice than I
> believed at the time . . . this was the first time I identified myself with the
> adult, with the father, to the extent that at the end of the editing, I dedi-
> cated the film to Jean-Pierre Léaud because this passage, this shift, became
> perfectly clear to me.[10]

The progression from Bazin/Truffaut to Truffaut/Léaud, symbolized
by Itard/Victor, tells a story of love through work ties rather than
blood ties, or the power of adaptation through adoption. By directing Victor in front of the camera as well as behind it, Truffaut
enacted the creation of character and relationship—terms which are
for him inseparable. Apart from teaching the wild child a language
or his own name, Itard teaches him to accept and return affection.
In this regard, one of the most poignant moments in the film is that
of Victor holding Itard's hand to his face, pressing his fingers against
his skin in a physical echo of the patting motion with which he
formerly expressed his connection to water and the moving wheel-
barrow.

On another level, it is difficult to ignore Truffaut's compressing
the events of Itard's chronicle into a nine-month period. *The Wild
Child* thus presents the rebirth of Victor through the labor of Itard.
This "feminine" identity is, paradoxically enough, the one that permits the parent to be most "masculine." As Marsha Kinder and
Beverle Houston have pointed out, the only major grown-up men in
Truffaut's films are the roles he plays himself, Dr. Itard and the
director in *Day for Night*.[11] They alone take and fulfill responsibility, precisely because they are not distracted by immature romantic
involvements. And it is in this love of work displayed by Itard and
Ferrand—and more specifically of showing individuals (Victor or the
actors) how to communicate—that Truffaut most directly expresses
himself.

Moreover, Truffaut's role in Steven Spielberg's *Close Encounters
of the Third Kind* (1977) develops the image and concerns that he
enacts before his own cameras. The young American director of

Jaws asked him to play a French scientist who directs an international attempt to make contact with extraterrestrial beings. The result of this casting is that Spielberg's science-fiction extravaganza is enriched by the theme of language on both a personal and cosmic scale. As Lacombe, Truffaut uses an interpreter since he speaks mostly French; this limitation in communicating is counterpointed by his ability to "speak" with the creature who emerges from the spaceship. At the beginning of *Close Encounters*, Lacombe is the first to realize that music is one of their means of communication (balancing Itard's statement to the wild child, "But language is also music") and, at the film's climax, he embarks upon the first exchange with the aliens through hand signals (like a teacher of the deaf) and an infectious smile. Vincent Canby's perception in *The New York Times* of November 20, 1977 attests to how Lacombe grows out of Truffaut's earlier roles:

This man, as played by François Truffaut . . . is someone of such compelling wisdom and understanding that he seems as much prophet as scientist. I suspect that part of this effect must be the result of our knowing who the actor is. In our world artists and scientists are the only prophets who remain.

Like Lacombe, both Itard the scientist and Ferrand the artist are so totally committed to their respective creations, the education of Victor and the making of the film, that these are truly labors of love. Unsurprisingly, Truffaut attributes to his work the same devotion:

I certainly love the cinema more than one loves one's profession. In effect, I really do put the cinema in competition with experience and I have been reproached at different periods in my life for preferring the cinema to real life. . .[12]

Implicit in *The Wild Child* is the desire to allow the actor to discover things for himself. Itard/Truffaut is more gratified by the child's imaginativeness than by his obedience, as when Victor invents a chalk holder. He also makes a point of building upon the child's natural propensity for ordering objects. *Day for Night* further literalizes Truffaut's premises and methods of direction. Ferrand handles his actors in a similar manner, guiding with sensitivity the older "children" of *Day for Night*. He too works from improvising the action to recording it; like Itard, he follows his subject's natural tendencies by having Julie repeat in costume what she had said about her own life. His belief in bringing out rather than imposing recalls Renoir's perception, "the film-director is not a creator but a midwife. His business is to deliver the actor of a child that he did not know he had inside him."[13]

Truffaut's respect for the actor is evident from the opening of Day for Night: he dedicates it with his own voice to the great actresses of the silent screen, Lillian and Dorothy Gish. Homage is later paid to another monumental actress, Jeanne Moreau, when we hear the broadcast of a film history quiz. Beyond these overt references, Truffaut's techniques alert us not only to his presence but to his sympathy for performers. For example, when Séverine is distraught after ruining a number of takes, part of the screen is blacked out with a wipe that pauses to frame Alexandre comforting her. As Monaco has observed in The New Wave, this "isolates and cradles his characters." The personal quality of this device is strengthened by the shot into which it leads: the director is tossing in a nightmare that turns out to be a stylized image of his childhood. This conjunction of wipe and entry into Ferrand's dream is repeated in the middle of the film, suggesting that cinematic continuity in space is related to personal continuity in time. Thus, even Truffaut's montage seems to express the director's personality.

Monaco suggests that the editing is modest and a bit shy:

He often cuts a little too soon as if to convey the impression that a scene is perfunctory, making those "privileged moments," when the camera gazes in reverie, all the more pointed. This cinematic idiom is a mirror of the awkward, touching gestures of Truffaut's alter ego Léaud.[14]

In another sense, Truffaut's perspective in showing us the editing room reinforces the way that montage allows us a privileged moment: because we are sneaking a peek at the rushes, the camera moves in through the window. We then meet the editor, for in Truffaut's film about filmmaking, the individuals behind the scenes receive acknowledgment equal to that of the actors. An action characteristic of Truffaut can be seen after the stuntman drives Julie's car off the road: Ferrand runs over to make sure that he is all right, displaying the same concern for a stand-in as for his stars.

My own experience on the set of *The Man Who Loved Women* confirms that this is in fact the way that Truffaut works. He establishes a feeling of warmth among the crew; an undogmatic perfectionist who requests rather than demands, Truffaut seems to earn from co-workers a respect that is inseparable from affection. Jean-Pierre Léaud, the actor who was central to the work of both Truffaut and Jean-Luc Godard in the 1960s, expresses deep admiration for the rigorous quality of the latter's genius as opposed to the more humane or generous quality of Truffaut's.[15] The fact that he has already developed an "équipe"— a loyal team that works with him from film to film—supports this impression. As with Renoir and his crew, "family" would be a more appropriate term, particularly for individuals like Assistant Director Suzanne Schiffman, Producer Marcel Berbert, Cinematographer Nestor Almendros, Editors Yann Dedet and Martine Barraqué, Script Girl Christine Pellé, and Composer Georges Delerue. In *Day for Night*, this feeling is captured by the "family portrait" for which the group poses before Séverine's departure.

In a Paris television interview (April, 1977), Truffaut explains that his preference for shooting in the provinces stems from the "family" experience that being on location permits. In Paris, people go to the set in the morning as if to an office; however, when the group lives together in a place like Montpellier, a real closeness can develop. He likens this atmosphere to a summer camp, for work and pleasure are interconnected: individuals are brought together by a "mobilisation émotive."

As a filmmaker whose vision does shape the entire picture from scenario to post-production, Truffaut is called upon to answer everyone's questions about every detail. We see this burden in Ferrand as he walks through the set, constantly asked to make decisions about wigs, props, finances, and schedules. The use of a handheld camera as he walks makes the scene more personal, mirroring Ferrand's difficulty in getting things smooth. As in *The Wild Child*, his exterior is restrained, but voice-over commentary and Truffaut's troubled eyes reveal the characters' emotions. Ferrand confesses, "What is a film director? A film director is someone who is continually being asked questions . . . sometimes he has the answers. But not always" (*DN*, 36).

The voice-over recalls Truffaut's diary within *The Wild Child* and

Truffaut during the shooting of *Stolen Kisses*.

With Suzanne Schiffman (in front), Truffaut directs *The Man Who Loved Women*.

Truffaut prepares the mannequin for *The Man Who Loved Women.*

the actual diary he kept while making *Fahrenheit 451*. These three interweavings of lived experience, film, and written text are personally and singularly Truffaut's in the way that each of the three terms can "interinanimate" (to use John Donne's term from "The Ecstasy") the other two. Between the real Dr. Itard's written chronicle of the wild boy of Aveyron and Truffaut's filmed one is the diary of Truffaut/Itard within the film; between the fiction of Ray Bradbury's *Fahrenheit 451* and Truffaut's cinematic reconstruction of it is his real diary, now published in France together with the scenario of *Day for Night*. Perhaps Truffaut writes so much because these protagonists cannot write at all: in *Fahrenheit 451*, he compensates for Montag's lack of literacy and makes a book while the character is burning books; and in *The Wild Child*, his journal is not only his voice but that of Victor's inarticulate soul. A poignant corollary to borrowed characters like Marion or Adèle who express the director is Truffaut speaking for his heroes when they cannot speak for themselves.

The diary of *Fahrenheit 451* provides a rich counterpoint to the screenplay of *Day for Night* since it embodies the concept of the latter: a journal of the process of making a film. To read them side by side is to see a sensitive writer and filmmaker constantly translating images, improvising, worrying, and accommodating. Between "technical" titles which present a temperature that results in fire and a filter that creates darkness, the author of these scenarios seeks out and underlines the quirky human touches that make cinema his passion. Moreover, continuities are truthfully acknowledged. In the introduction, we learn how the first sparks of *Day for Night* were lit: while he was making *Jules and Jim*, there was a "serious rehearsal" of a scene with Moreau, Werner, and Serre. Moreau, in character, said her line, "Isn't there anyone here who'll scratch my back for me?" whereupon the prop man, deceived by the actress' realistic delivery, entered the frame to fulfill her request. After the general outburst of laughter, and in the light of numerous incidents similar to this one, "the director is forced to admit that filming 'the film of the film' would prove more amusing and certainly more vital than filming *the* film" *(DN*, x.) (Moreau is also the source for one of *Day for Night's* memorable scenes: Julie locks herself in her dressing room and insists upon fresh country butter before she can return to the set. It was during the shooting of Joseph Losey's *Eva* that Moreau made the same demand.)

If one looks closely at Truffaut's interview with Hitchcock in the early 1960s, the critic already articulates his idea for a comedy on the making of a movie; however, it is Hitchcock who really proposes the contours of *Day for Night*!

A.H. It's a pretty good idea, and the way I'd do it is to have everything take place inside a film studio. But the drama would not be in front of the camera, but off the set, between takes. The stars in the picture would be minor characters and the real heroes would be the extras. In this way you'd get a wonderful counterpoint between the banal story being filmed and the real drama that takes place off stage. (*H*, 115-16)

The idea took shape nearly a decade later when Truffaut was having *Two English Girls* edited in Nice so that he could be near where his daughters were vacationing. Walking through the Victorine Studios every day, he saw a tremendous outdoor set which had been constructed a few years earlier for *The Madwoman of Chaillot*. Filled with building exteriors, a fountain, and a subway station, the set was in serious disrepair, and he learned that the only reason it was still

The set of *Day for Night*.

there was that striking it would be too expensive. The more he observed it, the more appealing it became, and his desire to make a movie about filmmaking returned.

The result was *Day for Night*, one of the most lyrical biographies of a film, as truthfully idiosyncratic as Fellini's *8½* and Preston Sturges' *Sullivan's Travels*. It strives to be as personal an experience for the audience as for the artists, "to make of each spectator of our film an observer on the set as well. An apprentice, if you will; one who will observe all that goes on for seven weeks' time . . ." (*DN*, xii). And whereas the use of actors Marcello Mastroianni and Joel McCrea distanced the other self-reflexive films from the aforementioned directors, Truffaut breaks down the art/life distinctions by playing the director himself. He is described in the scenario notes as someone who "never acts high-handedly, and seems not to care in the slightest about giving the impression of being the 'Big Chief.' Shooting a film always makes him happy. . . . To Ferrand improvisation can only deepen the resonances of a movie script" (*DN*, 12). The role of Ferrand requires as little acting from Truffaut as did Itard because the parts are so consistent with his own personality.

The extent to which this role is personal can be seen in the hearing aid worn by Ferrand. Besides suggesting a preoccupation with communication, the device is explained in the scenario: "Ferrand did his military service in the artillery; and during maneuvers lost the use of one ear, his left, the right having been impaired since childhood" (*DN*, 12). In an article that appeared in *La Voix du Sourd* ("The Voice of the Deaf") after Truffaut included an attractive deaf-mute in *The Man Who Loved Women*, he reveals that his ear was ruined in the artillery. One ear had already been damaged since childhood, but the other was then affected during maneuvers.[16] It would have been unlikely (and unnecessary) for the audience to know this fact, but it reinforces with subtlety the extent to which Truffaut brings elements of autobiography to bear on his art.

An equally central aspect of cinema in the first person singular is the way that Truffaut punctuates *Day for Night* and his other films with allusions to both his previous work and that of revered directors. This can be interpreted in the light of the paternity theme discussed above—for instance, Léaud is the father of the newborn Alphonse in *Bed and Board* and then plays Alphonse in *Day for Night*—or perhaps as simply continuity. He has called this film a "crossroads where the major characters of my other films meet," and specified how Julie Baker becomes the synthesis of the four British actresses with whom he has worked, particularly Julie Christie in *Fahrenheit 451*.[17] He "quotes" an entire sequence from his *Soft Skin* in *Meet Pamela*: Pamela and her father-in-law have run away to a motel and place their breakfast tray outside so as not to be disturbed, precisely as did Pierre and Nicole at La Colinière. The outer frame of *Day for Night* uses this episode to show the difficulty of getting the cat to drink the milk on the tray. Truffaut thus builds his past efforts into the present one with the humor and sincerity of an eye winking at the audience. When he quotes from Jean Vigo in *Les Mistons* and *The 400 Blows*, he is again acknowledging where his roots are, or that *Zéro de Conduite* is the ancestor of his films. When Louis and Marion go to see Nicholas Ray's *Johnny Guitar* and find that beyond the genre conventions is a "love story," they illuminate the core of *Mississippi Mermaid*; in addition, the allusion keeps the past work alive and inserts the new film into a rich tradition.

The most direct and lyrical expression of Truffaut's loving debts occurs in *Day for Night* when Ferrand opens a package of books that he ordered. At this moment he is on the telephone with the composer who is about to play the music for *Meet Pamela*'s ball sequence. Delerue's tender melody accompanies close-ups of monographs that point to the chosen fathers of the director: Dreyer, Lubitsch, Bergman, Godard, Hitchcock, Rossellini, Hawks, and Bresson.[18] I believe that this is the most naked and deeply felt love scene in Truffaut's work, an impression intensified by the realization that the same music was used in *Two English Girls* for that film's only happy romantic sequence. The idyll of Claude and Anne on their island is wrapped in these tones, specifically before Claude introduces Anne to amorous pleasure. It is therefore appropriate that the melody return in *Day for Night*, for Truffaut learned about love from the cinema, and this music serves to celebrate his teachers. Nevertheless, it is characteristic of the director that sentimentality is scrupulously avoided: his face is excluded from the frame so that if a reciprocal "love scene" is being represented, the passion is between the books and the camera.

The kind of modesty exercised in this shot is alluded to when Ferrand directs a kiss between Alexandre and Julie. Given the comparative absence of overt eroticism in Truffaut's films, the admonition, "Not too romantic, Alexandre," rings true for all the kisses stolen from his celluloid. The director's reticence is also brought into question by the little agent who badgers Ferrand, "Why don't you make political films? . . . Why don't you make an erotic film? I also have here with me a fascinating script dealing with pollution . . ." (*DN*, 52) and who introduces him to two ladies who could serve in any of the above. Truffaut thus exorcises his doubts about his choice of material by comically lumping together all the criticisms levelled against him.

He refuses the "topical" themes, but there may of course be an auto-critique implied by Ferrand's choice to make a banal film like *Meet Pamela*. Why such a trite script? Does Truffaut purposely shrug off the "what" of the film in order to let us dwell on the "how"? His own response was that he and co-scenarists Suzanne Schiffman and Jean-Louis Richard chose a simple story (which actually happened) because only excerpts of it would be included and they did not want the audience to be confused between "scenes of real life" (the chronicle of the shooting) and "fictional scenes" (those of *Pamela*). They decided to show primarily dramatic clips to contrast with the comic tone of the outer frame. Truffaut claims to have

liked the fact that the story functioned with two couples, two gener-
ations, and a well-defined plot so that no matter which moment
would be excerpted, the audience could always situate it (*DN*, ix-x).
In an interview in *Cinématographe*, he remarks, "I can add, to
defend the anecdote of *Meet Pamela*, that . . . all the conflicts of
Day for Night and *Meet Pamela* concern the problems of identity
and paternity."[19] While these explanations are convincing enough,
they do not sufficiently answer why all of the talented artists within
Day for Night should have been so committed to an ultimately
insignificant story.

The director, however, deals with this question within the film by
declaring that *Meet Pamela* signals the end of this kind of motion
picture. Ferrand acknowledges, "Along with Alexandre, a whole era
of moviemaking is fast disappearing. Films will soon be shot in the
streets—without stars, without scripts. There will be no more films
like *Meet Pamela*." In fact, this bears a striking resemblance to the
young critic's own declaration of emancipation that preceded his
first films:

Young filmmakers must decide not to walk in the imprints of the "old
cinema"; the point is not to make films of fifty million that ape luxury and
the foolishness of large productions . . . expensive studios should be abandoned . . . films should be made in the streets and even in real apartments.
(*Arts*, 8 janvier 1958)

The fact that Ferrand's lines are spoken off-screen while we watch a
hearse weaving through a square heightens the first-person quality
on two levels: visually we are presented with a real car in an artificial
set (one recalls poet Marianne Moore's brilliant metaphor for her
art, "an imaginary garden with real toads"), and freedom of movement within well-defined limitations, both of which are emblems of
Truffaut's cinematic style; orally we have the tone of a diary as
Ferrand records the personal and historical implications of an event.

Monaco is right to point out that *Day for Night* is in one sense a
bit facile in its concern with an isolated group of individuals who are
free to make temporary liaisons. Nevertheless, he goes on to realize
that ". . . Truffaut has turned this cliché to good advantage, since a
major theme of the film is the impermanence of relationships."[20]
When Alphonse repeats to Julie, who has just spent the night with
him, "Stay with me," or when Séverine laments, "we meet, we

Truffaut with Françoise Dorléac.

work together, we make love and then pouff," we can understand that the film itself is an anchor in the "tourbillon" of life; *Day for Night* is the response of art to the "pouff" (what Robert Frost called a momentary stay against confusion). Truffaut's visual devices identify with, or attempt to answer, the characters' needs: for example, he freezes a shot of the hallway during the lovemaking of Antoine and Julie and turns a two-shot of Alexandre and his young man into a still. But implicit in these scenes is that only by freezing the moment through art can the relationship be sustained—as proved by the end of the film. On the movieola, Ferrand could run the scene of the automobile crash in reverse and bring a character back to life, but not when Alexandre's car crashes. (This is also true for the painfully biographical source of the accident; Françoise Dorléac lives on in *The Soft Skin*, but the actress died in 1967 when her car overturned on the way to the Nice airport.)

This self-reflection of art as a record which resists transience brings us back to an equally, if less overtly, personal film, *Two English Girls*. Its credit sequence illustrates another aspect of Truffaut's vision: if *Day for Night* (like *Jules and Jim*) presents the ten-

dency to freeze what is mobile, to make a statue out of a human
being, to capture fleeting moments in "takes," the beginning of this
film tries to animate a stationary image, namely Roché's novel. (Of
course, it is equally true that *Day for Night* celebrates the movement of cameras, celluloid, and dials while the rest of *Two English
Girls* is permeated with the "statue impulse" discussed in Chapter
3.) Rows of *Les Deux Anglaises et le Continent* (the book) are presented from different angles, the camera moving closer as it did to
the statue of *Jules and Jim;* in both cases, the rhythm of the cutting
almost imputes a heartbeat to the object. It is appropriate that the
credits are superimposed on this image, as Truffaut is literally pointing to where credit is due; if *Fahrenheit 451* was an homage to all
books, this film is an homage to one (which even today leads the
director to extol Roché's virtues).[21] Truffaut, who has a profound
and occasionally excessive admiration for books, wanted to present
not only the story of the characters, but the books as vital beings.
This may be one of the reasons that *Two English Girls* often seems
to deal as much with the transcription of experience into text as with
the affective fluctuations of the characters.

Roché's book is then opened to reveal Truffaut's notes on the
pages—his visualization or animation of the words—thus incorporating the process by which the film came into existence. Claude's
voice begins, "I relived our story. Some day I will write about it" (a
line that appears much later in the novel); but his voice soon yields
to that of Truffaut, whose narration can be perceived as an oral
continuation of the written directions we glimpsed. As in *The Wild
Child,* he enters the film to explain or direct the action from within.
The credit sequence thus alerts us to the fact that *Two English Girls*
is simultaneously Roché's story and Truffaut's reflection on his own
art.

Claude writes *Jérôme et Julien:* "Through the emotions of a
woman who throughout her life, loved two men simultaneously, it
was easy to recognize, barely transposed, the story of his love for the
two sisters."[22] In *Jules and Jim,* this novel was called *Jacques et
Julien;* Claude completes and transcribes in Truffaut's twelfth film
the story begun in his third one. The continuities of Truffaut's presence are established in this manner, particularly when we see that
both films present novelists who transcribe the events as they tran-
spire on the screen. Claude brings together Jules (who was writing a
novel) and Jim (who was a journalist) in that he becomes an art critic

and then a novelist. It is difficult not to sense here Truffaut himself, the film critic-turned-storyteller whose art feeds upon his own experience.

Claude's diary rejoins Itard's; Muriel's diary looks forward to Adèle's. These characters do not need the camera in order to be "frozen." People who define themselves by writing and thus become books constitute the other side of Truffaut's art objects—books, statues, and films which become human. (Montag's great discovery upon reading for the first time is that "behind each of these books, there is a man.") It is in these transformations that the subtle but pervasive influence of Jean Cocteau—another man of letters and visual images, diaries and statues—can be appreciated. It is no accident that Truffaut produced Cocteau's last and searingly personal film, *Le Testament d'Orphée* (1960), for this fiercely independent artist meant a great deal to the young man.[23] The marble faces that line the wall of the castle in *Beauty and the Beast* (1945) were literal representations of what was to become Truffaut's metaphor: sculpture that breathes. Cocteau's mythical and magical images become psychological processes in Truffaut's work.

Death in Cocteau's *Blood of a Poet* (1930) is a statue that becomes a woman—as would be figuratively true of Catherine in *Jules and Jim*. The Poet succumbs to her injunction, "Follow me," which is no less the command of Albert's slide, fulfilled by Jules and Jim who go to the island to find the statue. Catherine will prove as implacable in her games as the enigmatic woman who plays cards with the Poet. Moreover, Cocteau hovers behind the continuity in the roles Truffaut gave Moreau, for in *The Bride Wore Black*, her white dress, black gloves, and black cape are the clothes worn by Death at the end of *Blood of a Poet;* both women are alternately human and frozen, and fundamentally revenge figures.

From Cocteau's work Truffaut might also have learned the visual/oral counterpoint that pervades *Two English Girls*. The impulse behind its tone (as well as that of *Jules and Jim* and *The Wild Child*) can be recognized in Cocteau's remark about *Blood of a Poet* (which was narrated by the director) from *Entretiens autour du cinématographe* (1951):

André Fraigneau: I notice that in this film which has become, in spite of you and itself, the archetype of the poetic film, its accompanying text is dry, quite the contrary of what one might call a poetic text . . .

Cocteau: To avoid redundancy. To not superimpose a poetic text on an image that I already blame for being so, in the sense that what is seen is apparent. . . . (pp.72–73)

As one of the first examples of cinema in the first person singular, *Blood of a Poet* centers on an artist, explained by the director's voice-over, who suffers in Cocteau's place. *Two English Girls* inserts itself in this self-conscious tradition; for example, Claude's response to publishing his book is, "I feel that the characters have suffered in my place." Beyond this frame, the characters have perhaps suffered in Truffaut's place: Dominique Fanne reveals that in the original version of the film (before music and post-synchronization were completed) the last line was Truffaut's voice-over, "I look old this evening."[24] It is now Claude who expresses this sentiment.

He then enters the Musée Rodin, taking refuge among figures that will not age. Earlier in the film, he and the two sisters had played "statues," each whirling the others around and then "freezing" them in the last pose. We now leave Claude amid real statues: he is "frozen" by the loss of both Anne and Muriel, after having been the first lover of each. When the last shot of the museum door through which he passes becomes a still, Claude's "statue game" becomes that of the director, who has animated and then frozen his characters.

The statue motif also suggests that Truffaut may actually have been resurrecting the first film that made him aware of the magical power of the cinema. In the opening paragraph of *Les Films de ma vie*, he tells us that at the age of ten, he was so impatient to see Marcel Carné's *Les Visiteurs du soir* (1942) that he decided to skip school the day it came to his neighborhood theater. The film was enchanting for the boy, who was unaware that his aunt would be stopping by that very evening to take him to the same movie. Truffaut could not confess to having seen it, so that he says of the re-viewing: "It is precisely then that I realized the magic of entering more and more intimately into an admired work, to the point where you can believe you are reliving the creation" (*FV*, 13).

"Reliving the creation" is a deeply appropriate metaphor for this film in which the love of a young man is reborn after a jealous Devil (magnificently played by Jules Berry) has bewitched him into forgetting. The Devil's power is therefore equated with the loss of the memory of love—that which Truffaut's diaries, books, and films serve to preserve. At the end, he turns the lovers who now resist him into statues. But the Devil is foiled: he can hear their hearts still beating. His "art" is thus as alive and immortal as himself, mocking the creator in vital solidity. Claude's—and Truffaut's—underlying struggle is with this very Devil, for they attempt to hold on to the memory of love; their creations consequently provide comfort and invite recollection of the past, and the re-living of themselves.

The phrase that provokes the Devil's downfall is spoken by Gilles when he drinks from Anne's hands: "Comme cette eau est fraîche" ("how fresh is this water"). It is the line of recognition, for he had said the same words to Anne before the Devil made him forget her. In both instances, it is the prelude to the kiss that seals their love. The fact that this phrase resurfaces in *The Wild Child* is intriguing. When Dr. Itard is trying to enable Victor to recall sounds and finds that the boy responds to "O," he intones, "Comme cette eau est fraîche." To teach Victor a language, Truffaut borrows a line from a work that actually taught him a new language. Despite the fact that its context is romantic in *Les Visiteurs du soir* and pedagogical in *The Wild Child*, in both cases its function is to spark memory, to break a spell that consists in discontinuity. And even if the director was not aware of the connection, the phrase reinforces the love that pulsates beneath Itard's static features.

In Truffaut's work, it is difficult to distinguish teaching from love. Even as a critic, the hyperbolic and fundamentally didactic quality of his articles resulted from a passion so great that rave or rage were the only channels. *The Wild Child* makes explicit the assumptions that underlie not only true education, but most of Truffaut's films: devotion to what is being presented/taught, and affection—if necessarily restrained—for the audience/student. His allusions constitute a crash course in cinema history; his multilevelled films imply a generous attitude toward audiences by being basically accessible to large numbers and yet stimulatingly complex for those who wish to take them more seriously. Through the story of the wild boy of Aveyron, he brings together the roles of actor and director on the one hand, and of teacher, writer, and father on the other—whose unitary whole is greater than the sum of its parts. As Dr. Itard, he fulfills two desires long familiar to him: "I believe there was a time in my life when I hesitated between wanting to be a novelist and wanting to be a lawyer—there was already the idea of persuading, yes, I like the idea of convincing."[25] Although he plays neither a novelist nor a lawyer, the latter role comes through in Itard's writing the journal (documentation and defense) while the former role is evident in his teaching: he invents situations to elicit the flow of language. And as we saw in Chapter 5, through his Journal he creates a persona, a character named Victor who often assumes more reality than the child himself.

The roles of instructor and father and the themes of teaching and love return in the form of Monsieur Richet and *Small Change*. Truffaut's decision to cast Jean-François Stévenin as the schoolteacher continues in the tradition of *The Wild Child*: Stévenin had been Assistant Director on *Day for Night* and was now moving to the other side of the camera. Richet is a gentle and engaging young man who, like Antoine in *Bed and Board*, is about to become a father. He shares with the early Truffaut hero a slight awkwardness, perhaps an over-earnestness; nevertheless, he differs in being more fulfilled in his work and more in harmony with his wife. His Truffautesque impulse to capture and record a magical moment— namely, to photograph the birth of his child—gives way to an equally Truffautesque incapacity when he is too deeply moved to do so. A close-up of his awestruck face conveys how at this moment life almost resists the intervention of a camera, too rich to be recorded.

In *Bed and Board*, Antoine's first moments as a father were spent posing with his son for a photograph. When Christine then asked him to leave, he wandered around Paris, pathetically looking for someone to whom he could announce his paternity. By contrast, Richet finds a rich channel for his excitement: in his class the next morning, the flushed and triumphant father makes his experience the source of his teaching. He tells the students about his son, proudly writes his name on the blackboard, and answers their questions about the birth with a naive happiness that rivals their own. He then puts aside his subject, geography, and asks that the pupils perfect oral communication of their own experiences. Like Itard, Richet's goal in teaching is to enable students to express themselves.

His farewell to his students shows again how Truffaut, through the voice of a teacher, truly speaks in the first person, especially when Richet explains, "It is because I have bad memories of my youth and that I don't like the way children are treated that I chose to be what I am: a teacher." As at the end of *Day for Night*, a group that has been working together is about to disintegrate: the classroom will become as empty as the studio set—until the next group forms. Richet displays the kind of moral imperative in his classroom that Truffaut admits to having felt in making *Small Change*, namely to take a strong position on children's rights with respect to political benefits and personal freedom. Whereas Truffaut's traditional cinematic counterpoint had employed the oral dimension to tone down the emotionally charged visual, here he uses a deliberately static or prosaic camera in order to focus on the words.

Richet points out to his class that political parties don't care about children because children can't vote. His earnest attempt to raise their consciousness and ours is a powerful plea on behalf of the one group that politicians unilaterally ignore. And in Richet's last words to the class, Truffaut gives voice to what must be his most deeply felt wisdom, for it suffuses all his films:

You'll see, time passes very quickly—and one day you will have children of your own . . . they will love you if you love them; and if you do not, they will carry their love or their affection and tenderness to someone or something else, because life is such that we cannot do without loving or being loved.

Richet's relationship to, and goals for, his class are affective, as is true for Truffaut and his audience; John Donne's image of "a naked thinking heart" (from "The Blossome") seems to crystallize this interdependence of lucidity and tenderness.

Fahrenheit 451 becomes more central to Truffaut's oeuvre in this context; the very concept of memorization that defines the bookpeople at the end is in fact a "learning by heart." They become what they behold out of the same impulses that animate Truffaut's films: love for the text combined with a desire to teach and a need to preserve. These sentiments recur in Claude's first lines of *Two English Girls*, "I relived our story. Some day I will write about it. Muriel thinks the account of our difficulties will help others." He wants both to set it down (to express himself) and to pass it on (to teach others)—and thereby hold on to his story. In Truffaut's art, one paradoxically holds on to the experience *by* passing it on. Continuity of self and culture are interdependent for his characters; the French word *garder* better expresses their need in the dual sense of guarding and keeping the experience alive. Montag needs to recite

Edgar Allan Poe not only for others to hear it, but in order not to
lose it himself. In this manner, text is also a pretext for self-
continuity. In Bradbury's novel (which Truffaut altered con-
siderably), Montag's decision to open himself to the world is expressed thus: "While none of it will be me when it goes in, after
awhile it'll all gather together inside and it'll be me . . . I get hold of
it so it'll never run off. I'll hold onto the world tight some day."[26]

There is another teacher in Truffaut's universe who attempts to
gather, record, and hold on to experience: Stanislas Prévine of *Such a
Gorgeous Kid Like Me*, who tries to turn Camille Bliss into a book,
Criminal Women. In an interview of 1975, the director confessed
that this film is secretly but definitely autobiographical, and that he
made it *against* himself:

> I am the two characters: Camille Bliss and Stanislas, the sociologist. I mock
> someone who insists on seeing life in a romantic fashion; I side with the girl
> who is a kind of brat, who learned to defy the whole world and to struggle to
> survive. I oppose one to the other, but I love them both.[27]

This is revealing in the light of the affective contradictions between
his films: he is aware that he tends to follow a "romantic" film with
one that destroys this romanticism (*The Soft Skin* after *Jules and
Jim*, or *Such a Gorgeous Kid Like Me* after *Two English Girls*). The
Man Who Loved Women can be seen as a response to *The Story of
Adèle H.*: if Truffaut's heroine was melodramatic in her single-
minded obsession with one man, Bertrand is comic in his kaleidoscopic obsession with *all* women. If Adèle's memoirs recount an
unrequited love and remove her from humanity, those of the new
protagonist chronicle successful conquests and humanize their
author.

Adèle's book, like Antoine's novel in *Bed and Board*, is rooted in
revenge—specifically for Pinson's rejection of her. Bertrand's decision to write his memoirs is partially revenge, after being rebuffed
by Hélène who only wants younger men; but more profoundly, it is
to combat the Devil of *Les Visiteurs du soir:* after having loved so
many women, he is afraid of forgetting them. When he can no
longer identify their photographs, when the images have no names,
Bertrand embarks upon a Proustian voyage; he will recapture the
fragments of his amorous past and weave them into a continuity that

will be known as Bertrand Morane. Unlike Adèle's impenetrable prose, his book will attempt to demystify, elucidate, and share his experience.

The Man Who Loved Women and Books

The Man Who Loved Women begins with a funeral attended only by women. As the coffin is lowered, a female voice-over comments that Bertrand is now well positioned to look at what he loved best in these women: "our legs!" She remembers his phrase, "Women's legs are compasses which measure the globe in all directions, giving it its balance and harmony" (*HAF*, 14). This line is uttered in Bertrand's voice and leads into the flashback where he is eyeing a shapely pair of legs. The film's opening thus establishes the power of verbal continuity; Bertrand's voice and words dissolve the barriers between present and past, or death and life, as will later be true of his entire book.

Bertrand is a small, dark, fortyish engineer in Montpellier who has only one pastime when he leaves work every day: the pursuit of women. In essentially humorous sequences, we witness his conquest of a variety of attractive, willing, and sensitive young ladies; but once the "unknown" becomes known to him, he says *au revoir*. Hélène, the "older" beautiful woman who runs the lingerie shop, proves to be the exception; Bertrand's own voice-over narration begins with his impression that "one day something will happen between this woman and me." What happens is the inspiration for his book when Hélène rejects him. And he begins his novel with another woman who led him to books because she didn't want him—his mother.

Bertrand's book takes root at a point that should by now be familiar to us: his childhood is characterized by the absence of a father and the presence of a mother who has little love for him. In a grainy black-and-white sequence that signifies the past, we see the awkward boy who "suffers from being an only child," and the cold, attractive mother "whose behavior seems to say, 'I would have been better off breaking my leg the day I bore this little idiot' " (38). Truffaut further hardens her image by cutting from a prostitute walking briskly, to the mother in the same position—and casting the same actress in both roles. From this we see that Bertrand's book is inspired by a deeply insecure relationship to a parent—like the motivation for Adèle's writing; in both cases, much of their obsessive behavior can be traced to the sense of being unwanted. Truffaut's Foreword to the "cinéroman" of *The Man Who Loved Women* proposes, "if one sentence could serve as the common denominator to the loves of Bertrand, it would be this one from Bruno Bettelheim in *The Empty Fortress*: 'It appeared that Joey never had any success with his mother' " (pp. 11-12).

If Adèle's actions and writing mirror those of her father,[28] Bertrand's experiences and memoirs echo his mother's affairs and records of them. In the second flashback, the boy finds *her* collection of photographs, as well as a detailed list of all her lovers. Bertrand now realizes that in writing his book he is reenacting her amorous accounts; this parallel is visually established when the child climbs up to reach his mother's memorabilia in exactly the same manner that Bertrand pulls down the typewriter to record his own. Bertrand's Underwood and Mme Morane's lists fill the same visual and emotional space. The third flashback shows how his mother forbade him to move or make a sound, only permitting him to read if the pages were turned silently—a command we should recall from Truffaut's childhood. She walks around him half-nude, "not to provoke me but rather, I suppose, to confirm to herself that I didn't exist" (83). Consequently, Bertrand's book, like his romantic exploits, can be seen as attempts to prove his existence and to make himself accepted, understood, and loved. (His last wish before dying is to be accepted by an all-female island: "Yes, they will accept me, I'll explain to them . . .") This interpretation is supported by another quotation from Bettelheim in *Small Change:* paving the way for Truffaut's next film, Richet reads out loud that a baby's relationship to his mother determines his future relationships with women.

The two primary concerns of the film—women and writing—are thus linked by the feeling of rejection at the source of his book; these preoccupations come together at the end of his manuscript through *its* acceptance. A young and vivacious editor at Editions Bétany convinces the director to publish *The Man Who Loved Women* (defending it in terms that obviously apply to the film of the same title). The crucial point is that in accepting the manuscript, Geneviève Bigey is also accepting its author. She realizes the inseparability of the man and his work and subsequently adds to her professional involvement with Bertrand a romantic one. It is her voice that resumes the narration at the end of the film when we return to the funeral; she calls herself his accomplice, "maybe because I am the only one here to know everything about him." Having presented his work to the world—and herself to him—Geneviève is responsible for Bertrand's life after death. She thus fulfills the same function for the film as for the book: Geneviève puts a verbal enclosure around his narration the way she put jacket frames on his written text.

The penultimate sequence of Bertrand's death depicts the inevitable culmination of his search for the unknown. After Geneviève has to return to Paris, Bertrand can't bear to be alone and goes out to look for another "inconnue." When he spots a tempting new shape, he runs blindly after her and is suddenly hit by a car. Even when critically ill in the hospital and forbidden to move, Bertrand fatally repeats himself: noticing a new nurse, he reaches his arms out "to these legs which attract him like a magnet" (*HAF*, 122). The blood-feeding system snaps as Bertrand embraces the ultimate "unknown," death. The fact that Truffaut frames *The Man Who Loved Women* with Bertrand's funeral intensifies the sense of fatality: events in a flashback necessarily lead to a predetermined point.

Like his parent, Bertrand is a collector of lovers; nevertheless, as one might expect of a Truffaut hero, this Don Juan is a rather atypical seducer. He is far more nervous and solitary than one would assume of a playboy. He has neither friends nor family; the space one fills with the name of the person to notify in case of accident is left blank. The source of his appeal is not virility but rather a childlike obstinacy—a seriousness that Bernadette recognizes: "I think it would be difficult to refuse you something. You have a special way of asking. It's as if your life depended on it" (*HAF*, 25). The *séducteur enfantin* aspect of Bertrand is humorously illustrated by the sequence in which he follows an attractive *derrière* through a department store. When the woman places a notice on a bulletin board, Bertrand jots down the information, which turns out to be "baby-sitting." Uta shows up at his apartment and, while he is in the kitchen, peeks into the bedroom to see the sleeping baby. She finds only a doll in the bed and confronts Bertrand, "But where is the baby?" "L'enfant, c'est moi!" (It's me!) answers Bertrand.

In this regard, he recalls Antoine Doinel, the perpetual adolescent who seeks the absolute (*The 400 Blows*), the impossible (*Stolen Kisses*), the unknown (*Bed and Board*). Even Bertrand's job links him to his ancestor: in *Bed and Board*, Antoine maneuvered toy

Delphine (Nelly Borgeaud) is in the mood for love.

Bertrand sees Hélène (Geneviève Fontanel) and her mannequin.

Bertrand becomes the mannequin in his nightmare.

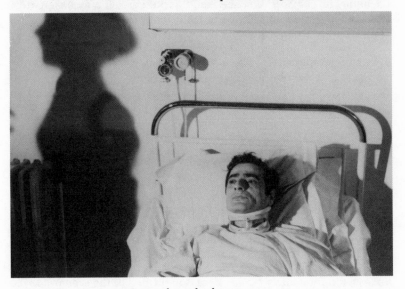

Bertrand sees his last *inconnue*.

boats; in *The Man Who Loved Women*, Bertrand directs miniature boats and planes which ultimately represent his own movements. Mirroring the tiny plane with which he is first associated, Bertrand flies in romantic circles, repeating the same patterns until, like his plane, he falls. In the second scene at the lab, he tinkers with a miniature boat; a pan from the controls to this vessel reveals the mechanical waves that propel it—not unlike the automatic system that triggers Bertrand's pursuit of women. He too floats in the rhythm of moving legs.

The first time we meet Bertrand, he glimpses an attractive pair of legs and goes to extreme lengths to find their owner. With a great deal of agitation, he notes her license plate number as the car recedes, and then traces it to a rental place. They won't reveal the driver's name if there hasn't been an accident; Bertrand therefore rams his car into a wall and smiles with satisfaction. He enjoys these complications, or the challenge of what he calls "la splendide inconnue." However, the sum of these comic incidents is quite serious and sad, for it is neither sex nor the hope for a lasting relationship that spur him on, but a need to escape from his solitude. Like Pierre Lachenay in *The Soft Skin*, he could quote Pascal on man's greatest misery being the inability to stay in a room alone.

As Charles Denner pointed out in a French television interview, his character's real reason for jumping from one woman to another is a fear of getting too close, a fear of being hurt.[29] He resists the intimacy of a developing relationship in order to control the situation and to retain his independence. Bertrand needs to spend an evening with a woman, but then also needs to sleep alone, even when the woman is as close to him as his mistress Fabienne. When he calls for a taxi to take her home one night, Fabienne ends their one-way relationship and predicts that he will suffer in his turn. "How do you know I haven't suffered already?" he responds. It is a good question for, as Truffaut reveals in the latter part of the film, Bertrand's frenetic flirting must be traced not only to the rejection by his mother, but to his painful separation from the one woman he truly loved.

The scene where he accidentally meets Vera is markedly different from the rest of the film. When he glimpses her in a hotel, the man who always runs after women tries to run away. She follows him and forces a tender confrontation. Vera is identified in the scenario as "la revenante" (the ghost), for while she is more than an apparition, she has haunted the hero for five years. He confesses that he survived her absence through pills ("It's not very romantic but I find it amusing that love stories which finish badly can be cured by pharmacy") but the humor does not mask his bitterness. Bertrand's grave features express the unsubdued torment he feels in her presence and the continued hold she has upon him. Even her name with its root *ver* (truth) suggests her crucial role in his life. In addition, this moment of truth is visually dominated by a large lamp. Its presence in each shot literalizes the notion of lucidity, for the encounter with Vera constitutes a breakthrough for Bertrand. He suddenly realizes that he has written the book on account of her, but that she is never mentioned—or that what is closest, deepest, and most significant cannot even be articulated. It seems particularly appropriate that this encounter takes place in the coatroom—the area where one leaves one's covers; in this *vestiaire*, they have divested themselves of roles and pretense. The comic hero assumes a degree of tragic intensity, as the scene with Vera tones the subsequent ones like a dark filter.

By shooting this in extreme close-ups which stress the isolation of the character, Truffaut creates more sympathy for Bertrand. As in *Shoot the Piano Player*, we are brought closer to the vulnerability of a face: like Charlie Kohler, Bertrand is a man who is trying to cut himself off from romantic involvement because he has already been scarred by it. This deepens the identification that Truffaut invites through Bertrand's voice-over commentary—which makes his emotions more accessible to us—and through the subjective camera: we share in his dreams by seeing the legs and faces that he imagines (a kind of "eye-over" observation).

The degree of the director's affectionate understanding of his character can be better appreciated if *The Man Who Loved Women* is compared to Fellini's *Casanova*. Released within a few weeks of each other, both films can be seen as personal meditations on art, love, and life through the figure of a seducer. Truffaut called the film Fellini's most beautiful, "which proves that he is the greatest visual artist—along with Orson Welles —of the sound film."[30] *Casanova* is nonetheless emotionally sterile; where Fellini presents a cold performer for whom style is self and mechanical narcissism is sex, Truffaut's protagonist constantly interrogates himself about his life and loves.

Casanova's erotic exploits move increasingly into the realm of

Bertrand's most important women: the editor Geneviève (Brigitte Fossey) (top); Vera (Leslie Caron) returns (bottom).

Confronted by nothing but men at the airport, Bertrand imagines this fetching scene.

spectacle and dehumanization, culminating in the magnificent sequence where he "makes love" to a life-sized doll. By the end of the film, he becomes as mechanized and frozen as his last partner. Bertrand's nightmare is like an inverted mirror of *Casanova* for it is precisely the fear of becoming a wooden spectacle that he is expressing. Bertrand dreams of an elegant mannequin in his own image, on display in Hélène's shop window. Women begin to gather and giggle at this unusual sight, and within the window Hélène runs her hand along the dummy's body. One interpretation might be that Bertrand envisions the only way that Hélène will have him, namely frozen in youth. The nightmare can also be seen as a foreshadowing of his death, for all these women will gather once again around another embalmed image of Bertrand—at his funeral (where they will fulfill his last wish to be accepted by an all-female community). However, the nightmare takes on deeper resonance through Bertrand's own presence as a spectator. With mounting horror, he observes himself as a lifeless sex object, till he must finally cover his eyes. In a film that is permeated with voice-over commentaries that provide mediation and continuity, this sequence is silent, and consequently more horrifying. Perhaps it is to counteract the fear of becoming such an object that Bertrand turns himself into the subject of an autobiographical novel. Truffaut thus deepens our comprehension of Bertrand's book by illustrating his need for contact as opposed to spectacle, and for continuity rather than silent stillness.

The complex narrative structure of *The Man Who Loved Women* mirrors the creative attempts of both Bertrand and Truffaut. The film is truly a "composition en abime," a self-reflective work in the manner of Gide's *Counterfeiters* or Renoir's *Golden Coach*, since it presents the artistic seams by which it is woven and held together. The various voice-over commentaries (Geneviève, Bertrand, and even M. Bétany whose reading of the baby-sitting sequence engenders and accompanies its visual presentation) fulfill the impulse of Bertrand's writing: they constitute the imposition of frames upon fragments of experience. Truffaut and Bertrand both tell a story retrospectively, moving backwards in time to a point of origin before bringing it up to the point of departure: the director leads the film from Bertrand's funeral to a year earlier, and then back; Bertrand leads the book from Hélène's rejection to his childhood, and then returns to the present.

Furthermore, the central problem posed by Bertrand is the same one that the director has been treating since *The 400 Blows*, namely how to make autobiographical art: "How should one speak of oneself?" is no less the question of a director for whom the mask of the third person permits him to speak in the first. Bertrand realizes that there are no rules for this particular game and comes to the same conclusion reached by Montag in *Fahrenheit 451* (and by Truffaut with respect to films): "Each book expresses the personality of its author. Each page, each sentence of any writer belongs to him . . . as personal as his fingerprints" (p. 91). Can we then assume that *The Man Who Loved Women* is as "personal" for Truffaut as Bertrand's art is for him? The answer might be yes if we consider that Geneviève's defense of Bertrand's book extends implicitly to the film of the same title. One of the readers criticizes the manuscript for being contradictory and not taking a stand for or against the character. She responds,

He is simply a man. Of course the book is full of contradictory details but . . . these are the contradictions of life. You say, "What is he trying to prove?" But he doesn't want to prove anything. He tells his story, without hierarchy between the significant details and those which simply illustrate the absurd quality of life. . . . It is a sincere and instinctive manuscript. (*HAF*, 96-7)

This perception applies to the bulk of Truffaut's work, particularly the narrative texture of *Stolen Kisses, Day for Night*, and *Small Change*.

    The Man Who Loved Women is obviously personal for the director but in an oblique way. While it is true that Bertrand is of the same physical build and coloring as Truffaut (and even the same astrological sign of Aquarius), it is overly reductive to assume a one-to-one relationship. It is misleading to read Truffaut into the Don Juan part of Bertrand; he is, however, intimately connected to his artistic identity. In sprinkling the film with allusions to his previous work, Truffaut's presence becomes more tangible, but only indirectly— and only for those who are already familiar with his oeuvre. For example, Bertrand is an extension of Fergus, the character played also by Denner in *The Bride Wore Black*, another playboy/artist who is killed in the pursuit of love. Denner's second role for Truffaut was Arthur in *Such a Gorgeous Kid Like Me,* a man who could make love only in dangerous or accidental situations, always followed by a sermon. This character feeds into Delphine whose ardor flames only when there is a chance of being caught; afterwards, she always scolds, "Is this really reasonable?" A delightful example is her pulling Bertrand onto a bed in a crowded department store. Bertrand's death reenacts the story told by one of the gangsters in *Shoot the Piano Player*: Ernest's father was killed by a car because he was looking at a woman while crossing the street.

    Geneviève is a new and autonomous figure but her characterization is enriched with echoes of Truffaut's earlier heroines. After she and Bertrand make love, she picks the breakfast tray up from the bed and places it outside the door—as did Françoise Dorléac as Nicole in *The Soft Skin* and Jacqueline Bisset as Julie in *Day for Night*. And whereas the question in the latter film was how to get the cat to drink the milk on the tray, in *The Man Who Loved Women* there is an insert of a black cat contentedly licking the bowl. The effect of this allusion is simultaneously distance and closeness. Truffaut detaches us from the romantic connection on screen to remind us of an artistic one beyond it. He thereby fulfills Geneviève's desire to control things after confessing to Bertrand how she was attracted to him: "Maybe because she speaks so directly to him, Geneviève feels the need to put a certain distance between her and Bertrand. She picks up the tray . . ." (*HAF*, 114). At the same time, this "quotation" serves to bring us closer to the man behind the scenes.

The Man Who Loved Women is thus a film that draws continuities, with Bertrand building the fragments of his love life into an autobiographical novel and Truffaut including the fragments of his cinematic experience into a personal film. Bertrand's ostensible goal is to understand himself as a lover; Truffaut's might be to understand himself as an artist. Geneviève encompasses these ultimately inseparable identities since she is the messenger figure between life/romance and art/immortality. In moving the breakfast tray, she momentarily yokes together Truffaut's past and present, as she will conclusively unite those of Bertrand. In this context, Geneviève also recalls Stanislas Prévine: in *Such a Gorgeous Kid Like Me*, it was his professional, and increasingly personal, concern with Camille that framed her own account. This describes Geneviève's relationship to Bertrand since her narration contains his own. However, she is a far more successful "accomplice" than Stanislas, especially because she effaces herself and permits Bertrand's tale to be told intact.

There is a progression from *Such a Gorgeous Kid Like Me* to *The Story of Adèle H.* to *The Man Who Loved Women* in that the relationship between narrator and subject grows closer: the movement is from the third to the first person singular. Stanislas writes up Camille; Adèle composes a persona, perhaps an example of the second person singular given that Adèle is essentially speaking to herself; Bertrand presents a "sincere and authentic" record of his own life—the subject and object of the book (and film) are one. Stanislas' text passes through hands which change it; Adèle's text is inviolate because incommunicable; *The Man Who Loved Women* synthesizes the better part of these antithetical situations by depicting the passage of the manuscript through numerous hands while the text is never tampered with. Truffaut repeats a crucial montage sequence of past event/present recording/transcribing for future (Camille's experience/Stanislas' tape recorder/Hélène's typing) when he cuts from Bertrand's memories to his act of composing them, and then to a secretary typing the manuscript. By punctuating the film with these processes, Truffaut reveals that one of his major concerns in this "comedy" about a playboy and his women is the relationship between experience and text.

The key incident in this respect is the encounter between Bertrand and Juliette, a little girl with a book in her lap who is crying because her sister is mean to her. Like Martine in *Small Change*, Juliette is a pivotal figure for she embodies the Truffautesque trinity of Child, Female, and Book. Bertrand tries to console her, "If I had such a pretty red dress as yours, I surely wouldn't cry." He repeats this line during the composition of his novel. And when he watches the book being printed, he reads this sentence again and we see a replay of the original shot. This time it is framed by more black space around the edges, so that memory is bracketed from the present. Bertrand asks the typist if he can still change a word and proceeds to replace "red dress" with "blue dress." We see the same shot with Juliette now in blue. The repetition of this sentence in its stages of transformation from experience to art illustrates the creative considerations shared by Truffaut and Bertrand: this imaginative coloring serves to distance the work from its author.

Art is often used by Truffaut's characters to distance and fantasize. For example, Antoine in *Stolen Kisses* is more comfortable reading Balzac and writing a pneumatique than being with Fabienne; Claude's first letter to Muriel in *Two English Girls* testifies to how he is absorbed by a mental image of her, and we see him falling in love as he writes. Like Claude, Bertrand is more enamored with the idea of love than the actual relationships. He also shares with Claude the need to compensate for the chaos and loss of experience with artistic order and continuity. On a more complex level, Bertrand needs to balance his search for the unknown with the preservation of the known—to follow the sure rhythm of typewriter keys as single-mindedly as the mysterious music of legs. In Truffautesque terms, he must weave his provisional encounters into a definitive frame.

It is nevertheless an oversimplification to dichotomize women/unknown versus text/known, since the real unknown in Bertrand's case seems to be his own identity. His pursuit of women can be seen as a pursuit of self, a desire to prove his existence, to touch and be touched into vital being. As Geneviève points out to him, Bertrand has to learn to love himself better before he can love others; in a sense, he begins to do so when he sees himself in print. He can be likened to the sixteenth-century French philosopher who drew himself into being through pages of personal observation—Montaigne. His *Essais* propose. "Painting myself for others, I have painted my inward self with colors clearer than my original ones. I have no more

made my book than my book has made me—a book consubstantial
with its author, concerned with my own self, an integral part of my
life."[31] And in Montaigne's last volume, he articulates one of Bertrand's deepest impulses: "I have done what I wanted. Everyone
recognizes me in my book, and my book in me." The degree to
which Genevieve recognizes Bertrand in his book suggests that, for
Truffaut, a text is not merely a repository of the past but a stimulus
or foreword (a pre-text?) to romance. Bertrand's novel succeeds so
well as sincere personal expression that Geneviève is seduced by it;
the vital connection between art and experience exists not only in its
creation but in its effect. It engenders new relationships while
commemorating old ones.

In addition to tracing the origins and consequences of a book,
Truffaut captures the excitement of the object itself as it emerges
into being. While he consistently shies away from graphic depictions of physical contact, he returns in numerous films to the physical delight of graphics, to the "feel" of the printed word. As early as
Antoine and Colette, he began developing the "hot off the press"
theme which will become a recurring motif in his work. Antoine's
job at a record plant allows Truffaut to include a close-up of an
album in the process of being printed. In a film that is rich with
musical selections, we are made aware of how materials must be
shaped and cut before Bach can be heard on the soundtrack.[32]

The uncut version of *Mississippi Mermaid* is far richer than the
released copy and contains a sequence that adds to this theme.
Marion makes a one-minute recording of her voice in which she
explains to Louis that she loves him, but that she can't stand poverty. It is one of the rare moments in the film when she can articulate her deepest—and conflicting—feelings, precisely because it is
distanced from direct confession. Mediated by the machinery visible in the frame, including a clock which ticks oppressively, her
message is a moving condensation of her capacities and needs. We
see the record being printed, an object that constitutes a definitive
statement of her love, but it turns out to be as vulnerable as her
attachment to Louis: when she steps outside, the record is smashed
by a speeding car. It is like the oral counterpart of the wedding
picture which the detective cuts up: documents of unique and irreplaceable moments, they prove fragile rather than permanent.

On the other hand, *Mississippi Mermaid* presents another form of
printing that combines love and technology (and wealth). Louis

owns a cigarette factory and after marrying "Julie," he makes his product more personal: a long shot of the plant reveals hundreds of packets with her picture on them, as the machines rhythmically reproduce her beautiful face. This stacking of images recalls a similar shot from the credit sequence of *The Bride Wore Black:* photos of Julie Kohler are ejected hot off the press, as mechanically as their subject will go after her victims. These machines also convey the urgency of being flooded with images, as palpable in the instruments as in artists.

Truffaut's obvious delight in mediating/creative processes is also manifest in *Stolen Kisses* when Antoine sends the pneumatique to Fabienne. As discussed in Chapter 3, the "aesthetic" element is not only in the message but in the rhythms of its delivery. *Day for Night* expands upon this concern with its triumphant scenes of rushes, editing tables, and actual shooting. But it is in *Two English Girls* that Truffaut first celebrates the sensuous quality of a *book* "hot off the press." Claude experiences a sense of relief as his text emerges, perhaps like a mother suddenly emptied of a precious burden. The author/mother analogy is actually verbalized in *The Man Who Loved Women* by Dr. Bicard: "Nothing is more wonderful than seeing the appearance of a book you have written . . . except of course the birth of a baby that you have carried for nine months . . ." (*HAF,* 89). The printing scene from *Two English Girls* is developed in the later film: along with Bertrand, we witness the solidification of his experience into text through various stages in the printing plant, including the collaboration of Geneviève. The title, jackets, and format are her contributions, suggesting that if Bertrand is the book's mother, perhaps Geneviève is the midwife who delivers it.

The end of the film reinforces the idea that part of the value of an art object is its permanence. At Bertrand's funeral, Geneviève explains that something will remain of him: "It is called a book." As Bertrand had done throughout his novel, she gives a name, while a close-up of her face dissolves into the book. The final credits unroll over two superimposed images: a row of copies of *The Man Who Loved Women*—suggesting how one solitary manuscript is endlessly recreated—and a pair of legs strolling back and forth, the same image that Bertrand mentally superimposed over the highway at the beginning of the film. By means of this double exposure, Truffaut shows how Bertrand's vision and consciousness have been retained through the text.

In 1973, Truffaut told an interviewer that he wished one day to make a film that would be the story of a book, from composition to publication.[33] *The Man Who Loved Woman* can be considered this film since we follow the manuscript from the first draft to the finished object. But there are deeper and darker implications in the tracing of this process than the pleasure of the text in all its stages. Bertrand's voice-over begins with a prediction about Hélène: "Some day something will happen between this woman and me." His book begins when Hélène resists his advances, and proceeds to move backward to his first sexual experience. Voice is thus a function of fantasy, frustration, and memory. What these events suggest—and what the entire composition of the book supports—is a discomfort with the present. Bertrand needs not only temporal continuity but the intensity that seems to grow only in anticipation or in retrospect. Like the texture of Truffaut's films, Bertrand's present is consumed by recollection in a future-oriented project, which is why the imperfect tense is so perfect. Likewise, his pursuit of women is more exactly the thrill of projecting and fantasizing than the physical aftermath; "l'inconnue" is the imaginative space *between* Bertrand and the desired object. It is noteworthy that he shows no interest in picking up the leggy hitchhikers on the road, but prefers to daydream about the brief encounter he had and hopes to repeat, with Bernadette. Like Henry James' Bernard in *Confidence*, he could say, "I like the beginning—I delight in the approach of it—I revel in the prospect," (an analogy strengthened by the fact that James will provide the source for Truffaut's next film).

Even Bertrand's interchange with the little girl in red points to this phenomenon. He asks her how old she would like to be and she responds seventeen. He calculates that she will be seventeen in 1985 and feels like he has made "a kind of date, an option on the future" (*HAF*, 82–83). His other projections are of course more reasonable; for example, he notes Uta's number because "you have to stock up for winter, pose the snares, fling the fishing rods, take options" (*HAF*, 30), options for dreams—and to counter-act the pain of separation, for Bertrand can't bear not having something or someone to look forward to. Truffaut's montage eloquently expresses Bertrand's need during Geneviève's departure. While she is still waving goodbye to him, the soundtrack introduces a telephone being dialed. There is a cut to Bertrand calling the women listed in his little black book. The overlapping sound represents his consciousness: he cannot bear to say goodbye to her without the compensating thought of someone to call. The editing recalls his imagined superimpositions throughout the film; all of these devices express Bertrand's tendency to anticipate or his need to project.

It is here that Truffaut may be presenting a slightly distorted but profoundly revealing image of himself, if we substitute film for woman, and his own notes for Bertrand's black book. He has admitted that the way he compensates for the feeling of disintegration at the end of shooting is by looking forward to a new project; the way that he guards against being too vulnerable to criticism when a film is released is by already having his next one in preparation. Perhaps like his hero, he can only wave goodbye if he hears the phone that signifies new business. Truffaut is as prolific as Bertrand is promiscuous, and as committed to (or even obsessed with) each project as Bertrand is to each woman. Even when he claims that he separates himself from a film once it is finished, it is apparent that every one of them is "unique and irreplaceable" to him.[34]

Bertrand takes time out from his flirting to gather, record, and share his encounters with beautiful women; Truffaut paused from filmmaking between 1973 and 1975 to put together *Les Films de ma vie* which chronicles his most significant encounters with films. It seems relevant here that the only two words we see in close-up while Bertrand types are "vision," and later "hibernation." The conjunction of these nouns implies that in order to see, you have to withdraw yourself for awhile. These literary parallels between director and character suggest that Truffaut's response to his painful experiences—to his difficult childhood, to romantic disillusionment, to the death of friends—is a withdrawal into projection: not merely anticipation, but the literal projection of dreams onto a screen. *The Man Who Loved Women* could equally well be titled *The Man Who Loved Books* and refers back in either case to François Truffaut, the man who truly loves books and films. The most enduring female for both men can be found in a sentence that Truffaut added to the *cinéroman:* Bertrand explains, "No woman here with me tonight; my new mistress is called Mademoiselle Underwood" (*HAF*, 49). The nights he spends with her result in the creation of his "offspring" and his immortality.

To spend some time in Truffaut's presence is to realize that his passion for art in no way diminishes his sincere interest in and affection for people. If he seems most alive when the conversation turns to cinema, it is really the individuals within and behind the moving pictures that he talks about. He has integrated the best parts of his masters by becoming a skilled craftsman in the manner of Hitchcock, a humanist poet in the manner of Renoir, and a generous man of letters in the manner of Bazin. If these people brought him closer to the cinema, it is equally true that their work then led Truffaut into their personal lives. For this lover of books and films, the primacy of the text has always been a function of the human presence preserved and communicated within it.

The scene that best crystallizes the heart of Truffaut's work might be the dream sequence of *Day for Night*. As the director Ferrand, Truffaut is haunted by a recurring image of a little boy with a cane, walking down a dark and deserted street. His destination turns out to be a movie theater, from which he pries loose the photographs hanging in front. He gathers the stills from *Citizen Kane* (a film about a boy whose parents sent him away, who became a famous figure and always got everything he wanted, except love) and he runs away with them; on the soundtrack, organ music rises and renders the scene a religious experience. The director is haunted by a boy with stolen pictures rather than kisses. The child is Truffaut, the cinema is his life. And our own sensitivity to love, art, and the space they share, is enriched by his projections, recollections, and lasting presence.

Jean-Pierre Léaud in *Love on the Run* with three images of his younger self.

7

Images on the Run

FOR A CRITIC approaching Truffaut's last five films, it would have been tidier if the director had made *The Woman Next Door* and *Confidentially Yours* earlier and ended with *The Green Room, Love on the Run*, and *The Last Metro*. There is a finality to these three films—a sense of closure resulting from the theme of death in his adaptation of Henry James's work; the idea of the last portrait of Antoine Doinel; and even the title of his greatest international hit, *Le Dernier Métro*. But art is (mercifully) never as neat as the categories in which critics would sometimes like to contain it, and Truffaut's two final films provide an unsettling coda, a return to the thematic and stylistic concerns that marked his previous—and not necessarily best—work. Following the mature female characters that graced his films beginning with *The Man Who Loved Women*, the heroine of *The Woman Next Door* could be seen as a throwback to the self-destructive *femme fatale* of the early 1960s Truffaut. And whereas Barbara in *Confidentially Yours* is a gorgeously feisty protagonist, the film recalls a cinematic universe more of style than of substance. Lighthearted but lightweight, *Confidentially Yours* doesn't quite constitute the signature that would complete the mosaic, the final stroke that proclaims a life's work consummated. Perhaps *La Petite Voleuse (The Little Thief)*—the last screenplay Truffaut wrote (with Claude de Givray) and planned to direct—would have offered a more cohesive summation, as it recounts the tale of a female Antoine Doinel, an unwanted adolescent who finds her identity first in delinquent activity and finally in the art of photography. (In good legacy form, the direction of *La Petite Voleuse* was assumed by Truffaut's former assistant, Claude Miller.)

Truffaut's last five films suggest that his cinema was like an ever-growing rear-view mirror: as the oeuvre moved forward, it was marked by a looking back—not only an awareness of what preceded,

Truffaut directing Fanny Ardant in *Confidentially Yours*.

but a re-framing. Whether peering over his shoulder at a previous era—as in *The Green Room* and *The Last Metro*—or at preexisting images (from the clips of young Antoine to the black-and-white tones of *Confidentially Yours*), he enlarged the rear-view mirror until the windshield could hardly frame what lay ahead. Nevertheless, the striking features of Fanny Ardant in the final two films suggest a more anticipatory perspective: in centering these stories around the woman he adored (who would become the mother of his last child, Josephine), Truffaut lovingly acknowledged his future.

To watch *The Green Room* with the knowledge that the director would die six years later, at age fifty-two, raises the question of whether this drama is not indeed prescient, looking both backward at the beloved-departed, and forward to Truffaut's own untimely demise. When he decided to cast himself as the central character, Truffaut claimed that it would be more personal: "It seemed to me that if I played Julien Davenne myself, it would be like writing a letter by hand rather than typing it."[1]

Ten years after the end of World War I, Julien works at a fading provincial magazine, where his forte is obituaries. That he is haunted by the carnage of the war—from which he has returned unharmed—

is suggested by the superimposition of his somber face in a close-up over battle footage during the opening credits. That he is obsessed with the loss of a particular person becomes increasingly apparent: his young bride Julie Davenne-Vaillance died a few months after their marriage eleven years before. If the pain of Julie in *The Bride Wore Black* manifested itself in revenge, Julien's pain takes the form of reverent memory: as he tells his friend Mazet, whose wife has just passed away, "The dead belong to us if we belong to them." In his house, a green room serves as a memorial, replete with candles and altar that recall *The Story of Adèle H.* and *The 400 Blows* (especially when the room catches fire). While looking for a ring that belonged to Julie, Julien meets Cecilia Mandel (Nathalie Baye), a kind young woman who shares with him the need to remember a dead love. She tries to lead him toward life, but Julien cares only about restoring an old chapel and dedicating it to his dear ghosts. He is devoted to all "my Dead," save one, Paul Massigny, a celebrity whose betrayal he never forgave. But Massigny turns out to be the very man Cecilia worships faithfully—a bond Julien cannot accept. This realization leads him to withdraw and wither, eventually dying among the flickering candles in the very chapel he created. As she lights a candle for him, Cecilia will carry on his work.

A subplot in *The Green Room* strengthens this film's connections to Truffaut's previous work: in Julien's charge is George (Patrick Maléon), a mute boy who recalls Victor in *The Wild Child*. Although his origins are never explained, George's presence mitigates the film's image of Julien as one who cares only for the dead. He may not be a very good father—for example, he shows slides (which he calls "beautiful") of war atrocities to the child—but he has obviously learned to sign in order to communicate with him. Truffaut's performance (as in *The Wild Child*) is restrained, but becomes moving when he explains things to the boy in sign language; for instance, when he tells George how pleased he is that the church has granted permission to rebuild the chapel, the characters are framed on either side of an open window, resembling those of Dr. Itard's home. The themes of deprivation and compensatory communication—finding an appropriate language—are once again intertwined; moreover, George is perhaps a graphic embodiment of Julien's own "inability to hear," or isolation. When the boy accidentally breaks some slides and Julien sends him to bed without dinner as punishment, George runs away, smashes a store window, and takes a female mannequin's head. Is this not an extension of Julien's own morbid possessiveness in the

Truffaut as Julien communicating with George (Patrick Maléon) in *The Green Room*.

green room, as exemplified by the wooden hand on which he placed Julie's ring? Julien's self-absorption is especially visible when he entreats Cecilia to light a candle for him after his death; "If I light one for you," she asks, "who will light one for me?" There is no reply. As Truffaut told David Sterritt of *The Christian Science Monitor*, "Ultimately, the notion of communication is parallel to that of survival. One survives not by himself but thanks to others. I think I've never praised solitude in a picture. When I show a loner, I'm criticizing him."[2]

If the "hero" of Truffaut's previous film, *The Man Who Loved Women*, was a loner who compulsively tried to connect with women—albeit superficially—Julien's obsession is with a single figure rather than with womanhood. It is tempting to assume that one of the sources of *The Green Room* is Truffaut's own grief over the death of twenty-five-year-old Françoise Dorléac in 1967. However, the origin of this film is more precisely Henry James's "Altar of the Dead" (and secondarily "The Beast in the Jungle"), as well as James's mourning following his fiancée's death. In a more formal context, the film is rooted in the imagery of candles; like the books of *Fahrenheit 451*, they are endowed with life, and Julien speaks of their flickering as "breathing." An appreciative review in the French magazine *Télérama* referred to the hero as *"l'homme qui aimait les flammes."* As Truffaut explained in early press material:

In all my period films, there were actors carrying tapers or candles. I always loved this liturgical aspect and wanted to take it to its limit. Without being a believer, I too—like Julien Davenne—love the dead. I think we forget them too fast, we don't honor them enough. Without going as far as Davenne— who is obsessed, loving the dead more than the living—I find that remembering the dead permits one to struggle against the transience of life.

It is not surprising that Truffaut was drawn to the work of Elie Wiesel, which is also concerned with memory and the responsibility of the living toward the dead. Already in 1960, his letters expressed interest in Wiesel's *Dawn,* which he called "quite close to what I would like to film, but perhaps too close to *Hiroshima mon amour"* (*Correspondance,* p. 177).

The Green Room is equally rooted in the music of Maurice Jaubert. It was the fourth time that Truffaut used a score by this composer, who died in 1940 at the age of forty—one of the relatively few Frenchmen killed in military action. He is probably best known to film enthusiasts through his scores for Jean Vigo and Marcel Carné; he was certainly known in this capacity to Truffaut, who used to memorize the soundtracks to favorite films—among which *Zero for Conduct* and *L'Atalante* occupied a significant place. Thus, if his films about children, especially *The 400 Blows, The Wild Child,* and *Small Change,* are to some extent an homage to Vigo, *The Story of Adèle H.* begins his homage to Vigo's composer. Indeed, all of Truffaut's films from 1975–78—*Small Change, The Man Who Loved Women,* and *The Green Room*—continued this process of adapting Jaubert's music to new cinematic contexts. For *Adèle H.,* all the music was recorded one month before shooting commenced; Truffaut thus directed Isabelle Adjani and the film not only from a literary blueprint that originated in the actual diary of the daughter of Victor Hugo, but from a musical one that originated in the soundtrack of *L'Atalante* and other films.[3]

For those familiar with *L'Atalante's* melodies, Jaubert's music not only serves the obvious dramatic function in *Adèle H.:* it adds another level of appreciation—a temporal layer which renders the film more complex. The soundtrack recreates the past of the cinema, the 1930s of "poetic realism"—of visual and oral harmonies which affected Truffaut so deeply as a child of the '30s who was addicted to

Truffaut with photo of Maurice Jaubert.

films. In *The Green Room*'s climactic scene at the altar—filled with
burning candles and photographs to retain the presence of the
departed—Julien stops before a picture of a young man conducting
an orchestra. He explains to Cecilia that upon hearing this man's
compositions, "I realized that his music full of clarity and sunshine
would be the best to accompany the memory of all these dead." The
subsequent close-up of this photo of Jaubert includes the reflection of
numerous candles—a muted explosion of light against glass, rhyming
with the soaring soundtrack—as if he were conducting the gentle
flames. Jaubert's music (mostly the "Concert Flamand" of 1936) vividly colors *The Green Room*, underscoring the fact that Truffaut is the
most nostalgic of the New Wave directors, and the most classical.
This is especially palpable when Julien looks at the photos of Julie on
the wall of the green room, and in the chapel scenes where the
orchestral crescendo engenders camera movement. Here we see
photographs of those he mourns, including Henry James—about
whom Julien says, "He taught me the importance of respecting the
dead"—Cocteau, Oscar Wilde, a little boy, a shy man, a couple
devoted to each other, an old man who played a small role in *Two*

Jean Dasté and Truffaut in *The Green Room*.

Truffaut in *The Green Room*.

English Girls, and a German soldier whose face is none other than Oskar Werner's—perhaps in his role from *Jules and Jim.* (Sadly enough, this actor would die two days after Truffaut.) The score alternates between restraint and violence, thereby expressing Julien's personality.

Despite the emotional weightiness of *The Green Room,* Truffaut's directorial style has a lightness and a modesty that render the film less lugubrious. In the scene where Julien forces a sculptor to destroy the wax statue he had made of Julie, the camera is placed outside the window, as if a closer perspective would be too brutal. When Julien stands at Julie's grave, the camera pans away to others in the cemetery, following them out and providing us with a needed respite from Julien's hold on our attention. And when he calls his editor Humbert (Jean Dasté) from the newspaper office late at night in order to know if Cecilia was Massigny's mistress, the high-angle camera not only keeps us at one remove from the character, but captures him behind a pattern of bars, suggesting his emotional imprisonment. The camera thus comments upon Julien in a manner that anticipates Truffaut's admission, "I am for the woman and against the man. As this century approaches its end, people are becoming more stupid and suicidal, and we must fight against this. *The Green Room* is not a fable, not a psychological picture. The Moral is: One must deal with the living! This man has neglected life. Here we have a breakdown of the idea of survival. . . ."[4] As in *The Man Who Loved Women,* our protagonist dies, leaving the woman to carry on his memory through her love and devotion to his ideals.

Just as *Small Change* constituted Truffaut's attempt to free himself from the oppressive tale of Adèle H., so *Love on the Run (L'Amour en fuite)* provided a welcome shift of tone from *The Green Room.* The latter films are nevertheless linked by the theme of the past pulsating into the present—the burden of memory in *The Green Room* and the weight of the flashbacks in *Love on the Run.* As Truffaut once said about Antoine Doinel (with respect to his love life), "This boy is too anxious to take advantage of the present. Consequently, he's always projecting himself into the past or the future." *Love on the Run* would be the last of the Antoine Doinel series, the fifth film built around the semi-autobiographical character who grew up on celluloid from *The 400 Blows* through *Antoine and Colette, Stolen Kisses,* and *Bed and Board.* This recapitulation interweaves flashbacks which in effect present the past of its characters. Truffaut "quotes" from his earlier films, permitting us to follow not only Jean-Pierre

Léaud, but his young female co-stars in their movement through adolescence.

The film's American premiere took place in February 1979 when The American Film Institute honored Truffaut on his twentieth anniversary as a filmmaker. The director was on hand (along with myself as translator) to launch the retrospective of his films in Washington and Los Angeles, and he explained how *Love on the Run* grew out of his realization that he'd filmed these individuals at various stages: "I didn't have to search for a child actor to play young Antoine Doinel: he already existed on screen. This is a rare opportunity in cinema; the only comparable situation would be to have Mickey Rooney today playing Andy Hardy!" The inspiration to make *Love on the Run* came from Copenhagen, where a theater ran an "Antoine Doinel Day"—*The 400 Blows* at 2:00, *Antoine and Colette* at 4:00, and so on—and viewers who had the patience could witness this character grow up, fall in love, and age before their eyes, all in one day. When Truffaut heard this story, he was seized by the desire to make a last Doinel film. As Gregg Kilday noted in the Los Angeles *Herald Examiner,* "The challenge of constructing a film that moved among the different stages of Doinel's life appealed to Truffaut, even though, he conceded, 'there is something limiting, problematic about building a film from pieces that exist.' "5

Antoine is now in his late thirties, divorcing Christine (Claude Jade), who remains a good friend, and writing his second novel. (He also works in a printing plant, and when he wakes up at his desk one morning, we can recall how the printing plant was a place of refuge for the runaway of Truffaut's first film.) In the course of *Love on the Run,* Antoine has a series of encounters that lead him to relive moments from his past, and to come to terms with them. He runs into Colette (Marie-France Pisier, who also collaborated on the screenplay), with whom he was infatuated in *Love at Twenty,* and Liliane (Dani), his girlfriend in *Day for Night* (although Léaud's character there is called Alphonse). And he also meets Monsieur Lucien (Julien Bertheau), who was his mother's devoted lover for many years; this sequence is a troubling and haunting one, as Antoine is led to accept a mother (now dead) who never really accepted him. Nevertheless, not all of *Love on the Run* is a remembrance of things past. Antoine's new love is Sabine, played by the French television personality Dorothée in her film debut. As Truffaut wryly pointed out, "In order for the ending to be not too sad, I had to introduce a new woman."

What made this filmic mosaic so appropriate for a Truffaut retro-spective is that it spans not only the Doinel cycle, but the director's obliquely personal "dramatic comedies" from *Shoot the Piano Player* to *The Man Who Loved Women.* Beyond the fact that there are clips from films outside the series—*Day for Night, Such a Gorgeous Kid Like Me, The Man Who Loved Women*—Antoine extends the portrait of skirt-chaser Bertrand Morane: he is a writer surrounded by a variety of attractive women who invariably prove stronger and wiser than he is. When asked by women at the Los Angeles screening to comment on this situation, Truffaut focused on the emotional drama: "My films share a basic tension, between characters who can accept the provisional or temporary nature of love, and those who demand that love be definitive. Of course we see the absolutists as mad; yet we admire them because we sense behind the madness a certain purity. They have gone to the extreme of their emotions."

Twenty years after lighting a candle to Balzac, Antoine remains a romantic. His amorous experiences are still literary, theatrical, and extreme: he pursues Sabine less like a lover than a detective (his profession in *Stolen Kisses*), or an artist infatuated with his creation (like the heroes of *Jules and Jim*). After jumping onto a moving train in which he glimpsed Colette, Antoine recounts to her the "fictional" basis for his next novel: in a telephone booth, a man finds the torn fragments of a woman's photo; he pieces them together, falls in love with the image, and tries to find the woman. We see Antoine acting this out while narrating (but twice he "steps out of the frame" by speaking directly to the camera from the phone booth). The playful self-consciousness is embellished when Antoine subsequently tells Sabine the same story—only this time he is confessing that it was *her* face, and that his "fiction" was in fact quite real. The film's multiple points of view thus overlap through Truffaut's typically intricate narrative structuring. Antoine's act of piecing together the image is a delectable objective correlative for the editing that is so central to this particular cinematic collage (and its mixture of "real" and "false" flashbacks). Unlike the linear progression of *The Story of Adèle H.* and *The Green Room,* the kaleidoscopic *Love on the Run* required a lengthy sixteen weeks of editing.

One of Truffaut's solutions was unity of sound, particularly the continuity provided by voice-over narration: Antoine and the other characters are constantly telling stories. The verbal commentaries function both as a formal linking device and as an illustration of a prevalent theme in Truffaut's work—the delight (or need) in telling

Truffaut directing Jean-Pierre Léaud in *Love on the Run*.

Jean-Pierre Léaud and Dorothée in *The Green Room*.

one's tale, and ultimately in recollecting and revising one's past. Antoine's autobiographical novel, moreover, points to Truffaut's own creative enterprise, for it actually records the Antoine Doinel cycle in book form. When Colette opens the novel, there is a cut to a painful scene from *The 400 Blows* which ends in Antoine's being slapped—leading to Colette's slamming the book shut. Printed text and moving celluloid interanimate one another throughout *Love on the Run,* as word engenders picture, and image embraces what can be spoken or written.

In addition, Antoine's job as a proofreader allows for reverent shots in the printing plant, as the camera acknowledges the mechanical processes involved in creation. The last scene of the film conveys the exhilaration shared by making art and making love, as the camera pans increasingly faster from Antoine and Sabine kissing, to an unknown couple in the same act, and then to the scene from *The 400 Blows* where Antoine rides in the whirling rotor: this joy of movement is no less an image of the cinema itself, as the rotor recalls the kinetoscope (precursor of film). The dizzying visual rhythm blends past and present, characters and camera, kinetics and kisses—and the love of images on the run.

Love on the Run might have been stronger if Truffaut had used its train images more centrally as a narrative thread. He admitted in Washington,

I think I would have liked the entire film to take place on a train because it lends itself beautifully to flashbacks. There is nothing easier than to begin the flashback, but nothing harder than to end it. When you come back, nine out of ten times there is a quality of deception that the audience perceives. You need a link, a bridge, so the story moves forward. A train is the perfect setting because it is moving forward itself. I think the audience makes an unconscious association between the movement of a train and the movement of film in the projector.[6]

Nevertheless, *Love on the Run* depends too heavily on pre-existing material which was more dramatically effective in the original context. If the flashbacks can be seen as beads on the string of present-tense narrative, this string isn't strong enough to hold them. The story of Antoine and Sabine is another variation on the adolescent-Antoine-coupled-with-a-mature-woman theme that has been woven throughout Truffaut's work. Although Stanley Kauffmann is right to say about *Love on the Run,*

Still when Truffaut uncorks his cinematic surges, the fount of romance and the adoration of women, the springs in his spirit that have remained youthfully, egocentrically hot, he's hard to resist. He never moves better than out of the exultant pain of high-spirited desire . . . quick followings, sudden puppy-like emphasis by large close-ups, impatient but lucid cutting between sequences, brief fascinated concentrations on purely peripheral characters (like the beautiful woman who is the judge in the divorce proceedings). Truffaut is at his best when he is drunk on the very Idea of woman; it keeps him fetchingly silly,[7]

the film is more an experiment than a self-contained work. At its best, it stimulates the viewer's desire to see the older Doinel films again.

At an American Film Institute seminar at the Center for Advanced Film Studies in Los Angeles, Truffaut proposed about the women in *Love on the Run*, "In questions of love, women are professionals where men are amateurs. I think women live their love stories in a double sense: they experience them and reflect on them at the same time. Men do not reflect upon what they're feeling . . . until it's too late."[8] By the time of *The Last Metro*, he would develop the notion of the stronger female even beyond the arena of romance, and create his most commercially successful film. Although it constitutes another look backwards—to the period of the German Occupation—*The Last Metro* centers on a modern woman who is smart, responsible, and courageous. The character played by Catherine Deneuve may have the same name, Marion, as her role in Truffaut's *Mississippi Mermaid*, but she shares only physical beauty with that duplicitous heroine.

Le Dernier Métro takes place in 1942 Paris, just as the Free Zone is about to be invaded. Lucas Steiner (Heinz Bennent), a German-Jewish stage director, is forced to go underground amid mounting anti-Semitism. He entrusts the management of the prestigious Theatre Montmartre to his wife Marion: she must surmount the subtle threats of the pro-Nazi drama critic Daxiat (Jean-Louis Richard), the romantic appeal of her new leading man Bernard Granger (Gérard Depardieu), and the curfew that requires their curtain to come down in time for the night's last subway service. The limitations imposed by war define the possibilities of theater. Marion's central preoccupation, however, is her husband: he is not in South America, as everyone believes, but hidden in the cellar of the theater. The play the

company puts on is *La Disparue* ("The Woman Who Disappeared,"
which was the original title of *The Green Room*), but it is really
Marion who disappears every night—under the stage. Role-playing,
improvisation, and a vivid imagination enable both Lucas and Marion to survive as well as mount a successful play. The 813 days he
spends literally underground are bearable only because Lucas de-
vises a way to participate in the performances above: through a
utilities duct in the wall, he can hear the rehearsals, and he prepares
notes that become Marion's suggestions to her director, Jean-Loup
Cottins (Jean Poiret). While the set is being constructed onstage,
Lucas builds his "apartment" below with props. And when the
French police arrive to search the cellar, he quickly strikes the set so
that the Gestapo find no trace of a hidden Jew. Theater is a cover in
The Last Metro—literally for Lucas who is really underground and
wants to be onstage, and figuratively for Bernard who is onstage but
wants to be in the Resistance.

Throughout the film, Marion is outwardly calm, but expresses
herself violently on three occasions: she hits Lucas on the head to
stop him from leaving the cellar; inexplicably slaps Bernard when he
tells her he is joining the Resistance; and—after a big show of calm to
a nervous Lucas—throws up just before going onstage for the premiere. Critic Geoffrey Hartman calls attention to "her training as an
actress which enables her to remain formal, even haughty, whatever
she actually feels. Truffaut communicates a temperament at once
passionate and inviolable. The entire movie participates in Deneuve's makeup; it is *porcelaine de Paris,* and the medium of film
gives merely an extra gloss to the sense that everything in Paris is an
extension of Deneuve and her kind of theater, despite the trivial
'Norwegian' (i.e., Nordic, non-Jewish) or pseudo-Ibsenian play being
rehearsed during the film."[9]

In the press book for his nineteenth feature, Truffaut explained,
"In filming *The Last Metro,* I wanted to satisfy three long-time
dreams: to take the camera backstage in a theatre, to evoke the
climate of the Occupation, and to give Catherine Deneuve the role of
a responsible woman." Perhaps the oldest of these dreams was the
second, for, as he explained in a *New York Times* interview, "I always
thought of making this film. At the beginning of my career, I couldn't
do it, because it was too close to *The 400 Blows*—not in terms of the
Occupation, but my own age at that time." Having been reluctant to
make two consecutive movies about a child, he thought of tackling a
love story set during the Occupation, but the release of *The Sorrow*

and the Pity led him to ask, "How can I make a fiction film that could measure up to a documentary like that?"[10] He was subsequently hindered by the spate of mid-1970s films about the era, and it was only a re-immersion into the written word that brought *The Last Metro* into being. In the introduction to the published script in *L'Avant-Scène du Cinéma*, Truffaut admitted, "While writing a preface to André Bazin's first articles, published under the title *The Cinema of the Occupation*, I had to reanimate the memories of early filmgoing. Suddenly the memories of this era came back with a rush, forcing me to make my oldest dream come true" (AS, p. 5). In this preface, he chronicles the details that would feed into *The Last Metro*, from obtaining a banned copy of *Gone with the Wind*, to an actor's slow diction which threatened to keep spectators past the last metro's departure. As Mirella Jona Affron summarized in her introduction to the published script in English, "He describes the role of the cinema and the theater . . . and the sanctuary theaters provided a deprived population until the day the Germans began to scour entrances and exits for recruits for their labor camps. He evokes the air-raid sirens that interrupted performances and the air-raid shelters that offered safety to audiences reluctant to leave their seats. He recalls the blacking out of Jewish names on screen credits. . . ."[11]

Truffaut's attraction to the tense war years continued with films like *Jules and Jim* and *The Green Room* for, as he maintained, "The war of 1914–18 and the Occupation of 1940–44 have every chance of appearing, in twenty years' time, like the two most turbulent and romantic periods of the twentieth century—consequently the most fascinating and inspiring" (AS, p. 4). More significantly, however, the Occupation was the time in which the director's personality was shaped. Much as Louis Malle would express in interviews following *Au Revoir les Enfants* in 1988, Truffaut recalled the Occupation as a period when "everything was paradoxical. We were told to be honest while surrounded by examples of the dishonesty needed to survive. For example, without food tickets, we would have starved. We had false tickets—badly made, obviously—so children were sent to the grocers: 'They'll close their eyes and wouldn't dare send back kids,' we said. I'm sure that my profound wariness of all certitudes stems from this period."[12]

His coscreenwriter and assistant director, Suzanne Schiffman, had also been a French child during the war—but a Jewish child. Although he didn't know her then, Schiffman lived near him in 1942: "Her father, who was a Polish Jew and spoke French with a thick

accent, remained hidden in the apartment. She had to wear the
yellow star when she went to school. Just as the girl does in the film,
she tried to conceal it under a scarf, "[13] Truffaut recalled about the
scene in which fourteen-year-old Rosette explains how she goes to
the theater. (And when Arlette [Andrea Ferreol] tells Marion that
Rosette's father stays in the attic while the mother manages everything, we presume Marion experiences a silent identification.) The
entire film, despite its obvious stylization, is filled with such authentic examples of daily resourcefulness, from the black market ham
Marion buys—hidden in a cello case—to the auto headlights whose
energy (created by stagehands riding bicycles for current) is used for
footlights. When a little boy's head is patted by a German soldier, the
boy's mother forces him to wash his hair—as Truffaut was forced by
his grandmother. In a close call with the Gestapo, Bernard is given a
signal not to acknowledge a Resistance comrade at their rendez-vous
in a church—precisely the signal Truffaut's uncle gave at a train
station.

Because of the significance of this wartime context, *The Last Metro*
is rather different from *Day for Night*, to which it bears obvious
similarities. Both go behind the scenes, an arena more compelling
than the spectacle they are preparing and performing (*Meet Pamela*
and *The Woman Who Disappeared*). Both center on a director whose
control is in question: if Ferrand (played by Truffaut) wears a hearing
aid but sees everything, Lucas can *only* hear. Indeed, his reliance
upon the spoken word at the expense of sight makes him a fascinating
complement to the boys in *The Wild Child* and *The Green Room* who
are deprived of hearing. Like Victor and George, Lucas compensates
for his loss, communicating indirectly. But *The Last Metro* goes even
further in its depiction of art as refuge or even salvation, and love as
difficulty or even pain.

The romantic elements are presently obliquely, eschewing
graphic eroticism for pungent suggestivity. The most literal scene
consists of a view of the legs of Marion and Bernard as we hear her
repeat "yes" off-camera. The tentative love between them is indeed
so subtle that some viewers have a hard time believing in their
attraction. Part of the problem might be that Lucas is too powerfully
romantic a figure for the beefy Bernard to pose a threat. As *The New
York Times*'s Vincent Canby pointed out in his review, "The sorrowful
love scenes of Marion and Lucas Steiner . . . are among the loveliest
moments in all of Mr. Truffaut's works. . . ."[14] And when Lucas tells
Bernard that Marion loves him, it almost seems as if he were carrying

Truffaut directing Catherine Deneuve in *The Last Metro*.

Catherine Deneuve and Heinz Bennent in *The Last Metro*.

his role of *metteur en scene* into "real" life, setting up the characters for maximum drama. Is it to keep Bernard from leaving *La Disparue?* Is Lucas already preparing his next play in which—as we will see—Marion plays a woman who deceives her husband with the man played by Bernard? The first half hour of the film convincingly sets up deprived Lucas and devoted Marion, whereas Bernard is relegated to flirtation and to the Resistance. When he tries to pick up Arlette in the first scene, they stop in mid-walk, start, stop, and so on—like a metro (all in one take). If, as Marion later puts it, Bernard is reminiscent of Jean Gabin in *La Bête humaine,* Lucas invokes Louis Jouvet. As Peter Pappas pointed out in his insightful review of *The Last Metro* in *Cinéaste,*

the most extraordinary performance of the film, the one true revelatory appearance, belongs to Heinz Bennent, playing the role of Lucas Steiner. Bennent's performance is evocative in the most Proustian sense of the word: it is the madeleine which pulls us into the obscurely remembered past. Through Bennent's portrayal of Steiner, which is to say, through Steiner's every delicate movement of his body, every aristocratic nuance of his hands, every measured step of his feet, we are swallowed into a Paris that no longer exists: the city of Sacha Guitry, Alain Cuny, the young Jean-Louis Barrault, and, of course, Louis Jouvet. [15]

Although Lucas is not presented as an actor, he is able to create a set/home, to improvise, and ultimately to embody the theater. He is thus the real hero of the film, waiting and preparing—much like Montag at the end of *Fahrenheit 451*—for a dark age to end.

If literature is what must be saved in the latter film, the stage is the focus in *The Last Metro,* for it provides more than entertainment. Although many viewers were aware that Truffaut had never been drawn to the theater, his *Correspondance* reveals that he planned in 1963 to direct Jean-Paul Belmondo and Marina Vlady in a French stage version of William Inge's *Picnic* (p. 248). His celebration of theater in *The Last Metro* is rooted in how—like the cinema in *Day for Night*—it accommodates everyone, from the concierge's son Jacquot who becomes an actor, to the Jewish adolescent attending opening night, to the gay director Jean-Loup and lesbian set designer Arlette. Indeed, Stuart Byron in *The Village Voice* perceptively called attention to the director's "unworried acceptance of homosexuals" as "evidence of the supreme humanism of François Truffaut." [16] The backdrop of World War II for the exploits of a theater troupe obviously recalls *To Be or Not to Be,* Lubitsch's dark farce of 1942; in both, valiant actors resist by performing, both onstage and off. Moreover, neither director condemns the heroine for adultery. Lubitsch endorses a style of understatement and indirection that is as vital to his heroine as to the tone of his work. Those like the hyperbolic ham Ravitch are mocked for their exaggerated acting, while the masters of innuendo like Carole Lombard's Maria are applauded within and beyond the film. In fact, the styles of Lubitsch and Maria intersect in the last scene through all that is *not* stated but deliciously implied: as her husband Josef (Jack Benny) begins his soliloquy—which had been the signal for the handsome young flier Sobinski (Robert Stack) to get up and visit Maria in her dressing room—he keeps his eye on Sobinski, who finally remains in his seat. But another young man suddenly gets up! *To Be or Not to Be* thus ends on a note of sustained comic tension with Maria directing her own "script" as deftly and mischievously as Lubitsch.

Similarly, Marion spends the night with a buffoonish admirer, and subsequently repeats an urgent "yes" as Bernard embraces her on the floor of his dressing room. Nevertheless, she succeeds in both saving a theater and saving a Jew—her work and her husband—and is consequently applauded at the end by both the theater audience and the movie house. This refusal to judge is perhaps even more redolent of Renoir's influence than Lubitsch's, and it is hard *not* to invoke *Rules of the Game* when an actor dressed in a gameskeeper costume rehearses Schumacher's line, "I thought it was a poacher, so I shot. . . ." The casting of Paulette Dubost—who played Christine's feisty maid Lisette—as Marion's dresser Germaine provides a nostalgic reminder of Renoir's tolerance: when sending gloves off to her man, a prisoner of war, Germaine admits that they're not for her husband, but "my number two." As in *Rules of the Game*, downstairs is more vital than upstairs (and the film moves up and down those stairs to fine dramatic effect: in a particularly Truffautesque moment, Lucas admits to Marion that he let her precede him on the stairs so he could look at her legs).

The real drama of *The Last Metro* is below—not only will Lucas be discovered, but how can a man survive 813 days in an airless cellar? It is hardly a coincidence that prior to making this film, Truffaut asked for a book by Ronald Fraser entitled *In Hiding: The Ordeal of Manuel Cortes.* It tells the true story of the former mayor of a Spanish village who—aided by his wife—concealed himself inside his own house from 1939–69 to avoid execution by the Franco regime. Lucas Steiner towers over the other characters—even from the basement—

Heinz Bennent in *The Last Metro.*

and it is significant that the thunderous applause for the play that closes *The Last Metro* becomes a standing ovation only when Lucas emerges from the shadows to take a bow.

The final sequence is sneaky: "Our story awaits its epilogue," announces the narrator, and locates us in the summer of 1944. Marion enters a hospital room, approaches a wounded and sullen Bernard, and says, "He's dead now." We assume the reference to be to Lucas, especially when she asks Bernard to make a new start with her. As the scene progresses, the window behind them (showing people moving) is suddenly a painted backdrop; their faces seem more heavily made up; and the eruption of applause reveals that this has been a play. Truffaut suggests how easy it is to confuse "theater" with "reality," and then elicits a sigh of relief when Lucas is spotted. As E. Rubinstein notes in the introduction to the English-language screenplay, "Thanks to the fact that we were so taken in by Truffaut's ruse, we realize too that the hospital scene has been inserted not only as a way of delaying, and so of intensifying the actual happy resolution of the film, but as a device for reminding us how things *might* have gone in those grim years of the early 1940s—for reminding us that, as in any fictional narrative, alternative endings are always available, and the happiest at least as arbitrary as the most doleful."[17]

Perhaps this ending is no more of a cheat than the film's opening, which moves from "real" archival images of the period to a photo of Lucas Steiner; nevertheless, it is an unexpected rupture of tone from a director who seems to equate theater with a certain license. When our three protagonists take a final bow together, the triangle—so fatal in Truffaut's earlier films (not to mention those of other directors)—is redeemed: no longer must the woman choose between husband and lover, for each has recognized the existence of the other. If most of *The Last Metro* suggested that "everyone has his secrets" (as in Truffaut's Hitchcockian films), the close-up of her hand clasping Bernard's and then Lucas's implies Renoir's line from *Rules of the Game*, "Everyone has his reasons."

The phrase that resonates from *The Last Metro*, especially in the context of Truffaut's subsequent films, is "Wait, wait," "I'm waiting," exchanged by Marion and Lucas. These words are uttered in the intimacy of an embrace—to extend the sensual moment—and refer as well to the patience Lucas must embody until the Liberation. They recur four times in *The Woman Next Door*—but the waiting turns out to be for death rather than freedom. In this tale of contemporary suburban passion, Truffaut returns to the intertwining of love and murder that characterized his earlier work. *The Woman Next Door* begins in Grenoble with the voice of Odile Jouve (Véronique Silver), the manager of a tennis club. This attractive, middle-aged woman introduces herself to the audience, even asking the camera to move back: we see that she limps and walks with a brace. "Let's sit down here," she proposes warmly, thereby introducing the blended tones of lightness and sorrow that will mark the film. She tells us that the story began six months ago, as we see Bernard (Gérard Depardieu) posing with his wife Arlette (Michele Baumgartner) and son in front of their house. The empty house next door will soon be occupied (prompting Bernard to quip comically to Arlette, "No more outdoor sex!").

When they meet the new neighbors Mathilde (Fanny Ardant) and Philippe (Henri Garcin), the tension between Bernard and Mathilde is expressed by a close-up of her troubled face, and by the freeze frame which later follows Bernard's declaration, "What's she doing here?", as he turns off the light. That they have a turbulent history together becomes apparent when Mathilde calls Bernard and—invoking the past of other Truffaut characters—pleads, "Wait, wait." Bernard responds, "I'm waiting." She repeats these words to him in the hotel room a few sequences later and, after their love-making,

Fanny Ardant in *The Woman Next Door.*

Fanny Ardant and Gérard Depardieu in the climactic scene.

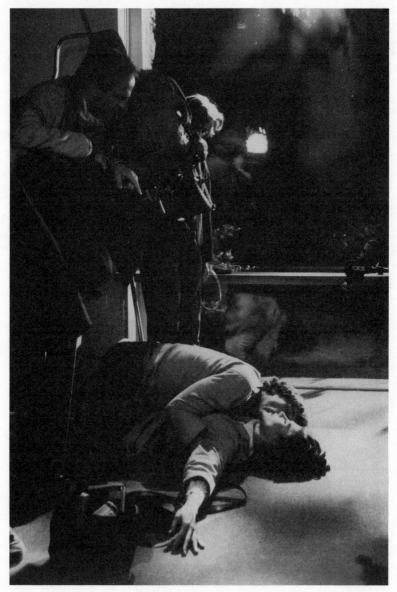

Truffaut shooting the scene.

Bernard whispers, "Wait, wait," as he kisses her again. Both characters try to resist the passion, presumably because of their irreproachable spouses. Bernard is the insistent one as the adulterous relationship resumes, and once the affair is in the open, it turns out that Mathilde cannot live without him. She is hospitalized with a nervous breakdown, until she seems cured and moves into an apartment with her husband. But she is no more at peace than the enigmatic Catherine at the end of *Jules and Jim:* like her cinematic predecessor, Mathilde lures Bernard out of bed and into the empty house for a last embrace—shooting him and then herself.

What elevates *The Woman Next Door* above tawdry romance is Truffaut's elegant treatment of the melodramatic material. In particular, Odile Jouve is not merely a narrator but a narrative counterpart to Mathilde.[18] She confesses to Bernard that her crippled leg is the result of having tried to kill herself when she was desperate over her lover: she jumped out of a window twenty years ago, and he never knew about it. At the tennis club a few scenes later—accompanied by romantic music—Bernard (and the fluid camera) watches a delivery boy with a telegram searching for Odile. She is visibly troubled by its contents. She then leaves town for a few days. The audience subsequently ties the threads together when a man comes to the club looking for her—presented with the same searching camera and lyrical music as in the telegram scene. We realize that Odile went away precisely to avoid what Mathilde is now experiencing—the turbulence of an old love after having achieved some kind of *repos* (not unlike the heroine of Madame de Lafayette's *Princesse de Clèves*). The parallel is rendered more concrete by Bernard's glimpsing Mathilde's scarred wrist, suggesting a suicide attempt after their separation eight years before.

For all the violent passion that pervades *The Woman Next Door,* the style is as discreet as Odile. Her playful harmony with the camera is established in the first scene as her voice accompanies a high-angle tracking shot of a police car before there is a dissolve to her face in direct address. Like Odile, the camera is omniscient, both sympathetic to and distanced from the protagonists. For example, it follows Mathilde and Philippe leaving Arlette's house and entering their own, and then moves back to Bernard hiding in the shadows before he goes home. As in *Jules and Jim,* the decision to pan and track rather than cut not only respects spatial unity but conveys the tense proximity of these characters. Once Bernard and Mathilde meet in the hotel, the camera does *not* follow them into the room for a titillating scene, but gently mocks our voyeurism by holding on a maid with a laundry cart moving down the corridor. When Bernard throws caution to the winds and attacks Mathilde during a party at Odile's club, the camera stays behind a window, framing other characters watching the couple; this makes us more aware of the spectacle than of the fight—more sensitive to the surprised and embarrassed spectators than to the lovers themselves. Truffaut also employs such self-conscious devices as the freeze frame on Bernard, and an iris on Mathilde after Philippe acknowledges that he loves a liar. The iris is repeated on Mathilde when she says, "Take me away, my love": although her husband is in the hospital room at this moment, it is obvious from the close-up of her closed eyes and from the iris that she is not speaking to him. Rather than allow for facile identification, these touches remind us of the mediation of the storytellers—both Odile and Truffaut.

The Woman Next Door is consistent with the style and concerns that we have seen from *Shoot the Piano Player* to *The Last Metro*. For example, Odile's description of herself at the moment of attempted suicide—"Je me suis jetée comme un paquet de linge sale" ("I threw myself out like a sack of dirty laundry")—brings us back to Theresa's self-assessment given to Edouard just before she jumps fatally from the window in *Shoot the Piano Player. Jules and Jim* is invoked not only by Mathilde's final murder-suicide, but by the coroner's clinical voice-over description of how their bodies were found. When Odile closes the film with the suggestion of an epitaph, "Neither with you nor without you"—adding, "but I doubt they'll ask my advice"—we are reminded of the narration at the end of *Jules and Jim* to the effect that Catherine wanted her ashes scattered, but it wasn't permitted. If the fatally adulterous situation is also reminiscent of *The Soft Skin*, the house and the telephone are indeed actors in the drama of *The Woman Next Door*, especially when Bernard and Mathilde are both trying to call each other at the same time and grow frustrated by busy signals. When Philippe takes Mathilde to the tropics for a belated honeymoon, the movement into heat and light functions much as it does in *The Story of Adèle H.*, for both heroines are succumbing to a madness borne of frustrated love. That desire can be likened to violence is suggested earlier by at least three scenes: when Mathilde first calls Bernard, the camera moves back from a painting of a couple who appear to be exchanging blows (on the right side of the frame) to reveal Mathilde looking at his house; when Bernard and Arlette hear cats at night, he says they are fighting, whereas Arlette replies that

"They're making love, savagely"; and after Mathilde and Bernard have their first illicit tryst in the hotel, she observes while looking at the bed, "It looks like a real battlefield." This terrain coexists with the fact that Bernard—despite Depardieu's bulky frame—is related to Truffaut's childish heroes: like Bertrand in *The Man Who Loved Women*, he mans miniature boats; like Antoine Doinel, he hides from the woman who attracts him; like Alphonse in *Day for Night*, he wants all or nothing, insisting that Mathilde leave with him.

Similar to the other characters in *The Woman Next Door*, Bernard tries to behave decently, but cannot control his feelings: witness the party scene where he strikes Mathilde in front of their assembled friends. Likewise, Mathilde faints the first time Bernard kisses her in the parking lot; Arlette is understanding when she learns about the affair, but then throws up at night; Philippe finally yells at Mathilde for repeating Bernard's name in her sleep; Mathilde puts too much bloody red in her drawing for a children's book; and in the midst of signing copies of the finished text, she runs away and hurls herself down in a secluded grove, crying like a wounded animal. They try to be tolerant, reasonable adults, but are no match for passion. Perhaps we can find one reason for their failure by continuing the comparison with *The Last Metro*: Depardieu has the same name in both films, implying a continuity in the characters. If nothing else, they are decent men caught in the eternal bind between desire and pre-existing commitment. The main difference is that the protagonists of the former are strong in their professional/theatrical identities: a heroine like Marion can control her anger at Lucas and—displaying infinite wisdom—reply to his tantrum with "I'd rather not say anything, because I'll only regret it afterwards." In Truffaut's previous four films, the characters try to *create* something—Bertrand's book in *The Man Who Loved Women*, Julien's chapel in *The Green Room*, Antoine's book in *Love on the Run*, the play in *The Last Metro*. The only artistic enterprise in *The Woman Next Door* is Mathilde's book for children, which is relegated to the background. In this context, the most positive—or healing—character is not only Odile, but Roland (Roger Van Hool), whom she describes to Bernard as a wonderful, devoted friend. Indeed, this easy-going, handsome young man encourages Mathilde and publishes her book, and ultimately fulfills Stuart Byron's point about the accommodation of homosexual characters in *The Last Metro*: Roland is gay, and his lover is at the club, but Truffaut does not call much attention to sexual orientation. In a reversal of pernicious stereotyping, the director implies that a homosexual character can be more successful maintaining affective relationships than a heterosexual.

The most Truffautesque of the male characters seems to be Philippe, although he works as an airport controller rather than as a writer or artist. Diminutive and bespectacled, he admits to Bernard that when he saw Mathilde, "I knew it would be my last chance for happiness." If this suggests Truffaut himself vis-à-vis Fanny Ardant, it is indeed Philippe who utters the very phrase the director offered in 1979: "Men are amateurs in love." After the final gunshots, the film never returns to Philippe—nor to Arlette—but seals off the doomed lovers' tale by having Odile pick up the narration exactly where she left it at the film's opening. (She is speaking at the very moment the police car arrives at the scene of the crime.) The high-angle camera takes leave of the survivors, offering detachment rather than illumination. This distancing from the story of a less-than-compelling middle-aged man coupled with the stunning Ardant continues in *Confidentially Yours*, albeit in a more comic vein.

Here, real-estate agent Julien Vercel (Jean-Louis Trintignant) is accused of murdering his rather unfaithful wife (Caroline Sihol), a movie theater proprietor who was her lover, and an unsavory nightclub owner. His vibrant secretary Barbara (Fanny Ardant) believes in his innocence and sets out to prove it with energetic intelligence. Often bickering but ultimately kissing, this couple matches wits with policemen and an assortment of shady types that recall earlier films of the detective genre. Although a lighthearted murder mystery might sound like a contradiction in terms, *Confidentially Yours* (*Vivement Dimanche!*) is both a comedy and a detective thriller (not unlike *The Thin Man*). Truffaut was attracted to the original story—*The Long Saturday Night*, by Charles Williams—for three reasons:

I liked the idea of a *série noire* (detective novel) without gangsters. Second, the relationship between a secretary and her boss, which can be so amusing, has not been explored in recent films. And most of all, I wanted to make a detective film with Fanny Ardant. I read many novels by Williams and found that he created the best roles for women. I liked the idea of an "ordinary" woman from daily life conducting the investigation. Fanny represents in France a certain elegance and lyricism. I wanted to show that she could be a comedienne—in a popular role, behind a typewriter.[19]

There are obvious echoes of *Stolen Kisses*, where Antoine Doinel was often seen behind newspapers or doors as he tried to solve a mystery. The Lablache Detective Agency in *Confidentially Yours* is reminiscent of the Blady Agency in the previous film, right down to the boss's exhortation, "Detective work is ten percent inspiration and ninety percent perspiration" (paraphrasing Edison on invention). The bumbling private eye that Barbara catches in her hotel room is not unrelated to those who persuaded Antoine to let them into a room where they confronted an unfaithful wife. A more significant connection, perhaps, is the camera's presence as a curious but limited narrator. Just as it followed Antoine and Christine up the stairs to bed toward the end of *Stolen Kisses*—only to wander into the wrong room, retreat, find the right room, and discreetly exit—so Truffaut keeps the camera outside the house when Madame Vercel returns and fights with Julien. A neighbor out for a stroll, hearing the fight, says to his dog, "It's none of our business"—a line comically applicable to the viewer. And if one of the central threads in *Stolen Kisses* was the characters' need to tell stories—to recount themselves—the climax of *Confidentially Yours* offers another comic and poignant example: when the killer Clément (Philippe Laudenbach) admits his guilt, it is in a phone booth rather than a confessional, and the priest has been replaced by the detective. Clément explains (in typically Truffautesque language), "Everything I've done was for women. Women are magic . . . so I became a magician."

Ardant's Barbara shares with previous Truffaut heroines like Deneuve's Marion, Adjani's Adele, and Moreau's Catherine a strength and intensity that render the male protagonists a bit pallid by comparison. Similarly, Trintignant has a great deal in common with Léaud's Antoine, Aznavour's Charlie, and Denner's Bertrand, whose characters are diminutive and acted upon by attractive women. Like Lucas Steiner forced underground in *The Last Metro*, Julien is locked in the back room of his office while Barbara carries on his work outside. (In all cases, the hero has a proclivity toward women's legs: Barbara knowingly obliges by walking a few extra steps in front of the window where Julien is stuck.) The main difference is that—unlike the passion palpable throughout *The Woman Next Door*—this film is not persuasive as a love story.

Truffaut went against convention not only in the coolness of the romantic relationship, but in his decision to eschew color. *Confidentially Yours* is his first black-and-white film since *The Wild Child*—both shot by Nestor Almendros. Why not color? "Of all film genres," he maintained, "the detective thriller is best suited to black-and-white. Hollywood continues to make the same genre films as before the war—like Westerns and musicals—that gain from being in color.

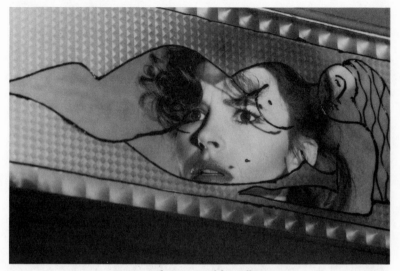

Fanny Ardant in *Confidentially Yours.*

Série noire films, however, lost something with color. I wanted to resist the tyranny of color. Each director should choose whether the subject warrants color or black-and-white."[20] This provided a challenge for production designer Hilton McConnico (who came to international prominence for the art direction of *Diva*). For his first film in black-and-white, he proposed to Truffaut and Almendros that all the sets and costumes be done in black, white, and gray, and then created thirty-five black-and-white paintings to hang all over the different sets. One of the most striking examples of his integrated production design is a window above a door in the nightclub: etched onto the glass is the shape of an ample, reclining woman's body, through which Barbara peers into the next room. The traditional female icon is filled not by a male gaze, but by Ardant's intelligent facial features. (McConnico has a cameo role as the man who tries to pick up Barbara when she poses as a prostitute.)

Another challenge for Truffaut was the translation of a novel—where everything transpires statically through telexes, telegrams, and telephones—into visual terms. Episodes were invented to render Barbara more active than in the novel, which is narrated chronologically by the real estate agent. Truffaut removed this first-person commentary and—in the spirit of Ernst Lubitsch—added two flash-

Jean-Louis Trintignant is aware of his wife's (Caroline Sihol's) legs in *Confidentially Yours*.

backs recounted by Julien and Barbara. The first is the wife's murder, which the audience, instead of seeing chronologically and "objectively," learns about from Julien's explanation. Had we seen him walk into the house and discover the body upon returning from the police station, we would have assumed his innocence. But just as the opening of *Confidentially Yours* creates a purposeful ambiguity by introducing Julien hunting and then *not* showing us the killer, so the flashback raises the question of whether its contents are not merely Julien's fabrication. Barbara's flashback is more playful, much like Antoine's in *Love on the Run* as he describes finding a woman's torn photo in a phone booth: she begins the narration in the police station, and then we see her in the lawyer's office earlier that afternoon. Barbara continues narrating *in* the flashback, winking almost complicitously at the viewer who is reminded that he is watching the *telling* of the story—not just the tale itself.

Hitchcock is another avowed influence in *Confidentially Yours*, from Barbara's nighttime drive to Nice in the rain, reminiscent of Marion's approaching the motel in *Psycho*, to the fact that the seemingly guilty character is innocent and vice versa. Truffaut acknowledged, "If you sense a Hitchcockian fragrance, it's from the English period [of *The 39 Steps* or *The Lady Vanishes*]. Whenever possible, I replaced ordinary scenes with arguments: the more Julien and Barbara fight, the more the audience will want them to be together."[21] The main problem is the plausibility of the relationship, for Julien never achieves the dimensions that would render him worthy of such a statuesque French Nancy Drew as Barbara. The only "Wait, wait" phrase is uttered by his wife and, significantly enough, he does not follow it with the Truffautesque reply, "I'm waiting." Once the mystery is solved and Clément shoots himself in the phone booth, there is an abrupt cut to a children's choir singing at the wedding of Julien and a very pregnant Barbara. *Confidentially Yours* ends with children's feet kicking a lens cap around, leading the viewer to wonder about such lighthearted music after all the corpses we have just witnessed. Although the film has maintained a comic tone throughout (and one of the most racy lines is not completely subtitled: we hear Julien's wife dismissively tell him that the now-deceased Massoulier "made love like an umbrella"), the sunny opening and closing frame seems hardly related to the nocturnal mystery that it brackets.

For many viewers, *Confidentially Yours* was proof that Truffaut's talents had diminished since his auspicious New Wave beginnings, especially because he was using an established star (Trintignant) while his amorous lens was celebrating the leading lady's compelling beauty. For others, it was a different kind of proof, namely that this director was capable of constant experimentation with everything from genre to film stock, and that he could offer the lightest of touches right after the gloomy vision of *The Woman Next Door.* Whatever the assessment, it would be his last film—although not his last work. The publication in France of Truffaut's *Correspondance* in May 1988 turned out be a coda to his output, a best-selling and critically acclaimed volume that fulfilled his identity as a man of letters as well as images. Simultaneously, production was begun by two of his former collaborators on films of their own, both clearly inspired by Truffaut: Claude Miller took over *La Petite Voleuse* (from a screenplay by Truffaut and Claude de Givray), while Suzanne Schiffman took on *The Paperback Woman* starring none other than Jean-Pierre Léaud. The director's presence was also preserved in a volume of essays entitled *Le Plaisir des yeux,* in which he wrote an important cautionary note to those who would study the cinema: "Let us never forget that ideas are less interesting than the human beings who invent them, modify them, perfect them or betray them. . . . Nothing ages faster than theoretical studies of art, probably because they are

Truffaut (*left*), Nestor Almendros (*center*) and Jean-Louis Richard as Daxiat on the set of *The Last Metro*.

done according to methods developed from ideologies which follow one another, contradict one another, and chase each other away . . ." (p. 38, p. 85).

What interested Truffaut above all was people, and if he seemed most alive when the conversation turned to cinema, it was really the individuals within and behind the moving pictures that he talked about. He integrated the best parts of his masters by becoming a skilled craftsman in the manner of Hitchcock, a humanist poet in the manner of Renoir, and a generous man of letters in the manner of Bazin. If these people brought him closer to the cinema, it is equally true that their work then led Truffaut into their personal lives. For this lover of books and films, the primacy of the text was always a function of the human presence preserved and communicated within it.

The scene that best crystallizes the heart of Truffaut's work might be the dream in *Day for Night*. As the director Ferrand, Truffaut is haunted by a recurring image of a little boy with a cane, walking down a dark and deserted street. His destination turns out to be a movie theater, where he pries loose the photographs hanging in front. He gathers the stills from *Citizen Kane* (a film about a boy whose parents sent him away, who became a famous figure and always got everything he wanted, except love) and he runs away with them; on the soundtrack, organ music rises and renders the scene a religious experience. The director is haunted by a boy with stolen pictures rather than kisses. The child is Truffaut, the cinema his life. And our own sensitivity to love, art, and the space they share is enriched by his projections, recollections, and lasting presence.

Notes and References

Abbreviations

Throughout the book, the following abbreviations are used to identify page references to these works by François Truffaut:

AD   *The Adventures of Antoine Doinel: Four Autobiographical Screenplays.* Trans. Helen G. Scott. New York: Simon and Schuster, 1971.
C   *Correspondance.* Paris: 5 Continents/Hâtier, 1988.
DN   *Day for Night.* Trans. Sam Flores. New York: Grove Press, 1975.
FV   *Les Films de ma vie.* Paris: Flammarion, 1975.
400 Blows   *The 400 Blows.* New York: Grove Press, 1969.
H   *Hitchcock.* Trans. Helen G. Scott. New York: Simon and Schuster, 1967.
HAF   *L'Homme qui aimait les femmes.* Paris: Flammarion, 1977.
J   *La Nuit Américaine et le Journal de tournage de "Fahrenheit 451."* Paris: Seghers, 1974.
SC   *L'Argent de poche.* Paris: Flammarion, 1976.
TEG   *"Les deux Anglaises et le Continent,"* *L'Avant-Scène du Cinéma,* No. 121, January, 1972.

Chapter One

1. André Bazin, *Le Cinéma de l'occupation et de la résistance* (Paris, 1975), pp. 20–21.
2. André Bazin, *What Is Cinema?* Trans. Hugh Gray (Berkeley, 1967), I:102.
3. Bazin, *Cinéma de l'occupation,* pp. 20–21.
4. C. G. Crisp, *François Truffaut* (New York, 1972), pp. 7–8.
5. Bazin, *What is Cinema?* Trans. Hugh Gray (Berkeley, II:37, 21, 1971), II:37, 21.
6. We feel Rossellini's influence when Truffaut says, "If in some of my films, I tried to follow a single character simply, honestly, in an almost documentary manner, I owe it to him" (*FV,* 289).

7. Graham Petrie, *The Cinema of François Truffaut* (New York, 1970), p. 12.

8. Andrew Sarris, *The American Cinema* (New York, 1968), p. 28.

9. All quotations from "A Certain Tendency of the French Cinema," *Cahiers du Cinéma in English*, No. 1, pp. 32–35.

10. André Bazin, "On the Politique des Auteurs," *Cahiers du Cinéma in English*, No. 1, p. 18. See also Sarris' attempt to place auteurism in proper perspective: "Ultimately, the auteur theory is not so much a theory as an attitude, a table of values that converts film history into directorial autobiography. The auteur critic is obsessed with the wholeness of art and the artist. He looks at the film as a whole, the director as a whole" (*The American Cinema*, p. 30). Equally useful is Sarris' article "The Auteur Theory Revisited," in *American Film 2* ix (July–August, 1977).

11. Alexandre Astruc, "La Caméra-Stylo," *Ecran Français*, No. 144 (30 mars, 1948). Reprinted in English in *The New Wave*, ed. Peter Graham.

12. Vincent Canby, "Truffaut's Clear-Eyed Quest," *New York Times*, September 14, 1975. Truffaut's stated opinion is that "it doesn't detract for anyone ignorant of the allusion, and it adds for someone who recognizes it" (Charles Samuels, *Encountering Directors*, New York, 1972, p. 39).

13. In conversation with the author, Truffaut explained that he chose the character's other name—Saroyan—because of his admiration for the American writer William Saroyan, especially his *Man on the Flying Trapeze*. Moreover, Aznavour, like Saroyan, is of Armenian descent.

14. François Truffaut, "Should Films Be Politically Committed?," in *Focus on "Shoot the Piano Player,"* ed. Leo Braudy (Englewood Cliffs, N.J., 1972), p. 135.

15. Dan A. Cukier and Jo Gryn, "A Conversation with François Truffaut," in *Focus on "Shoot the Piano Player,"* p. 13.

16. Don Allen, *Truffaut* (New York, 1974), p. 10.

17. The same issue of *Cahiers* that contained Rivette's review of *The 400 Blows* called attention to the Paris premiere of *The Quiet One*, a social documentary on childhood for which Agee wrote the commentary. It was filmed entirely on New York streets, in Harlem apartments, and at the Wiltwyck School for Boys. Bosley Crowther's review in the *New York Times* (February 14, 1949) attributes to this film the same qualities that Agee and Truffaut praised in others.

18. Preface to André Bazin and Eric Rohmer, *Charlie Chaplin* (Paris, 1972), pp. 7–8.

19. *Téléciné* 160 (mars, 1970), p. 4.

20. For a comprehensive discussion of this scene, see Karel Reisz and Gavin Millar, "The Technique of *Shoot the Piano Player*," in *Focus on "Shoot the Piano Player."*

21. "Through the Looking Glass," *Focus on "Shoot the Piano Player,"* p. 115.

22. Welles' influence is seen as particularly rich when Truffaut confesses that, at the age of fourteen, it was through Welles that he discovered Shakespeare and through the writer of the score for *Citizen Kane*, Bernard Herrmann, that he discovered Stravinsky!

23. *Film Quarterly*, 17:i (Fall, 1963), 6.

24. Don Allen, *Truffaut*, p. 11.

25. *Film Quarterly*, loc. cit., p. 5.

26. Truffaut told me that his main objection had been to Ford's treatment of women; he was repulsed by the proverbial scene of a woman being spanked.

27. Dominique Maillet, "Interview de François Truffaut," *Lumière du Cinéma*, No. 4 (mai, 1977), p. 24, and the author's conversation with Truffaut, May, 1977.

28. Samuels, *Encountering Directors*, p. 45.

29. Graham, *The New Wave*, p. 108. (Translated from *Cahiers du Cinéma*, No. 138, décembre, 1962.)

30. *Lumière du Cinéma*, loc. cit., p. 21.

31. Samuels, p. 34.

Chapter Two

1. In this context, see Eric Rohmer and Claude Chabrol, *Hitchcock* (Paris, 1957).

2. During the interview, Truffaut discusses the Hitchcockian theme of a man accused of a crime of which he is innocent, "a theme that satisfies the audience's fascination with the clandestine, while also allowing it to identify with the character" (*H*, 34).

3. Leo Braudy, "Truffaut, Hitchcock and the Irresponsible Audience," *Film Quarterly*, 21:iv (Summer, 1968), 23, 25–26.

4. In a later interview, Truffaut proved less adamant about dialogue: "I don't think that films are purer when the characters stop talking. One of my favorite Hitchcock films is *Dial M for Murder*, and people speak throughout it. And yet the mise-en-scène is fantastic in this film" (*American Film*, May, 1976, p. 36).

5. *Film Quarterly*, 17:i (Fall, 1963), 8.

6. *American Film*, May, 1976, p. 40.

7. *Cahiers du Cinéma*, No. 157 (juillet, 1964), pp. 49–50.

8. Author's conversation with Truffaut, Paris, May, 1977.

9. "Ray Bradbury on Hitchcock, Huston and Other Magic of the Screen," *Take One*, 3:xi (May–June, 1972), 22.

10. Dominique Fanne reminds us in her excellent study *L'Univers de François Truffaut* (Paris, 1972) that transfer is also part of the texture of William Irish's novels; his characters substitute for each other, are killed in one another's place, and love each other under assumed identities (p. 69).

11. Monaco is perceptive when he proposes that Julie "glides, like a nun, or more pertinently like Hitchcock's Mrs. Danvers in *Rebecca*, with whom she shares a demonic and destructive obsession" (*The New Wave*, p. 64). We may add that both women have assumed such an identity through their desire to keep alive the love of a dead person.

12. Peter Bogdanovich, *The Cinema of Alfred Hitchcock* (New York, 1962), p. 24.

13. Petrie, *The Cinema of François Truffaut*, p. 156.

14. *Téléciné* 160, p. 38.

15. Molly Haskell, *From Reverence to Rape* (New York, 1974), p. 198.

16. Braudy ends his article on *Hitchcock* with the impression of Truffaut's "unwillingness to leave the surface and plunge, however, uncertainly, into the dark and icy depths" (p. 27)—a comment that also characterizes the last shot of *Fahrenheit 451*. Despite the fact that Truffaut merits this response, the nightmares of his later films in which women fight these depths suggest a fear of madness. To some extent, his approach to Hitchcock's dark explorations might, therefore, be defensive (not unlike the evasions of Charlie Kohler vis-à-vis deep emotions).

17. *Téléciné* 160, pp. 5–6.

18. *Film Quarterly*, 17:i (Fall, 1963), 4.

19. Author's conversation with Truffaut, May, 1977.

Chapter Three

1. *L'Avant-Scène*, 162 (octobre, 1975), p. 7.

2. "From *The 400 Blows* to *Small Change*," *New Republic*, April 2, 1974, p. 25.

3. Jean Renoir, *My Life and My Films* (New York, 1974), p. 154.

4. André Bazin, *Jean Renoir*, Edited with an Introduction by François Truffaut, translated by W. W. Halsey II and William H. Simon (New York, 1974) pp. 238–39.

5. "Direction" in *Footnotes to the Film*, ed. Charles Davy (London, 1937), pp. 13–15.

6. Raymond Durgnat, *Jean Renoir* (Berkeley, 1974), pp. 12–13.

7. *My Life and My Films*, p. 128.

8. Leo Braudy, *Jean Renoir: The World of His Films* (New York, 1972), p. 208.

9. "On me demande. . . . ," *Cahiers du Cinéma*, No. 8 (janvier, 1952), p. 5.

10. *Village Voice*, November 15, 1976, p. 55.

11. Truffaut pointed out to the author that Fabienne is also referring to *Jules and Jim*, in which Catherine throws the key out the window before trying to kill Jim.

12. André Bazin, *Jean Renoir*, p. 258.

13. Ibid., p. 87.

14. Durgnat, p. 134.

15. Bazin, p. 84.

16. Penelope Gilliatt, *Jean Renoir* (New York, 1975), p. 69.

17. Without voice-over, this image is quite horrifying in its equation of love and violence. In a sense, it illustrates Truffaut's new understanding of Hitchcock, which he articulates in the 1975 foreword to *Le Cinéma selon Hitchcock*. Upon re-seeing clips from Hitchcock's work at a Gala of the Film Society of Lincoln Center, he was struck by its "sincerity and savageness" and realized that "all the love scenes were filmed like murder scenes and all the murder scenes like love scenes" (pp. 6–7).

18. Bazin, *Jean Renoir*, p. 259.

19. Ibid., p. 258.

20. Ibid., p. 87.

21. Leo Braudy demonstrates how the gentle self-consciousness of Renoir already exists in *A Day in the Country*, in which the director plays the innkeeper/cook and his editor plays the servant. They set up the situation for the characters and then withdraw, leaving them to work it out for themselves (Braudy, *Jean Renoir*, p. 174).

22. See also Monaco's insightful remarks about Ferrand's hearing aid in *The New Wave*, p. 90.

Chapter Four

1. See Kinder and Houston, "Truffaut's Gorgeous Killers," *Film Quarterly*, 27:ii (Winter, 1973–74), 2.

2. Yvonne Baby, "I Wanted to Treat *Shoot the Piano Player* Like a Tale by Perrault," *Focus on "Shoot the Piano Player,"* p. 23.

3. Crisp, *François Truffaut*, p. 95.

4. "Hitchcock vs. Truffaut," *Sight and Sound*, 38:ii (Spring, 1969), 88.

5. Truffaut is well aware of Moreau's qualities (see stills in this chapter): "She has a kind of moral authority . . . she is very physical, very carnal, but she prevents anything dirty from coming over on the screen. She is like love; she is not like lechery . . . when you know her, you find that she has the qualities of both a man and a woman, without the laborious reasoning side of men and without the coquettishness of women" (Sanche de Gramont, "Life Style of Homo Cinematicus," *New York Times Magazine*, June 15, 1969, p. 47).

6. Petrie, *The Cinema of François Truffaut*, p. 156.

7. For a comprehensive analysis of this problem of gender, see Michael Delahaye, "Les Tourbillons élémentaries," *Cahiers du Cinéma*, No. 129 (mars 1962), pp. 39–44.

8. Stanley Kauffmann, *A World on Film* (New York, 1966), p. 226.

9. Roger Greenspun, "Elective Affinities: Aspects of *Jules et Jim*" in *The Film*, ed. Andrew Sarris (Indianapolis, 1968), p. 29.

10. Fanne, *L'Univers de François Truffaut* (Paris, 1972), p. 150.

11. Michael Klein suggests in *"Day for Night:* A Truffaut Retrospective on Women and the Rhetoric of Film" *(Film Heritage,* 9:iii [Spring, 1974], 21–26) that Julie Baker is an attempt to reconcile the liberated/destructive woman and the earth mother—two aspects of earlier Truffautesque women.

12. Barbara Coffee's "Art and Film in François Truffaut's *Jules and Jim* and *Two English Girls" (Film Heritage,* 9:iii [Spring, 1974], 8) calls attention to the way that visual art is incorporated into narrative design, particularly in the Brown home: "There is a noticeable predominance of paintings and drawings of females . . . as if to reinforce the idea that Claude is continually being manipulated by women who seem to wield the greater power in the relationships."

13. *Film Quarterly,* 27:i (Winter 1973–74), 8.

14. "Dialogue on Film," *American Film,* May, 1976, p. 35.

15. *"The Story of Adèle H.* Is a Tribute to an Experience," *Village Voice,* October 27, 1975, p. 144.

16. The source for Truffaut's inspiration is Frances Vernor Guille's edition of *Le Journal d'Adèle Hugo* (Paris: Lettres Modernes Minard, "Bibliothèque Introuvable," 1968).

17. *New York Post,* January 10, 1976, p. 14.

18. Ibid., p. 35.

19. *Film Quarterly,* loc. cit., 9.

20. Truffaut explains the means by which he conveyed this impression: "I realized that Charles Denner would be visible for two hours. Therefore, when there is a scene with a woman, I almost always favor the woman, giving her twice as much dialogue and twice as many shots to re-establish the balance" (Dominique Maillet, *Lumière du Cinéma,* No. 4 [May, 1977], 21).

Chapter Five

1. "Du Côté de chez Antoine," *Cahiers du Cinéma,* No. 95 (mars 1959), 37.

2. Author's interview with Truffaut, New York, October 2, 1976.

3. Interview by Claude Beylie, *Ecran,* mars, 1976, p. 50.

4. Ibid, pp. 48–49.

5. Ibid, p. 50.

6. "Talk of the Town," *New Yorker,* February 20, 1960, pp. 36–37.

7. Anne de Gasperi, "Avec eux, pas de cinéma!," *Les Nouvelles Littéraires,* 18 mars 1976, p. 3.

8. Author's interview with Truffaut, October 2, 1976.

9. *Ecran,* loc. cit., p. 49.

10. *L'Avant-Scène* 107 (octobre, 1970), 8.

11. Ibid., p. 10. (See also *Téléciné* 160, p. 3.)

12. Ibid., p. 9.

13. Louise Sweeney, "Profile," *Christian Science Monitor*, June 18, 1973, p. 7.

14. *New York Post*, October 1, 1976, p. 23.

15. Interview by Joseph McBride and Todd McCarthy, *Film Comment*, 12:v (September–October, 1976), 54.

16. *L'Avant Scène*, loc. cit., p. 38.

17. Interview by Sylviane Gold, *New York Post*, October 1, 1976, p. 25.

18. Samuels, *Encountering Directors*, p. 51.

Chapter Six

1. The following biographical information comes primarily from three sources: *Aline Desjardins s'entretient avec François Truffaut*, transcribed from a 1973 broadcast of Radio-Canada (Ottawa) and subsequently noted as "Desjardins"; an interview with Michèle Manceaux from *L'Express*, April 23, 1959, and reprinted in *400 Blows*; and the author's conversation with Truffaut, December 27, 1976.

2. John Russell Taylor, *Cinema Eye, Cinema Ear* (New York, 1964), p. 207.

3. Gordon Gow, "Intensification: An Interview with François Truffaut," *Films and Filming*, 18:x (July, 1972), 19.

4. Desjardins, p. 17. Truffaut's introduction to the first American screening of Visconti's *Ossessione* at the New York Film Festival, October 2, 1976, confirms this position: in asking for a reassessment of the total oeuvres of the late Visconti and Fritz Lang, he added that cinéphiles pride themselves on loving films that critics and audiences did not like.

5. Desjardins, p. 28.

6. Ibid., p. 50.

7. François Truffaut, "I Wish" (as told to Donna Dudinsky), *Take One*, 4:ii (March, 1974), 8–10.

8. Truffaut explains why we never see the father: "Jean Hugo was rather apprehensive of any filmed representation of Victor Hugo. I promised to spare him the sight of a bearded actor claiming to be Victor Hugo and upon our assurance that his great-grandfather would never be seen on the screen, we got his permission to go ahead" (*L'Avant-Scène*, No. 165 [janvier 1976], 4).

9. Pauline Kael, "All for Love," *New Yorker*, October 27, 1975, pp. 130–32. A variation on the sisters theme results from Truffaut's decision to cast Julie Christie as both Linda and Clarisse in *Fahrenheit 451*, turning Bradbury's unrelated characters into what look like twin sisters.

10. Desjardins, p. 62.

11. *Film Quarterly*, 27:i (Winter, 1973–74), 7.

12. Desjardins, p. 42.

13. *My Life and My Films*, p. 128.

14. Monaco, *The New Wave*, p. 90.

15. Author's conversation with Jean-Pierre Léaud, Paris, May 2, 1977.

16. François Cuif, "Recontre avec François Truffaut," *La Voix du Sourd*, mars, 1977, pp. 10–11. Paradoxically enough, Truffaut claimed in an interview that the reason for the hearing aid was to distance himself from the role: "I knew that I was no longer quite myself. I was not really Truffaut, I was Ferrand" (*Cinématographe* 3, Summer, 1973, p. 17).

17. *Cinématographe* 3, pp. 14–15.

18. The only directors conspicuous by their absence are Renoir and Cocteau. Both are invoked in other scenes: Joelle compares herself to the cook in *Rules of the Game*, and a Cocteau tapestry hangs prominently in Julie's room.

19. *Cinématographe* 3, p. 16.

20. Monaco, *The New Wave*, p. 93.

21. When I suggested during an interview that the film was superior to the novel, Truffaut embarked on a passionate defense of Roché's genius.

22. *L'Avant Scène* 121, p. 58.

23. Truffaut made clear to me that Cocteau and Bresson had a tremendous impact on the New Wave in general and on him in particular, singling out *Les Dames du Bois de Boulogne*, scripted by Cocteau and directed by Bresson. (*The Wild Child* may be a good example of the Bressonian influence.)

24. *L'Univers de François Truffaut*, p. 177.

25. Desjardins, p. 45.

26. Ray Bradbury, *Fahrenheit 451* (New York, 1953), p. 144.

27. *Cinématographe* 15 ("Spécial Truffaut," octobre–novembre, 1975), 6–7.

28. Jack Kroll's enthusiastic review of *Adèle H.* (*Newsweek*, January 5, 1976) claims that Adèle's entire story is "an incredibly parodic replay of her father's sensibility." He compares Hugo's pursuit of Adèle's mother (also named Adèle) to the passion manifested by his daughter: "The young poet's flaming letters to the girl . . . sound scarily like his daughter's entreaties almost half a century later" (p. 74).

29. "Aujourd'hui Magazine," moderated by Jean-Louis Trintignant, May 2, 1977, and the author's conversation with Charles Denner.

30. *Lumière du Cinéma*, No. 4 (mai 1977), 24.

31. Michel de Montaigne, *Complete Essays*, trans. Donald M. Frame (Stanford, Cal., 1958), p. 504.

32. Relevant here is the credit sequence of *Shoot the Piano Player*, which focuses on the inside of Charlie's piano; we hear the honky-tonk tune while observing the "behind-the-scenes" creation of it. Moreover, the credit sequence of *Day for Night* contains a graphic representation of the sound track: two vertical lines move as the composer rehearses with his musicians.

33. Desjardins, p. 47.
34. See *Cinématographe* 15, p. 9.

Chapter Seven

1. Catherine Laporte and Danièle Heymann, *L'Express*, 13 mars 1978.
2. David Sterritt, "Film Is the Art of Going Forward," *Christian Science Monitor*, November 27, 1978, p. 20.
3. Annette Insdorf, "Maurice Jaubert and François Truffaut: Musical Continuities from *L'Atalante* to *L'Histoire d'Adèle H.*," *Yale French Studies* ("Cinema/Sound") No. 6 (1980), pp. 204–218.
4. Sterritt, p. 20.
5. Gregg Kilday, "François Truffaut Reconciling the Fathers of His Art," *Herald Examiner*, February 27, 1979, B1, B5.
6. *Ibid.*
7. Stanley Kauffmann, "Wring Out the Old," *New Republic*, April 28, 1979, pp. 24–25.
8. Transcript of American Film Institute Seminar with François Truffaut, February 28, 1979, p. 22.
9. Geoffrey H. Hartman, "The Dubious Charm of M. Truffaut," *Partisan Review* (50th Anniversary issue), 1984, p. 623. It is noteworthy that Deneuve comes from a family of performers: her father, Maurice Dorléac, was a theater actor; her mother, née Deneuve, was also an actress; and her sister Françoise Dorléac (who kept her father's name while Catherine took her mother's) brought her into the profession.
10. Annette Insdorf, "How Truffaut's *The Last Metro* Reflects Occupied Paris," *New York Times* (Arts and Leisure), February 8, 1981, p. 21.
11. Mirella Jona Affron and E. Rubinstein, eds., *"The Last Metro": François Truffaut, Director* (New Brunswick, N.J. 1985), pp. 4–5.
12. Annette Insdorf, "How Truffaut's *The Last Metro* Reflects Occupied Paris," p. 21.
13. Tom Buckley, "Truffaut Recollects When Nazis Were in Paris," *New York Times*, October 14, 1980, p. C5.
14. Vincent Canby, "Film: *The Last Metro:* A Melodrama of Sorts," *New York Times*, October 12, 1980.
15. Peter Pappas, "The Last Metro," *Cineaste* X, 4 (Fall 1980), p. 11.
16. Stuart Byron, "Truffaut and Gays," *Village Voice* (October 29–November 4, 1980), p. 64.
17. *The Last Metro*, p. 16.
18. In his article "The Great Womanizer" Andrew Sarris writes, "Truffaut tells me that this character is based on Helen Scott, an old friend and collaborator . . ." (*Vogue*, February, 1982, p. 351).
19. Annette Insdorf, "François Truffaut: A New Life, a New Film," *San Francisco Chronicle* ("Datebook"), March 4, 1984, p. 25.
20. *Ibid.*
21. *Ibid.*

Selected Bibliography

1. Books

ALLEN, DON. *Truffaut*. Cinema One Series. New York: Viking, 1974. A sensitive film-by-film analysis with detailed filmography, but no bibliography.

BRAUDY, LEO, ed. *Focus on "Shoot the Piano Player."* Englewood Cliffs, N. J.: Prentice-Hall, 1972. An excellent collection of essays about the film and interviews with Truffaut.

COLLET, JEAN. *Le Cinéma en question*. Paris: Les Editions du Cerf, 1972. A close reading of Truffaut's 1960s films in the context of other New Wave directors, stressing that he is a consummate storyteller.

————. *Le Cinéma de François Truffaut*. "Collection Cinéma Permanent." Paris: Editions Lherminier, 1977. A dazzling case for the richness and complexity of the films, although occasionally obfuscated by semiological approaches. Brilliant analysis of the writing motif in Truffaut's films, and of imagery—notably fire and flight.

CRISP, C. G., *François Truffaut*. New York: Praeger, 1972. An insightful film-by-film study up to *The Wild Child*, but the sources of information and quotations are never identified.

FANNE, DOMINIQUE. *L'Univers de François Truffaut*. Paris: Les Editions du Cerf, 1972. A well-documented and lyrical exploration of Truffaut's work up to *Two English Girls*, with an extensive bio-filmography.

GRAHAM, PETER, ed. *The New Wave*. Cinema One Series. New York: Doubleday, 1968. A collection of seminal articles. Especially valuable are translations of an interview with Truffaut, Astruc's "La Caméra-Stylo," and Bazin's "La Politique des Auteurs."

MONACO, JAMES. *The New Wave: Truffaut, Godard, Chabrol, Rohmer, Rivette*. New York: Oxford University Press, 1976. A penetrating, sympathetic, and comprehensive picture of Truffaut's work, with admirable attention to both context and structure.

PETRIE, GRAHAM. *The Cinema of François Truffaut*. International Film Guide Series. New York: A. S. Barnes, 1970. A warm and intelligent thematic approach to the films up to *Mississippi Mermaid*.

TAYLOR, JOHN RUSSELL. *Cinema Eye, Cinema Ear*. New York: Hill and Wang, 1964. A sensitive treatment of the early films with suggestive comparisons between Truffaut and the Romantic poets.

TRUFFAUT, FRANÇOIS. *The Adventures of Antoine Doinel: Four Autobiographical Screenplays*. Trans. Helen G. Scott. New York: Simon and Schuster, 1971. Originally published in Paris in 1970, contains first treatment of *The 400 Blows*, and complete screenplays of *Antoine and Colette, Stolen Kisses*, and *Bed and Board*.

_____. *Day for Night*. Trans. Sam Flores. New York: Grove Press, 1975. Script, supplemented with excellent footnotes by translator.

_____. *Les Films de ma vie*. Paris: Flammarion, 1975. A superb collection of critical writings from *Arts* and *Cahiers du Cinéma*.

_____. *The 400 Blows*. Ed. and trans. David Denby. New York: Grove Press, 1969. Contains informative interviews and articles. (A novelization of the film by Truffaut and Marcel Moussy, *Les Quatre Cents Coups*, was published in Paris [Gallimard, 1959].)

_____. *Hitchcock*. Trans. Helen G. Scott. New York: Simon & Schuster, 1967. A tribute to the master originally published in French as *Le Cinéma selon Hitchcock* (Paris: Robert Laffont, 1966). Revised edition (Paris: Editions Seghers, 1975) contains an intriguing reappraisal in the "Avant-Propos."

_____. *L'Homme qui aimait les femmes*. Paris: Flammarion, 1977. A "Cinéroman" (novelization) of Truffaut's latest film, without illustrations.

_____. *Jules and Jim*. Trans. Nicholas Fry. New York: Simon and Schuster, 1968. The script of the film.

_____. *La Nuit Américaine et le Journal de tournage de Fahrenheit 451*. Paris: Seghers, 1974. The script in French of *Day for Night* bound with Truffaut's journal of the making of the earlier film from Ray Bradbury's novel.

_____. *Small Change*. Trans. Anselm Hollo. New York: Grove Press, 1976. A novelization of the film, with photographs.

_____. *The Story of Adèle H*. Trans. Helen G. Scott. (English dialogue by Jan Dawson.) New York: Grove Press, 1976. A translation of the script of the film.

_____. *The Wild Child*. Trans. Linda Lewin and Christine Lémery. New York: Washington Square Press, 1973. The script of the film.

2. Periodicals

BRAUDY, LEO. "Hitchcock, Truffaut, and the Irresponsible Audience." *Film Quarterly*, 21:iv (Summer, 1968), 21–27. A provocative inquiry into Truffaut's *Hitchcock*, voyeurism in the cinema, and *Psycho*.

CANBY, VINCENT. "Truffaut's Clear-Eyed Quest." *New York Times*, September 14, 1975, p. 13. A perceptive and adulatory reappraisal of *The Soft Skin* and *Mississippi Mermaid.*

CAST, DAVID. "Style Without Style." *Film Heritage*, 7:ii (Winter, 1971–72), 10–14. An excellent formal analysis of *The Soft Skin* by an art historian.

COFFEE, BARBARA. "Art and Film in François Truffaut's *Jules and Jim* and *Two English Girls.*" *Film Heritage*, 9:iii, (Spring, 1974). Sensitive to how visual art reinforces the centrality of women in these films.

DELAHAYE, MICHEL. "Les Tourbillons élémentaires." *Cahiers du Cinéma*, No. 129 (March, 1962), 39–44. A close and rigorous analysis of *Jules and Jim* in terms of formal inversions in language, images, and roles.

GREENSPUN, ROGER. "Elective Affinities: Aspects of *Jules et Jim.*" *Sight and Sound*, 32:ii (Spring, 1963), 78–82. A sophisticated study of the "geometry" of the film, especially in relation to Catherine.

————. "Through the Looking Glass." *Moviegoer*, No. 1 (Winter, 1964). Another brilliant discussion of imagery and the need of characters to tell stories, this time in *Shoot the Piano Player.*

HASKELL, MOLLY. "*The Story of Adèle H.* Is a Tribute to an Experience." *Village Voice*, October 27, 1975, pp. 144–45. A profoundly intelligent review which places the film in a rich context of "women's films."

HOUSTON, PENELOPE. "Uncommitted Artist?" *Sight and Sound*, 30:ii, (Spring, 1961), 64–5. An articulate response to the objections of the "critics of the left" with respect to *Shoot the Piano Player.*

JEBB, JULIAN. "Truffaut: The Educated Heart." *Sight and Sound*, 41:iii, (Summer, 1972), 144–45. Traces Truffaut's "loving and crowded richness of characterization" through the 1960s films, culminating in an extended analysis of *Mississippi Mermaid* and *Two English Girls.*

KAEL, PAULINE. "All for Love." *New Yorker*, October 27, 1975, pp. 130–32. A sensitive and laudatory review of *The Story of Adèle H.*

KINDER, MARSHA, and BEVERLE HOUSTON. "Truffaut's Gorgeous Killers." *Film Quarterly*, 27:ii (Winter, 1973–74), 2–10. A thought-provoking appraisal of the destructive women in his films.

KLEIN, MICHAEL. "*Day for Night:* A Truffaut Retrospective on Women and the Rhetoric of Film." *Film Heritage*, 9:iii (Spring, 1974), 21–26. Analyzes Julie Baker's pivotal role in Truffaut's film.

————. "The Literary Sophistication of François Truffaut." *Film Comment*, 3:iii (Summer, 1965), 24–29. Discusses irony and dislocation in *Shoot the Piano Player* and *Jules and Jim.*

KROLL, JACK. "Truffaut: Romantic Realist." *Newsweek*, January 5, 1976, p. 74. Superb review of *The Story of Adèle H.*, advancing the well-supported claim that Truffaut is the "sanest" artist working in film today.

MAST, GERALD. "From *The 400 Blows* to *Small Change.*" *The New Repub-*

lic, April 2, 1977, pp. 23–25. A concise and sympathetic overview of Truffaut's work, with special attention to *Small Change*.

MILLAR, GAVIN. "Hitchcock vs. Truffaut." *Sight and Sound*, 38:ii (Spring, 1969), 82–88. Mostly about Hitchcock, particularly *The Lady Vanishes* and *Saboteur*, but ends by arguing that *The Bride Wore Black* is not really Hitchcockian because what interests Truffaut "is character and not situation."

REISZ, KAREL, and GAVIN MILLAR. "The Technique of *Shoot the Piano Player*," in *The Technique of Film Editing*. An excellent close analysis of a sequence from the film that illustrates Truffaut's "range of moods and technical dexterity."

RHODE, ERIC. "*Les Quatre Cents Coups*." *Sight and Sound*, 29:ii (Spring, 1960), 89–90. [Reprinted in *400 Blows*.] Praises how Truffaut, unlike Resnais, "conceals art" in the film and fulfills Bazin's theories.

RICH, FRANK. "The Passionate Liberation of Adèle H." *New York Post*, January 10, 1976, p. 14. Review from a feminist perspective, stressing Adèle's connections to earlier Truffaut characters.

―――. "Truffaut's *Small Change* Is a Bundle of Joy." *New York Post*, October 1, 1976, p. 23. A sensitive and glowing review with attention to recurring visual imagery.

RIVETTE, JACQUES. "Du côte de chez Antoine." *Cahiers du Cinéma*, No. 95 (May, 1959), 37–39. A lyrical tribute to *The 400 Blows*, which compares Truffaut to Proust, Flaherty, and Renoir.

SHATNOFF, JUDITH. "Franois Truffaut: The Anarchist Imagination." *Film Quarterly*, 16:iii (Spring, 1963), 3–11. A warmly intelligent analysis of the "dangerous talent" in Truffaut's first three films, with the superb remark that "he's an ex-j.d., a slum kid with a slum kid's energy and ability to thumb his nose and laugh and suffer simultaneously. He's also a French intellectual. . . ."

TÉCHINÉ, ANDRÉ. "*La Peau douce*." *Cahiers du Cinéma*, No. 157 (July, 1964), 49–50. A review that tries to come to terms with the ways in which *The Soft Skin* is a radical departure from *Jules and Jim*.

TRUFFAUT, FRANÇOIS. "A Certain Tendency of the French Cinema." *Cahiers du Cinéma in English*, No. 1 (January, 1966), 31–40 (translated from *Cahiers du Cinéma*, No. 31). The polemical article that made Truffaut the first major spokesman of what was to become the New Wave.

―――. Foreword to Volume II of *What Is Cinema?* by André Bazin. Berkeley: University of California Press, 1971 (trans. Hugh Gray).

―――. Introduction to *Le Cinéma de l'occupation et de la résistance*, by André Bazin. Paris: Editions 10–18, 1975.

―――. Preface to *Charlie Chaplin* by André Bazin and Eric Rohmer. Paris: Les Editions du Cerf, 1972. Truffaut weaves Bruno Bettelheim into a loving tribute to Charlot by comparing how autistic children and Chaplin relate to objects.

―――. Preface to *Le Cinéma de la cruauté,* by André Bazin. Paris: Flammarion, 1975. A collection of articles on von Stroheim, Dreyer, Preston Sturges, Bunuel, Hitchcock, and Kurosawa. [André Bazin. *Jean Renoir.* Paris: Editions Champ Libre, 1971, and New York: Simon & Schuster, 1973 (trans. W. W. Halsey II and William H. Simon). Also contains numerous articles by Truffaut.]

WOOD, ROBIN. "Chabrol and Truffaut." *Movie,* No. 17 (Winter, 1969–70), 16–24. This intelligent critic finds a connection between the indecisiveness of Truffaut's heroes and the director's need for artistic father figures. He concludes that Truffaut's view of life, though derived from Renoir, is more limited.

3. Interviews with Truffaut

ADLER, MELANIE. "François Truffaut: The Romantic Bachelor." *Andy Warhol's Interview,* March, 1976, pp. 8–10. Truffaut on *The Story of Adèle H.,* women, Howard Hawks, Henry Miller, and favorite contemporary American actors Al Pacino and Jack Nicholson.

ANON. "Dialogue on Film." *American Film,* 1:vii (May, 1976), 34–40. AFI transcript providing many insights into *The Story of Adèle H.* and its origins, and Truffaut's assessment of contemporary artists: he praises Milos Forman, and calls Nestor Almendros "the cameraman I admire most."

ANON. "François Truffaut." *Télécine,* No. 160 (March, 1970), 34–42. Transcribed from French television. A revealing interview, including Truffaut's lament that everyone ascribes "tendresse" to his films, whereas he thinks he is rather hard and clinical.

ANON. "Libre cours." [Speaking Freely.] *Télécine,* No. 160 (March, 1970), 2–9. An important discussion of both *The Wild Child* and *Mississippi Mermaid.*

ANON. "On Film." *New Yorker,* February 20, 1960, pp. 36–37. An engaging interview where Truffaut talks about children, *The 400 Blows,* and a film he was planning at the time, *Le Bleu d'outre tombe,* about conflict among teachers.

BEYLIE, CLAUDE. *Ecran,* March, 1976, pp. 48–50. Comprehensive interview about *Small Change,* including Beylie's affectionate appraisal of Truffaut's oeuvre.

COLLET, JEAN, MICHEL DELAHAYE, JEAN-ANDRÉ FIESCHI, ANDRÉ S. LABARTHE, and BERTRAND TAVERNIER. "Entretien avec François Truffaut." *Cahiers du Cinéma,* No. 138 (December, 1962), 40–59. Condensed and translated in *The New Wave,* ed. Peter Graham, pp.

9–23 and 85–113. A significant document that explores where the New Wave stood in 1962, how Truffaut saw his transition from critic to director, and why he defined himself as a popular entertainer.

CUKIER, DAN A., and JO GRYN. "Entretien avec François Truffaut." *Script*, No. 5 (April, 1962) 5–15. Truffaut talks about the camera that follows the woman with the violin in *Shoot the Piano Player* and declares that his masters are Renoir and Hitchcock.

DESJARDINS, ALINE. *Aline Desjardins s'entretient avec François Truffaut.* Transcribed from a broadcast of Radio-Canada. Ottawa: Les Editions Leméac, Collection Les Beaux-Arts, 1973. The most comprehensive and revealing interview, particularly with respect to Truffaut's childhood.

DUDINSKY, DONNA. "I Wish." Trans. Peter Lebensold. *Take One*, 4:ii: (March, 1974). A profoundly frank portrait of how Truffaut's "adapted" characters express him.

GOLD, SYLVIANE. "Truffaut's Small Charges." *New York Post*, October 1, 1976, p. 25. Concise but revealing, including Truffaut's claim that Charlie Chaplin has meant more to him "than the idea of God."

GOW, GORDON. "Intensification." *Films and Filming*, 18:x (July, 1972), 18–22. Contains a great deal of the interviewer's own fine insights. Special attention paid to biographical material, *Mississippi Mermaid*, and Hitchcock's influence.

GRAMONT, SANCHE DE. "Life Style of Homo Cinematicus—François Truffaut." *New York Times Magazine*, June 15, 1969, pp. 34–47. An engaging profile in which Truffaut is especially articulate about Jeanne Moreau and Jean-Pierre Léaud.

INSDORF, ANNETTE. "François Truffaut: Feminist Filmmaker?" *Take One*, 6:2 (January, 1978), 16–17. Truffaut speaks candidly about women in the cinema, *The Man Who Loved Women*, and his latest film, *The Green Room*.

MAILLET, DOMINIQUE. *Cinématographe*, No. 3 (Summer, 1973), 14–18. A wealth of information about *Day for Night*. Also includes Truffaut's perceptive remarks about Bertolucci and *Last Tango in Paris*.

———. *Cinématographe*, No. 15 (October–November 1975), pp. 2–9. Focus on *The Story of Adèle H.* and how the prospect of the opening "terrified" Truffaut.

———. *Lumière du Cinéma*, No. 4 (May, 1977), 19–25. A crucial exploration of *The Man Who Loved Women*, as well as his responses to the current cinema, the decline of American films, and his experiences on the set of *Close Encounters of the Third Kind*.

MANCEAUX, MICHÈLE. *L'Express*, April 23, 1959. Translated and reprinted in *400 Blows*. A candid account of how Truffaut's painful childhood memories were transformed into *The 400 Blows*.

MCBRIDE, JOSEPH, and TODD MCCARTHY. *Film Comment,* 12:v (September–October 1976), 42–45. An informative and entertaining interview in which Truffaut talks about the making of *Small Change* and the importance of children in his work.

SAMUELS, CHARLES TAYLOR. "Talking with Truffaut." *American Scholar,* 40 (Summer, 1971). (Reprinted in Samuels, *Encountering Directors.* New York: Putnam, 1972.) An interview of September, 1970, where he tells how he creates "units of emotions," especially in *Bed and Board.* He also claims, rather unconvincingly, that some of the technical innovations in *The 400 Blows* were accidents.

SWEENEY, LOUISE. "Profile." *Christian Science Monitor,* June 18, 1973, p. 7. Interesting comments about *Such a Gorgeous Kid Like Me* being a "derision of romanticism."

TRUFFAUT, FRANÇOIS. "Is Truffaut the Happiest Man on Earth? Yes." *Esquire,* 74:ii (August, 1970), 67. Yes, because "I make my daydreams come true and I get paid for it." An eloquent self-portrait sprinkled with praise for women, Orson Welles, and Mike Nichols, ending with a bit of nostalgia for pre-auteurist timers.

The author also interviewed François Truffaut in New York in October, 1976, and in Montpellier, France, in December, 1976. Further conversations with Truffaut and with Charles Denner and Jean-Pierre Léaud occurred in Paris in May, 1977.

Additional Reading

AFFRON, MIRELLA J., and E. RUBINSTEIN, eds. *"The Last Metro": François Truffaut, Director.* New Brunswick, N.J.: Rutgers, 1985.

ALMENDROS, NESTOR. *Un Homme à la caméra.* Paris: Hâtier, 1979. Also published as *A Man with a Camera.* New York: Farrar, Straus and Giroux, 1984. (Preface by Truffaut.)

BONNAFONS, ELIZABETH. *François Truffaut.* Lausanne: Editions l'Age d'Homme, 1981.

CAHIERS DU CINÉMA. *Le Roman de François Truffaut.* Paris: Editions de l'Étoile, 1985. (*Cahiers du Cinéma,* numéro spécial, décembre, 1984.) Reprinted in English as *The Films in My Life.* Trans. Leonard Mayhew, New York: Simon & Schuster, 1978; Touchstone, 1985.

DALMAS, HERVE. *Truffaut.* Paris: Rivages, 1987.

GILLAIN, ANNE, ed. *Le Cinéma selon François Truffaut.* Paris: Flammarion, 1988.

RABOURDIN, DOMINIQUE, ed. *Truffaut par Truffaut.* Paris: Editions du Chêne, 1985. Also published as *Truffaut by Truffaut.* New York: Harry N. Abrams, 1987. Reprinted in English as *The Films in My Life.* Trans. Leonard Mayhew. New York: Simon & Schuster, 1978; Touchstone, 1985.

SIMONDI, MARIO, ed. *François Truffaut* (essays by Vincent Amiel, Claude Beylie, Elizabeth Bonnafons, Edoardo Bruno, Jean Collet, Serge Daney, Vittorio Giacci, Annette Insdorf, Franco La Polla, Jean Narboni, Serge Toubiana). Florence: La Casa Usher, 1981.

TRUFFAUT, FRANÇOIS. *La Chambre verte*. Scenario in *L'Avant-Scène du Cinéma* 215, 1978.

————. *Correspondance* (Letters edited by Claude de Givray and Gilles Jacob). Paris: Hâtier/5 Continents, 1988.

————. *Le Dernier Métro*. Scenario in *L'Avant-Scène du Cinéma* 303–4, 1983.

————. *Hitchcock-Truffaut* (definitive edition). Paris: Editions Ramsay, 1984. New York: Simon and Schuster, 1985.

————. *Le Plaisir des yeux*. Paris: Cahiers du Cinéma, 1987.

WALZ, EUGENE P. *François Truffaut: A Guide to Reference and Resources*. Boston: G. K. Hall, 1982.

Filmography

UNE VISITE (16mm. private production, 1955)
Screenplay: François Truffaut
Photography: Jacques Rivette
Editors: Alain Resnais, François Truffaut
Cast: Florence Doniol-Valcroze, Jean-José Richer, Laura Mauri, Francis Cognany

LES MISTONS (Les Films du Carrosse, 1957)
Producer: Robert Lachenay
Assistant Directors: Claude de Givray, Alain Jeannel
Screenplay: François Truffaut, based on a short story in *Virginales* by Maurice Pons (Script in *L'Avant-Scène du Cinéma*, No. 4, May, 1961)
Photography: Jean Malige (1,33)
Music: Maurice Le Roux
Editor: Cécile Decugis
Narrator: Michel François
Cast: Gérard Blain (Gérard), Bernadette Lafont (Bernadette), and "les mistons"
Running Time: 26 minutes (later cut by Truffaut to 17 minutes)
Premiere: March 3, 1961, Paris
16mm. rental: Images, 2 Purdy Ave., Rye, N. Y. 10580

UNE HISTOIRE D'EAU (Les Films de la Pléiade, 1958)
Producer: Pierre Braunberger
Co-Director: Jean-Luc Godard
Production Manager: Roger Fleytoux
Screenplay: Jean-Luc Godard (Script in *L'Avant-Scène du Cinéma*, No. 7, September, 1961)
Photography: Michel Latouche (16mm)
Sound: Jacques Maumont
Editor: Jean-Luc Godard
Narrator: Jean-Luc Godard
Cast: Jean-Claude Brialy (lui), Caroline Dim (elle)

Running Time: 18 minutes
Premiere: March 3, 1961, Paris

LES QUATRE CENTS COUPS (THE 400 BLOWS) (Les Films du Carrosse/SEDIF, 1959)
Producer: Georges Charlot
Assistant Director: Philippe de Broca
Story: François Truffaut (for script, see *The 400 Blows* in Selected Bibliography)
Adaptation: François Truffaut, Marcel Moussy
Photography: Henri Decaë (Dyaliscope)
Camera Operator: Jean Rabier
Art Direction: Bernard Evein
Music: Jean Constantin
Sound: Jean-Claude Marchetti
Editor: Marie-Josèph Yoyotte
Cast: Jean-Pierre Léaud (Antoine Doinel), Albert Rémy (M. Doinel), Claire Maurier (Mme Doinel), Patrick Auffay (René Bigey), Georges Flamant (M. Bigey), Jeanne Moreau (Woman with dog), Jean-Claude Brialy (Man in street)
Running Time: 94 minutes
Premiere: June 3, 1959, Paris. Dedicated to André Bazin
16mm. rental: Films, Inc.

TIREZ SUR LE PIANISTE (SHOOT THE PIANO PLAYER) (Les Films de la Pléiade, 1960)
Producer: Pierre Braunberger
Production Manager: Roger Fleytoux
Assistant Directors: Francis Cognany, Robert Bober
Screenplay: François Truffaut, Marcel Moussy, based on the novel *Down There* by David Goodis
Photography: Raoul Coutard (Dyaliscope)
Camera Operator: Claude Beausoleil
Art Direction: Jacques Mély
Music: Georges Delerue
Songs: "Framboise," Bobby Lapointe; "Dialogues d'amoureux," Félix Leclerc
Sound: Jacques Gallois
Editors: Cécile Decugis, Claudine Bouché
Cast: Charles Aznavour (Edouard Saroyan/Charlie Kohler), Marie Dubois (Léna), Nicole Berger (Thérésa), Albert Rémy (Chico Saroyan), Daniel Boulanger (Ernest), Claude Mansard (Momo), Michèle Mercier (Clarisse)
Running Time: 80 minutes

Premiere: November 25, 1960, Paris
16mm. rental: Films, Inc.
Beta, VHS: Budget

JULES ET JIM (JULES AND JIM) (Les Films du Carrosse/SEDIF, 1961)
Producer: Marcel Berbert
Assistant Directors: Georges Pellegrin, Robert Bober, Florence Malraux
Screenplay: François Truffaut, Jean Gruault, based on the novel by Henri-Pierre Roché (Script: Paris: Editions du Seuil, 1971, from *L'Avant-Scène du Cinéma*, No. 16)
Photography: Raoul Coutard (Franscope)
Camera Operator: Claude Beausoleil
Costumes: Fred Capel
Music: Georges Delerue
Song: "Le Tourbillon," Boris Bassiak
Sound: Temoin
Editor: Claudine Bouché
Narrator: Michel Subor
Cast: Jeanne Moreau (Catherine), Oscar Werner (Jules), Henri Serre (Jim), Marie Dubois (Thérèse), Vanna Urbino (Gilberte), Boris Bassiak (Albert), Sabine Haudepin (Sabine)
Running Time: 110 minutes
Premiere: January 23, 1962, Paris
16mm. rental: Films, Inc.
Beta, VHS: Sheik

ANTOINE ET COLETTE (episode in **L'AMOUR A VINGT ANS—LOVE AT TWENTY**) (Ulysse Productions, 1962)
Producer: Pierre Roustang
Production Manager: Philippe Dussart
Assistant Director: Georges Pellegrin
Screenplay: François Truffaut (Script: see *The Adventures of Antoine Doinel* in Selected Bibliography)
Photography: Raoul Coutard (Franscope)
Camera Operator: Claude Beausoleil
Artistic Adviser: Jean de Baroncelli
Music: Georges Delerue
Editor: Claudine Bouché
Narrator: Henri Serre
Cast: Jean-Pierre Léaud (Antoine Doinel), Marie-France Pisier (Colette), Patrick Auffay (René), François Darbon (Colette's father), Rosy Varte (Colette's mother), Jean-François Adam (Albert Tazzi)
Running Time: 123 minutes (L'AMOUR A VINGT ANS)
Premiere: June 22, 1962, Paris

LA PEAU DOUCE (THE SOFT SKIN) (Les Films du Carrosse/SEDIF, 1964)
Producer: Marcel Berbert
Assistant Director: Jean-François Adam
Screenplay: François Truffaut, Jean-Louis Richard (script in *L'Avant-Scène du Cinéma*, No. 48, May, 1965)
Photography: Raoul Coutard (1, 66)
Camera Operator: Claude Beausoleil
Music: Georges Delerue
Editor: Claudine Bouché
Cast: Jean Desailly (Pierre Lachenay), Françoise Dorléac (Nicole), Nelly Benedetti (Franca), Daniel Ceccaldi (Clément), Sabine Haudepin (Sabine), Jean-Louis Richard (Man in street)
Running Time: 115 minutes
Premiere: May 10, 1964, Paris
16mm. rental: Swank Films

FAHRENHEIT 451 (Anglo Enterprise/Vineyard Films, 1966)
Producer: Lewis M. Allen
Associate Producer: Michael Delamar
Production Manager: Ian Lewis
Assistant Director: Bryan Coates
Screenplay: François Truffaut, Jean-Louis Richard, based on the novel by Ray Bradbury (Synopsis only of script in *L'Avant-Scène du Cinéma*, No. 64, October, 1966.)
Additional Dialogue: David Rudkin, Helen Scott
Photography: Nicholas Roeg (Technicolor)(1,66)
Camera Operator: Alex Thompson
Art Direction: Syd Cain
Design and Costumes: Tony Walton
Music: Bernard Herrmann
Sound Editor: Norman Wanstall
Sound Recordists: Bob McPhee, Gordon McCallum
Special Effects: Bowie Films, Rank Films Processing Division, Charles Staffel
Editor: Thom Noble
Cast: Oscar Werner (Montag), Julie Christie (Linda/Clarisse), Cyril Cusack (the Captain), Anton Diffring (Fabian), Bee Duffell (the Book-woman)
Running Time: 112 minutes
Premiere: September 16, 1966, Paris
16mm. lease and rental: Universal 16; rental only: Swank and others

LA MARIÉE ÉTAIT EN NOIR (THE BRIDE WORE BLACK) (Les Films du Carrosse/Artistes Associés, Dino De Laurentiis Cinematografica, 1967)
Producer: Marcel Berbert
Production Manager: Georges Charlot
Assistant Director: Jean Chayrou
Screenplay: François Truffaut, Jean-Louis Richard, based on the novel by William Irish (Cornell Woolrich)
Photography: Raoul Coutard (Eastmancolor) (1,66)
Camera Operator: Georges Liron
Art Direction: Pierre Guffroy
Music: Bernard Herrmann
Musical Director: André Girard
Sound: René Levert
Editor: Claudine Bouché
Cast: Jeanne Moreau (Julie Kohler), Claude Rich (Bliss), Jean-Claude Brialy (Corey), Michel Bouquet (Coral), Michel Lonsdale (Morane), Charles Denner (Fergus), Daniel Boulanger (Delvaux)
Running Time: 107 minutes
Premiere: April 17, 1968, Paris
16mm. rental: United Artists 16

BAISERS VOLÉS (STOLEN KISSES) (Les Films du Carrosse/Artites Associés, 1968)
Producer: Marcel Berbert
Production Manager: Claude Miller
Assistant Directors: Jean-José Richer, Alain Deschamps
Screenplay: François Truffaut, Claude de Givray, Bernard Revon (Script: see *The Adventures of Antoine Doinel* in Selected Bibliography)
Photography: Denys Clerval (Eastmancolor) (1,66)
Camera Operator: Jean Chiabaut
Art Direction: Claude Pignot
Music: Antoine Duhamel
Song: "Que reste-t-il de nos amours?", Charles Trenet
Sound: René Levert
Editor: Agnès Guillemot
Cast: Jean-Pierre Léaud (Antoine Doinel), Delphine Seyrig (Fabienne Tabard), Claude Jade (Christine Darbon), Michel Lonsdale (M. Tabard), Harry Max (M. Henri)
Running Time: 91 minutes
Premiere: September 6, 1968, Paris
Beta, VHS: RCA/Columbia

LA SIRÈNE DU MISSISSIPPI (MISSISSIPPI MERMAID) (Les Films du
Carrosse/Artistes Associés/Produzioni Associate Delphos, 1969)
Producer: Marcel Berbert
Production Manager: Claude Miller
Assistant Director: Jean-José Richer
Screenplay: François Truffaut, based on the novel, *Waltz into Darkness* by
William Irish (Cornell Woolrich)
Photography: Denys Clerval (Dyaliscope Eastmancolor)
Camera Operator: Jean Chiabaut
Art Director: Claude Pignot
Music: Antoine Duhamel
Sound: René Levert
Editor: Agnès Guillemot
Cast: Jean-Paul Belmondo (Louis Mahé), Catherine Deneuve (Julie
Roussel/Marion), Michel Bouquet (Comolli), Nelly Borgeaud (Berthe
Roussel), Marcel Berbert (Jardine)
Running Time: 123 minutes
Premiere: June 18, 1969, Paris. Dedicated to Jean Renoir
16 mm. rental: United Artists 16

L'ENFANT SAUVAGE (THE WILD CHILD) (Les Films du Carrosse/
Artistes Associés, 1969)
Producer: Marcel Berbert
Associate Producer: Christian Lentretien
Production Manager: Claude Miller
Assistant Director: Suzanne Schiffman
Screenplay: François Truffaut, Jean Gruault, based on *Mémoire et Rapport
sur Victor de l'Aveyron* by Jean Itard (1806), (Script in *L'Avant-Scène
du Cinéma*, No. 107, October, 1970)
Photography: Nestor Almendros (1,66)
Camera Operator: Philippe Théaudière
Art Direction: Jean Mandaroux
Costumes: Gitt Magrini
Music: Antonio Vivaldi, played by Michel Sanvoisin (recorder) and André
Saint-Clivier (mandolin)
Musical Director: Antoine Duhamel
Sound: René Levert
Editor: Agnès Guillemot
Cast: Jean-Pierre Cargol (Victor), François Truffaut (Dr. Jean Itard), Fran-
çoise Seigner (Mme Guérin), Jean Dasté (Prof. Pinel), Claude Miller
(M. Lémeri)
Running Time: 85 minutes

Premiere: February 26, 1970, Paris
16 mm. rental: United Artists 16

DOMICILE CONJUGAL (BED AND BOARD) (Les Films du Carrosse/
Valoria Films/Fida Cinematografica, 1970)
Producer: Marcel Berbert
Production Manager: Claude Miller
Assistant Director: Suzanne Schiffman
Screenplay: François Truffaut, Claude de Givray, Bernard Revon (Script:
see *The Adventures of Antoine Doinel* in Selected Bibliography)
Photography: Nestor Almendros (Eastmancolor) (1,66)
Camera Operator: Emmanuel Machuel
Art Direction: Jean Mandaroux
Costumes: Françoise Tournafond
Music: Antoine Duhamel
Sound: René Levert
Editor: Agnès Guillemot
Cast: Jean-Pierre Léaud (Antoine Doinel), Claude Jade (Christine Doinel),
Hiroko Berghauer (Kyoko), Daniel Ceccaldi (Lucien Darbon), Claire
Duhamel (Mme Darbon), Daniel Boulanger (Tenor)
Running Time: 97 minutes
Premiere: September 1, 1970, Paris
16mm. rental: Swank Films

**LES DEUX ANGLAISES ET LE CONTINENT (TWO ENGLISH
GIRLS)** (Les Films du Carrosse/Cinetel, 1971)
Producer: Marcel Berbert
Production Manager: Claude Miller
Assistant Director: Suzanne Schiffman
Screenplay: François Truffaut, Jean Gruault, based on the novel by Henri-
Pierre Roché (Script in *L'Avant-Scène du Cinéma*, No. 121, January,
1972)
Photography: Nestor Almendros (Eastmancolor) (1,66)
Camera Operator: Jean-Claude Rivière
Art Direction: Michel de Broin
Costumes: Gitt Magrini
Music: Georges Delerue
Sound: René Levert
Editor: Yann Dedet
Narrator: François Truffaut
Cast: Jean-Pierre Léaud (Claude Roc), Kika Markham (Anne Brown),
Stacey Tendeter (Muriel Brown), Sylvia Marriott (Mrs. Brown), Marie
Mansart (Mme Roc), Philippe Léotard (Diurka)
Running Time: 108 minutes, cut from 132 minutes

Premiere: November 26, 1971, Paris
16mm. rental: Janus Films
Beta, VHS: CBS/Fox

UNE BELLE FILLE COMME MOI (SUCH A GORGEOUS KiD LIKE ME) (Les Films du Carrosse/Columbia, 1972)
Producer: Marcel Berbert
Production Manager: Claude Miller
Assistant Director: Suzanne Schiffman
Screenplay: François Truffaut, Jean-Loup Dabadie, based on the novel *Such A Gorgeous Kid Like Me* by Henry Farrell
Photography: Pierre William Glenn (Eastmancolor) (1,66)
Camera Operator: Walter Bal
Art Direction: Jean-Pierre Kohut
Costumes: Monique Dury
Music: Georges Delerue
Sound: René Levert
Editor: Yann Dedet
Cast: Bernadette Lafont (Camille Bliss), Claude Brasseur (Murène), Charles Denner (Arthur), Guy Marchand (Sam Golden), André Dussollier (Stanislas Prévine), Philippe Léotard (Clovis Bliss), Anne Kreis (Hélène)
Running Time: 100 minutes
Premiere: September 13, 1972, Paris
16mm rental: Swank Films

LA NUIT AMÉRICAINE (DAY FOR NIGHT) (Les Films du Carrosse/ PECF/Produzione Internazionale Cinematografica, 1973)
Producer: Marcel Berbert
Production Manager: Claude Miller
Assistant Directors: Suzanne Schiffman, Jean-François Stévenin
Screenplay: François Truffaut, Suzanne Schiffman, Jean-Louis Richard (Script-Paris: Seghers, 1974; New York: Grove Press, 1975)
Photography: Pierre-William Glenn (Eastmancolor) (1,66)
Camera Operator: Walter Bal
Art Direction: Damien Lanfranchi
Costumes: Monique Dury
Music: Georges Delerue
Sound: René Levert
Editors: Yann Dedet, Martine Barraqué
Cast: Jacqueline Bisset (Julie/Pamela), Valentina Cortese (Séverine), Jean-Pierre Aumont (Alexandre), Jean-Pierre Léaud (Alphonse), François Truffaut (Ferrand), Nathalie Baye (Joelle), Graham Greene and Marcel Berbert (Insurers)

Running Time: 115 minutes
Premiere: May 24, 1973, Paris
16mm. rental: Warner Brothers Non-Theatrical Division
Beta, VHS: Warner

L'HISTOIRE D'ADÈLE H. (THE STORY OF ADÈLE H.) (Les Films du
Carrosse/Artistes Associés, 1975)
Producer: Marcel Berbert
Production Manager: Claude Miller
Assistant Director: Suzanne Schiffman
Screenplay: François Truffaut, Jean Gruault, Suzanne Schiffman, with the
collaboration of Frances V. Guille, based on *Le Journal d'Adèle Hugo.*
(Script in *L'Avant-Scène du Cinéma*, No. 165, January, 1976)
Photography: Nestor Almendros (Eastmancolor) (1,66)
Camera Operator: Jean-Claude Rivière
Art Direction: Jean-Pierre Kohut-Svelko
Costumes: Jacqueline Guyot
Music: Maurice Jaubert (1900–1940)
Musical Director: Patrice Mestral
Musical Adviser: François Porcile
Sound: Jean-Pierre Ruh
Editor: Yann Dedet
Cast: Isabelle Adjani (Adèle Hugo), Bruce Robinson (Lt. Pinson), Sylvia
Marriott (Mrs. Saunders), Reubin Dorey (Mr. Saunders), Joseph
Blatchley (Mr. Whistler)
Running Time: 110 minutes
Premiere: October 8, 1975, Paris
16mm. rental: Films, Inc.
Beta, VHS: Warner

L'ARGENT DE POCHE (SMALL CHANGE) (Les Films du Carrosse,
1976)
Producer: Marcel Berbert
Production Manger: Roland Thenot
Assistant Director: Suzanne Schiffman
Screenplay: François Truffaut, Suzanne Schiffman
Photography: Pierre-William Glenn (Eastmancolor) (1,66)
Art Direction: Jean-Pierre Kohut-Svelko
Costumes: Monique Dury
Music: Maurice Jaubert (1900–1940)
Musical Director: Patrice Mestral
Musical Adviser: François Porcile
Song: "Les Enfants s'ennuient le dimanche," Charles Trenet
Sound: Michel Laurent, Michel Brethez

Editors: Yann Dedet, Martine Barraqué-Curie
Cast: Jean-François Stévenin (Jean-François Richet), Virginie Thévénet
    (Lydie Richet), Geory Desmouceaux (Patrick), Philippe Goldman (Ju-
    lien), Sylvie Grezel (Sylvie), Laura Truffaut (Madeleine Doinel), Eva
    Truffaut (Patricia)
Running Time: 105 minutes
Premiere: March 17, 1976, Paris
16mm. rental: Films, Inc.
Beta, VHS: Warner

**L'HOMME QUI AIMAIT LES FEMMES (THE MAN WHO LOVED
WOMEN)** (Les Films du Carrosse/Artistes Associés, 1977)
Producer: Marcel Berbert
Production Manager: Roland Thenot
Assistant Director: Suzanne Schiffman
Screenplay: François Truffaut, Michel Fermaud, Suzanne Schiffman
Photography: Nestor Almendros (1,66)
Camera Operator: Anne Trigaux
Art Direction: Jean-Pierre Kohut-Svelko
Costumes: Monique Dury
Music: Maurice Jaubert
Musical Director: Patrice Mestral
Sound: Michel Laurent
Editor: Martine Barraqué-Curie
Cast: Charles Denner (Bertrand Morane), Brigitte Fossey (Geneviève
    Bigey), Nelly Borgeaud (Delphine), Geneviève Fontanel (Hélène),
    Nathalie Baye (Martine), Leslie Caron (Véra), Jean Dasté (Dr. Binard),
    Roger Leenhardt (Monsieur Bétany)
Running Time: 118 minutes
Premiere; April 27, 1977, Paris
16mm. rental: Cinema 5, 595 Madison Ave., New York, N.Y. 10021
Beta, VHS: Columbia

LA CHAMBRE VERTE (THE GREEN ROOM) (Les Films du Carrosse/
    Artistes Associés. 1978)
Producer: Marcel Berbert
Production Manager: Roland Thenot
Assistant Director: Suzanne Schiffman
Screenplay: François Truffaut, Jean Gruault from "The Altar of the Dead"
    by Henry James
Photography: Nestor Almendros
Camera Operator: Anne Trigaux
Art Direction: Jean-Pierre Kohut-Svelko
Costumes: Christian Gasc, Monique Dury

Music: Maurice Jaubert
Sound: Michel Laurent
Editor: Martine Barraqué-Curie
Cast: François Truffaut (Julien Davenne), Nathalie Baye (Cécilia Mandel), Jeanne Lobre (Mme Rambaud), Jean Dasté (Bernard Humbert), Patrick Maléon (Georges)
Running Time: 94 minutes
Premiere: April 5, 1978, Paris
16mm. rental: Films, Inc.
Beta, VHS: Warner

While making this film about a man's devotion to the dead, Truffaut explains,

In all my period films, there were actors carrying tapers or candles. I always loved this liturgical aspect and wanted to take it to its limit. Without being a believer, I too—like Julien Davenne, the hero of *La Chambre verte*—love the dead. I think we forget them too fast, we don't honor them enough. Without going as far as Davenne—who is obsessed, loving the dead more than the living—I find that remembering the dead permits one to struggle against the transience of life.

L'AMOUR EN FUITE (LOVE ON THE RUN) (Les Films du Carrosse, 1979)
Producer: Marcel Berbert
Production Manager: Roland Thénot
Assistant Director: Suzanne Schiffman
Screenplay: François Truffaut, Marie-France Pisier, Jean Aurel, Suzanne Schiffman
Photography: Nestor Almendros (Eastmancolor) (1,66)
Art Direction: Jean-Pierre Kohut-Svelko
Costumes: Monique Dury
Music: Georges Delerue
Song: "L'Amour en fuite," Laurent Voulzy and Alain Souchon (lyrics)
Sound: Michel Laurent
Editor: Martine Barraqué-Curie
Cast: Jean-Pierre Léaud (Antoine Doinel), Marie-France Pisier (Colette), Claude Jade (Christine), Dani (Liliane), Dorothée (Sabine), Rosy Varté (Colette's mother), Marie Henriau (judge), Daniel Mesguich (Xavier)
Running Time: 94 minutes
Premiere: January 29, 1979, Paris
16mm rental: Janus Films
Beta, VHS: Warner

LE DERNIER MÉTRO (THE LAST METRO) (Les Films du Carrosse, TF1, SEDIF, SFP, 1980)
Producer: Jean-José Richer
Production Manager: Roland Thénot
Assistant Director: Suzanne Schiffman
Screenplay: François Truffaut, Suzanne Schiffman, Jean-Claude Grumberg (Script in L'Avant-Scène du Cinéma, No. 303–304, 1–15 mars, 1983)
Photography: Nestor Almendros (Fujicolor) (1,66)
Art Direction: Jean-Pierre Kohut-Svelko
Costumes: Lisèle Roos
Music: Georges Delerue
Sound: Michel Laurent
Editor: Martine Barraqué
Cast: Catherine Deneuve (Marion Steiner), Gérard Depardieu (Bernard Granger), Heinz Bennent (Lucas Steiner), Jean Poiret (Jean-Loup Cottins), Andréa Ferreol (Arlette Guillaume), Paulette Dubost (Germaine Fabre), Sabine Haudepin (Nadine Marsac), Jean-Louis Richard (Daxiat)
Running Time: 128 minutes
Premiere: Sept. 17, 1980
16mm. rental: Films, Inc.
Beta, VHS: CBS/Fox

LA FEMME D'À CÔTÉ (THE WOMAN NEXT DOOR) (Les Films du Carrosse, TF1, Soprofilms, 1981)
Producer: Armand Barbault
Production Manager: Roland Thénot
Assistant Director: Suzanne Schiffman
Screenplay: François Truffaut, Suzanne Schiffman, Jean Aurel
Photography: William Lubtchansky (Fujicolor) (1,66)
Art Direction: Jean-Pierre Kohut-Svelko
Costumes: Michèle Cerf
Music: Georges Delerue
Sound: Michel Laurent
Editor: Martine Barraqué
Cast: Gérard Depardieu (Bernard Coudray), Fanny Ardant (Mathilde Bauchard), Henri Garcin (Philippe Bauchard), Michèle Baumgartner (Arlette Coudray), Véronique Silver (Madame Jouve), Roger Van Hool (Roland Duguet)
Running Time: 106 minutes
Premiere: September 30, 1981, Paris
16mm. rental: United Artists
Beta, VHS: CBS/Fox

VIVEMENT DIMANCHE! (**CONFIDENTIALLY YOURS**) (Les Films du
Carrosse, Film A2, Soprofilms, 1983)
Production: Armand Barbault
Production Manager: Roland Thénot
Assistant Director: Suzanne Schiffman
Screenplay: François Truffaut, Suzanne Schiffman, Jean Aurel, based on *The
Long Saturday Night* by Charles Williams
Photography: Nestor Almendros (1,66)
Art Direction: Hilton McConnico
Costumes: Michèle Cerf
Music: Georges Delerue
Sound: Pierre Gamet
Editor: Martine Barraqué
Cast: Fanny Ardant (Barbara Becker), Jean-Louis Trintignant (Julien Vercel),
Philippe Laudenbach (Maître Clément), Caroline Sihol (Marie-Christine
Vercel), Philippe Morier-Genoud (Santelli), Xavier Saint-Macary
(Bertrand Fabre), Jean-Pierre Kalfon (Jacques Massoulier)
Running Time: 111 minutes
Premiere: August 10, 1983, Paris
16mm. rental: New Yorker Films
Beta, VHS: CBS/Fox

DISTRIBUTORS OF 16 MM RENTAL PRINTS

Films, Inc. 5547 North Ravenswood Ave., Chicago, IL 60640-1199
New Yorker Films. 16 East 61st St., New York, NY 10023
Swank Films. 393 Front St., Hempstead, NY 11550
United Artists 16. 729 7th Ave., New York, NY 10019
Universal 16. 445 Park Ave., New York, NY 10022
Warner Bros. Non-Theatrical Division. 4000 Warner Blvd., Burbank, CA
63166

Index